Milton

BOOKS BY HILAIRE BELLOC

Historical:
MILTON
CROMWELL
CHARLES THE FIRST:
  KING OF ENGLAND
NAPOLEON
RICHELIEU
WOLSEY
CRANMER
JAMES II
JOAN OF ARC
DANTON
MARIE ANTOINETTE
ROBESPIERRE
HISTORY OF ENGLAND
MINIATURES OF FRENCH HISTORY
ETC.

Essays:
CONVERSATION WITH AN ANGEL
SHORT TALKS WITH THE DEAD
HILLS AND THE SEA
THE PATH TO ROME
ON ANYTHING
ON NOTHING
ETC.

Novels:
THE POSTMASTER-GENERAL
BELINDA
THE MISSING MASTERPIECE
SHADOWED
THE HAUNTED HOUSE
THE EMERALD
THE GIRONDIN
THE GREEN OVERCOAT
ETC.

General:
THE CRUISE OF THE NONA
AVRIL
THE FOUR MEN
THE CONTRAST
ESTA PERPETUA
ETC.

Poetry:
VERSES 1910
SONNETS AND VERSES 1923

Children's Books:
BAD CHILD'S BOOK OF BEASTS
MORE BEASTS FOR WORSE CHILDREN
A MORAL ALPHABET
CAUTIONARY TALES
ETC.

Religious:
HOW THE REFORMATION HAPPENED
SURVIVALS AND NEW ARRIVALS
EUROPE AND THE FAITH
ETC.

JOHN MILTON
By Jonathan Richardson

Milton

BY

HILAIRE BELLOC

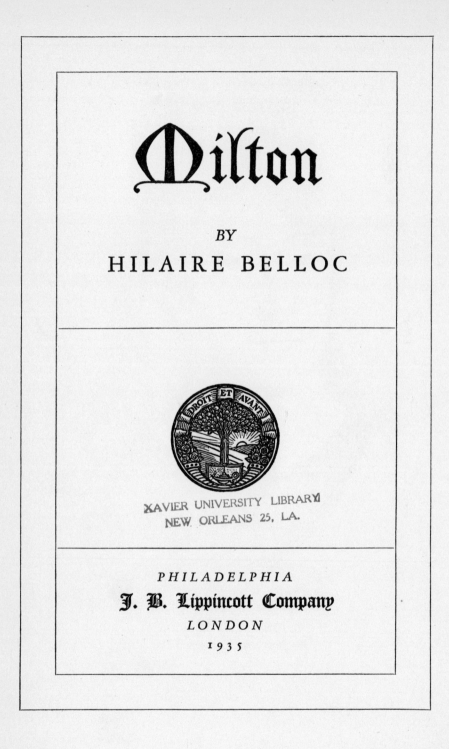

PHILADELPHIA

J. B. Lippincott Company

LONDON

1935

78707

TO
DIANA COOPER

Contents

[7]

CONTENTS

Part One

Time and Place

Time and Place

BORN in 1608, Milton's appearance as a master dates from his twenty-second year; dying in 1674, his memorable prose and verse fill the lifetime between 1629 and 1673.

These years were critical in the story of England. They form the decisive phase in that complete transformation which turned the English from Catholic to Protestant; from common obedience under a King to subjection by ranks under a Gentry (with King-ship forgotten); from a nation of owners to a nation of wage earners and therefore from a peasantry to a capitalist society.

In those years first vigorously appear above ground the English colonies, English banking, the expansion of London and the springs of what was to become so mighty an increase in English numbers and power: Modern England. Of such a development Milton was in part a prophet, in part a pioneer, in some degree a creator; whence his profound historical significance, and the importance, for the understanding of the England coming after him, that we should understand himself.

It is as a writer that he counts; therefore we must concentrate on his significant writing. Since his supremacy was in Poetry it is as a Poet that we must chiefly examine him, touching but briefly on only the salient matters in his career apart from letters, and considering those matters only as they affect his character and, above all, his Muse.

[11]

For this purpose we must first consider his environment: the time and place in which he moved: next the separate natures of the Poet and the Man, a contrast always present in the masters of high verse. These examined we can proceed to the main business of his works; and as these fall into three clearly distinct periods—Lyric until his thirty-fourth year, Polemic (that is, filled with public controversy) thenceforward till his fifty-second, Epic at the close—under these titles shall I deal with them. Such is the order of what follows.

·   ·   ·   ·   ·   ·   ·

John Milton's life and character begin to be influenced as a child in the years just following the death of Robert Cecil, first Lord Salisbury, who had completed his great father's work and imposed the results of the religious revolution upon the English State—though as yet not wholly upon the English people. The boy did not grow up in a Puritan England nor even in a Protestant England; he grew up in an England in which Protestant feeling was growing, had already become the tone of mind in a majority, and was secure of becoming the national tone of mind as a whole—but it was an England in which the struggle between the old culture and the new was still fierce, and remained fierce throughout the whole of Milton's own life.

The seventeenth century in England (as almost everywhere in Europe) was still—all the central part of it—a battlefield between the ancient traditions and the new religion. The true line of cleavage running through England between the Gunpowder Plot and the expulsion of the Stuarts—a long lifetime of eighty-three years which overlaps Milton's own lifetime from three years before his birth to fourteen years after his death—does not lie between those who were officially called Papists and the rest of the community. It does not even lie between those who might reluctantly admit themselves of Catholic sympathy and the others: it lies between those who felt a tenderness or regret for the age-long moral habit of the country, for what had been the immemorial national Catholic religion, and those who rejected and disliked those traditions and that religion. In either camp you had of course a whole range of moods running from indifference to enthusiasm; but the two moods remain distinct, and the number of neutrals in the centre, though considerable, was small compared with either wing.

The traditional side naturally held a larger proportion of older men; the innovating side a larger proportion of younger. The innovating side was growing, the traditionalist side was dwindling; and—what was of the first importance—the former had the driving power of national feeling to inspire them, the latter were apologetic and doubtful. The two stood, just before Milton was born, fairly equal; by the time he came to die they had grown to differ as three to one. Not more than a quarter of the English people looked back, by that time (1674), with any longing to the older England. Moreover a violent Civil War had intervened, wherein the religious question was tangled up with the main political conflict, and in that Civil War it was the growing thing which had won. To us of to-day, looking back across two hundred years of a completely Protestant England, it is a natural illusion to think of mid-seventeenth century England as something of the same kind. That illusion is only another example of the standing error which warps nearly all effort at historical vision—the error of reading our own times into the past.

If we appreciate that it was in a divided England of this kind, with a still vital tradition in it drawn from the last of Catholicism and struggling confusedly to survive, that Milton lived and wrote, we can understand the man and his work. If we think of him as living in a unitedly Protestant England, let alone a Puritan England, he and what he did are alike incomprehensible.

As for the Puritan feeling with which his name is associated, that is a particular part of the religious complexity of the time which needs careful statement. When we talk of the Puritan fraction among the English people we mean that body of them the individuals of which were under the influence of Calvin. We do not mean those of them who accepted Calvin's ideas of a highly organised Church, the Presbyterian discipline; we mean those whose minds were steeped in Election, Predestination and something terrible inherent in the Majesty of God.

It is a mood unmistakable in the individual who is possessed by it. The number of such individuals when Milton was a child was not, as yet, very great, but they were fervid, energetic, clear as to what they felt and would impose, and were expanding rapidly. By the time he was at the door of manhood they had grown formidable, especially in the City of London. There proceeded from them a continual protest against the organisation of the English Church under Prelates, that is, against a hierarchy, against the relics of priesthood and the sacramental idea as a whole. By the time Milton was thirty the lawyers and the great landowners (followed by a great number of the yeomen who, exasperated by new taxes, aimed at weakening the power of the Crown) had allied themselves with the Puritan zeal; and that zeal was often found mixed up in the same individual with the new attack on the Monarchy. The two feelings, revolutionary on the political as on the religious side, formed but one during the height of the conflict (1641-1660) and inspired, for a time at least, something like half-educated England.

Milton's own attitude towards Puritanism proper was peculiar; it was special to himself. He was attached to it because he was by nature rebellious, also by nature combative—and this was the rebellious and combative side of England. He was attracted to it because it was the marching wing against Papistry —and he loathed Papistry with all the loathing aroused by family quarrels. A father whom *his* Papist father had turned out of the house, a brother who was reverting to that Papist family tradition, were sufficient to feed this fire of anti-Popery in John Milton. Again, the conception of Divine Election was native to him, and very dear. He always thought of himself as a supreme example of God's special choice. It was a piece of megalomania which swelled in him steadily as his life proceeded, and reached its extreme at the very end. There was also something in him, after his character had been twisted by the tragedy of his broken marriage in 1642, which took a certain pleasure in the contemplation of suffering in others, and indeed in the mass of men. A religious atmosphere in which the mass of men were doomed was not uncongenial to him, nor a populous Hell into which he could thrust his enemies, his critics, the royalist populace of England—anything or anyone who offended his sensibilities—especially his inflamed pride.*

But one cannot carry on and say that Milton therefore fulfilled the Puritan programme, for that programme included a mingled ignorance of, and repulsion for, Pagan antiquity—Greece and Rome—and a corresponding passion for the Hebraic. And again, that programme directly attacked beauty and joy. By its definition beauty and joy were lures.

Now Milton was built up on the Greek and Roman classics: Scripture was in the making of him, and he was of those who took all the inspired Hebrew folklore literally in every detail of its text, but the Hebraic never ousted in him the Greek and the Latin classics. He drew not from the Levant, but from Athens and Rome. Joy in its more solemn form he would not abandon: and as for beauty, beauty was for him all his life an appetite, an object and a guide. Of all the English poets he is the one for whom sudden beauty in diction seems most in-

* In his later theological speculations he condemned them rather to annihilation than torment.

evitable, in whom you never know under what incongruous conditions beauty at white-heat will not appear, shining through an immortal line. He knew that he was the vehicle, and, after a fashion, the priest, of beauty; and he worshipped at that shrine all his life—to our immense advantage.

There is also this to be remarked in the modification of his Puritanism; that being always ready to attack whatever hand he felt weighing upon him, he was ready to turn in some degree against the very religion of his adoption.

In what has just been said I have used two words which must further be amplified in any preliminaries upon a judgment of Milton: these two words are "London" and "Yeoman."

Milton was a Londoner. He was born in, and all his early years were formed by, most of his central years surrounded by, the then distinctive and personal influence of London.

For the London of those days was a City; it was one thing, with a distinctive character—small enough to feel itself in contrast with the fields around, large enough to be a State within the State. The little England which moved the exalted patriotism of Milton held, when he was a child, perhaps five million people, or rather more. By the time he came to die some six million. It was an England of say a million families, slowly increasing by a rate which added perhaps a quarter to its numbers in a century.

Now this England was an England of peasants. The idea of a peasantry has disappeared from amongst us to-day; we discover it only in foreign travel, Irish, Belgian, French. In Milton's England peasantry was universal. The overwhelming mass of English people lived in villages; even the small minority who lived in towns lived for the most part in little places which were mainly markets or ports for the villages—and the villages were villages not of farmers and labourers, still less of landowners monopolising whole parishes; they were villages of yeomen.

Perhaps half the families of England numerically, at any rate the determining number of them, those who gave its character to the State, were yeomen families. They were possessors of the land which they tilled, and of the roofs under which they were born and lived; no small proportion were absolute owners. The bulk of the rest paid small unchangeable dues for their land, from which no one could turn them out; they held in freehold, being for the most part in what was called "fee-farm." The children inherited the land from their parents, continued on it, and that not by the grace of some rich master but of right. There were of course a certain number, even a large number, of day labourers; but they were not the mass, they did not give the tone to the society of the English village. In the same way the craftsman was, as a rule, the owner of his tools and commonly of the house in which he worked. He would begin as an apprentice but he would rise to independence.

All this must be understood of the society of England in Milton's youth.

Well, in the midst of such a peasant society, little more than a tenth in size of what England is to-day, London was unique. When Milton was a child it contained one-fifteenth, or possibly more, of the total population—if one includes Westminster and the parts about the Strand linking Westminster with the City, and Southwark beyond London Bridge. By the time of Milton's death it had grown to be nearly one-tenth of the whole kingdom. Its trade was three times larger than the trade of all the other ports put together; in it alone could you find wide converse, frequent and large assembly, and therefore the combined power of great numbers. In it were concentrated nearly all the major instruments of credit, which were growing vigorously during all this very period into the beginnings of English banking. It alone in England received immediately news from abroad, the chief foreign travellers, and therefore the influence of the Continent of Europe. In London alone was the Englishman constantly familiar with the face and manner of the foreigner, on which account London was aggressively national in feeling.

But London was not traditional; London was in the forefront of the religious revolution. It was also largely—though not universally—attached to the political revolution of the day, and the struggle of the wealthier classes to substitute their power for the King's.

We may not say that the bulk of London was disloyal; we cannot even say that the London of the Civil Wars would have been rebel if it had had to decide the issue by counting heads—but the chief financial and commercial forces were on that side. The direction of London was Protestant in religion, nourishing more than any other district the seeds of Puritanism, and much more than any other unit of all that made up England did it pit money-power against the Crown, in those days when the heart of the whole struggle was the question of who should rule—Money, or the King. Remember that in a capital where the mob was not a mob of proletarians but of apprentices, the mob—many owning some property, most expecting it—would on occasion demonstrate in favour of the greater owners and therefore of their money-power.

And in this very matter of class it is urgent to remember also the difference between Milton's England and ours. In that society the few very great landed families held a supreme position. It was a tradition inherited from an older time, though most of them were not of ancient blood, but men grown rich through quite recent legal and commercial accumulations, transformed into the Earl of this and the Marquis of that by the purchase, through forensic and mercantile wealth, of many manors: —a manor being a source of income drawn from the dues payable by the yeomen and from the rents of land held in freehold by the Lord of the Manor himself. The bond of this class was the peerage; a small body of less than a hundred at the beginning of Milton's life, nearly doubled by the end of it.

Below the peerage were the gentry, among whom the proportion of old wealth was larger, but who were, at least half
of them, new wealth. They were commonly men of one manor.
They had not as yet eaten up the yeomen—that was to come as
a consequence of the Civil Wars. The bond of their society and
of the lawyers, who were by this time inextricably mixed up
with them, was the House of Commons.

There was a distinction between these, the gentry (the
squires) and the burgesses, and this difference in rank comes
largely into Milton's own life at the moment of his marriage.
It was a traditional distinction which survived, although wealth
accumulated in commerce or at the law was at the basis of the
gentry as well as of the peers; but it is to be remarked that in
all this there was not, as there is to-day, still less than there was
in the nineteenth century, a strong class feeling in the sense of
one set of men living different lives from another set. There was
not (what grew up later) a sort of mystery about the way in
which a superior class carries on. The feeling was far more
domestic. To take a parallel, one may compare the feeling of
rank in those days to something like the feeling of status in a
school: the difference between big and small boys. The feeling
is strong, but it does not prevent a constant common life.

It is essential to grasp another profound difference between
that society and our own—the solidity and permanence of the
now well-established middle-class to which Milton himself belonged, its growing wealth, and its numbers.

These men (of whom Milton himself and his father before
him and grandfather before that, were types) did not suffer
from sharply changing fortunes. The families from which they
came had not, as a rule, arisen suddenly, but either by a slow
accumulation, or from a long yeoman descent. They also, like
the peasants below and the gentry above them, owned the
houses in which they lived and often would be born and die
under the same roof; and the proportion they bore to the rest

of the small community was more considerable by far than that which any corresponding class bears to-day. There is perhaps an equal proportion to-day of well-to-do salaried men to whom the term "Middle-class" is in modern phraseology also applied; but that is quite a different thing from a class of well-founded owners—and such was the class from which men like Milton derived. They took property as a matter of course; they took its reasonable stability as a matter of course; they took also as a matter of course their inheritance of it from their parents and the certitude that their children would inherit from them in turn. All this was as normal to the middle-class of the mid-seventeenth century in England as it is to the wealthy territorial class in England to-day. They were at no man's bidding: their livelihood was not at the mercy of an economic superior.

In connection with this last point it is important to estimate the value of money at the time. Money comes largely into Milton's affairs, and into all the discussions of the time—and yet it is the one point upon which our histories commonly give least satisfaction. Throughout this book I have quoted sums of money in modern terms, but seeing the way that currencies now dance about there is no very precise standard available. I have therefore followed a general rule and multiplied by six, writing down £60 where £10 is mentioned in Milton's time. When I say, for instance, that the dowry promised to Milton at his first marriage was £6,000 I mean of course that the actual sum promised in 1642 was £1,000. When I say that Christopher Milton's house was rated at about £240 a year or more, I mean that the sum mentioned in the claim for commutation was £40.*

Now this, of course, is only a very rough and ready rule of

---

* At the moment of writing, January 1935, the pound sterling and the dollar being nearly at parity, an American reader may multiply the sums given in the text by five without going far wrong. Thus he may reckon the dowry promised to Milton on his first marriage at 30,000 dollars—and so in proportion through the book.

thumb, and imprecise through a number of reasons. The purchasing power of money was declining throughout Milton's sixty-six years of life; a pound meant a great deal more in 1608 than it did in 1674. And again, it was a moment when prices fluctuated very largely, especially the prices of the necessaries of life, and in particular wheat, one reason for this being the social disturbances of which the time was full.

Then we have the very important disturbing factor that the *social* value of money was not the same thing as its actual purchasing power. A thousand a year has much more social value in a small poor community than in a large or rich one. An age and place where there are few purchasable commodities (a comparatively small number of things or services generally used) gives a much higher *social* value to money than does a time or place where there are many more such commodities. We have seen the proof of this during the last generation; the great number of new inventions offers not only increased opportunity for spending, on a scale unknown before they entered the market, but actually compels such expenditure: for instance, on transport.

I repeat therefore that this multiple of six is too loose and too much of a rule of thumb. £1,000 a year meant in Milton's boyhood much more than £6,000 a year to-day; in his old age it meant, perhaps, less than a modern £5,000; but the essential thing for the reader to remember is that a multiple of six for the whole lifetime is not too high. If anything, money represented on the average in Milton's lifetime something more than six times what it represents to-day in purchasing power—certainly not less.

A very good way of testing this is the central phase of Milton's life—the time of the Civil Wars, the nine years between the campaign of Edgehill and the final battle of Worcester (1642-51).

Milton enters that decade in the turning point of his life, his thirty-third year, the year of his first marriage. The succeeding time is filled with his most arduous activities, though not with his most famous verse—for his most exalted verse came both before and after those nine years. Now on those nine years we have a mass of economic detail, because estimates and levies were always being made for the purpose of carrying on the conflict; we have all sorts of details on the equipment and food of men and beasts, the cost of lodging, the salaries of the various professions, the wages of day labourers—and all the rest of it. If we compare the costings with ours to-day we shall find that this multiple of six continually reappears.

These pages are not suitable for any long economic description; so I will close with one example:

You could equip a cavalry soldier fully, including his great boots (but not including the furniture of his horse) for £2. You would hardly do it anywhere for £12 to-day. A serviceable horse picked for mounted troops, young and up to weight, for which to-day you must write £30 and upwards, could be got for five or six pounds.

And the last feature we have to remember, one which will enter continuously into any study of Milton, is the new religion of patriotism—the worship of the country by its citizens, the transference to the English image of that feeling which hitherto had attached to Princes and before them to what had been the common religion of Christendom.

Patriotism was gradually becoming in seventeenth century England that new religion which was to acquire such passionate intensity in the nineteenth century. It was nourished by the religious revolution, which depended upon it; by the isolation of the island; by the perpetual contrast and conflict with neighbouring Ireland; by the fact that the English Crown alone among the Crowns of Christendom (and it was still a minor one) had separated itself from the old religious inheritance. The Scandinavian kingdoms indeed had done the same, but they were small; and the petty Protestant Princes and Free Cities among the Germans, the Calvinist and Lutheran Swiss, the wealthy majority of the successful rebellious Dutch (who under leadership mainly Calvinist had set up their commercial republic separate from their original sovereign), were not kingdoms.

The word "King" still stood for real strength in those days: the King of Poland, the great Emperor of Germany, the King of a now united Spain, the King of France, all these, all the main political organisations of Europe, were Catholic. Official England, especially its monarch, held a sort of fort for Protestantism, continually menaced by the pressure of far wealthier and larger Catholic Continental powers, but saved by the rivalries among them.

For the rest, it is remarkable how typical the divisions of Milton's literary life were of England's own political fortunes. That life falls into the three phases I have mentioned, and they correspond nearly exactly to the three main phases of public life in this country as it ran between the Poet's boyhood and his old age. The long lyric phase when his mind was as yet undisturbed ran side by side with the long peace which England enjoyed, in growing prosperity, under the excellent personal rule of King Charles the First. By the time that Milton was writing his first great thing, the Christmas Ode, Charles's struggle with the rich men in Parliament and the money-power of the City of London had for the moment been settled in the King's favour; and all the supreme lyrical work of Milton, from that Nativity Ode to the *Lycidas*, was written during the Antonine Peace of the second Stuart.

The shock and catastrophe of his own life corresponded exactly with the opening of the Civil Wars. His marriage, which disturbed everything in him and left him embittered to the end, took place in the summer of 1642, his thirty-fourth year, the very moment when the armies were marching towards their first clash. His wife's desertion of him falls in precisely those autumn days when the untried swords of Englishmen were thrust into English flesh on the first great battlefield. Edgehill comes in the very hours when Milton at last fully appreciated his wife's determination to leave him, and suffered the ignominy of her family's jeers.

All his political Polemic work follows on the same model; it runs parallel with the outward political business of the Civil Wars, and the succeeding irrational welter under the despotism of Oliver Cromwell, from 1642 to the Restoration—nineteen years. With the Restoration in 1660 a third phase, completely new, opens: the Epic. Milton is no longer the violent controversial pamphleteer, the old lyrical phase is a score of years behind him; he is in opposition, diminished in fortune and alone. Standing so framed, he produces *Paradise Lost* and the *Samson Agonistes*—the last of which is the very protest of the cause apparently defeated, but a sort of symbol that the defeat was momentary and apparent rather than real.

For indeed not Milton himself (though he would like to have done so) but those forces which Milton had championed, superficially defeated by the Restoration and for the moment blinded and bewildered, had pulled down the pillars of the house. Monarchy was defeated and killed in the Civil Wars and the older England was ruined.

Though Milton himself did not fully appreciate what had happened, yet, before he died, that which he desired to see had been founded. He had argued for the tenure of Kings as servants—they had indeed become in England servants, and very soon they were to be mere puppets. He had argued for freedom of expression—with the exception (of course) of Catholic expression—and before he died such freedom was upon the threshold. He had desired the freedom of all Protestant organisations at large, each congregation to act as it would; the Stuart policy of toleration had introduced that conception— and before he died it was manifest to any far-seeing man that

Nonconformity would ultimately flourish at will. Every effort to cut down the growth would fail. He had regarded Catholicism, the Scarlet Woman, the Babylonian Woe (which some also called the Church of God and the Salvation of the World) as an abomination, and confidently expected the end of its last remains among his people: he did not quite live to see this consummation, but it was well on its way. Not long after his death the fury of more than half London over the Popish Plot was an earnest of what was to come; long before, even in the heat of the Restoration, the ruin of Catholic Ireland had been accomplished by the King's confirmation of the Cromwellian loot of Irish land.

One may imagine Milton complaining in old age to some young lad who can remember nothing before the Restoration, one who was (let us suppose) just coming of age in the poet's last year—and saying to that youth that all his life had been sacrificed to lost causes. Whereat the youth, had he been (what youth happily can never be) wise, observant and perceiving the curve of things—might have answered him:

"Sir, rest you content. The future of England is with you, and you are in no small part the maker thereof. Kingship is broken. Bishops mean less and less. The Papist cannot much longer endure. Ireland has been murdered: she shows no sign of life. While as for your cherished doctrine of divorce, it has already become the law of England. Is not that glorious? A plurality of wives, for which (in secret) you argue so eloquently, is not as yet widely established, but now that divorce is granted us we shall doubtless have polygamy in effect. And as for the supposed Divinity of Christ, that illusion is, I assure you, waning, and must in due time become a laughing stock."

So would the young man have spoken, and then might the old poet have closed his eyes in peace, hearing such good tidings. But I doubt whether he would have done so. For peace also was repugnant to him.

Part Two

The Man and the Poet

The Man and the Poet

THAT glorious instrument, the English tongue, had reached maturity when by the influence of a certain man, a poet, it nearly took on a final and a classic form. This man was John Milton.

He did not consciously intend that the language of which he was in verse a master should grow fixed in a perfect mould. That it all but did so in the lifetime of those who followed Milton was due to no plan of his or of any man's; nor was it even due to any model left by him. The accepted manner of rhymed ten syllable heroic verse which succeeded him and only just missed permanence, the manner of Dryden and Pope, was not Milton's own manner. It was neither the blank verse of his great epic nor the lovely intertwining of his lyrical rhythms. No; but his spirit overshadowing posterity commanded awe, and so brought the ideal of a standard poetic convention near to fruition. For Milton became the national poet, and the quality of his achievement made those who came after him ashamed of extravagance. He recalled them to rule by his glance, he imposed order by the serenity of his own triumph. But this influence faded; by the early nineteenth century it had disappeared. No classic tradition survived to attain that immortality which the genius of English deserved to share with Greek and Latin.

Now Milton not only nearly succeeded in a literary revolution; he did actually succeed in a political one. A new religion, arising from what depths we know not, having swept Europe, had come to occupy England; one man more than any other stamped the general literature of England with this new changed mood called *Protestant,* and that man was John Milton.

It was not due to him that English letters (especially where they enshrine historical tradition) are Protestant from the beginning of modern times; the mighty influence of the Authorised Version, supplemented by a host of greater and lesser writers, is responsible for that. But it was John Milton, coming just at the moment when the tide had fully turned, who gave to the Protestant temper in English writing the character of something to be taken as a matter of course. He furnished the repeated lines; his genius handed on (through the action of beauty) the religious temper which was already that of a majority, and was to become within a lifetime after him that of the whole nation. He was the leader of that advance upon a very wide front, he was the moderator of that large consensus whereby the literature of England became identical with the successful religion.

Dryden sufficiently soon, Pope from birth, were upon the other side; they were attached to the Roman communion. The sympathisers with the old religion were dwindling, but were still a formidable minority in Milton's own day. Had there arisen, contemporary with Milton, someone in that minority possessing the Power of the Word upon a scale comparable to his, such counter-literature would have aided that Catholic minority to survive. It is conceivable that two streams would have flowed henceforward through the region of high English verse, and that another spirit also would have communicated its contrasting influence to the drama, to fiction, and even to history. But the supereminent power of Milton in that which must always bear for men the authority of a revelation, the quality of something Divine—high verse—decided the issue; and on this account Milton's influence on his country has had even more political than literary power. For Milton dominates among those who made what is now England.

What then was this man who came so near (by indirect effect) to giving us a classical form which should endure? What was this man who did most amply succeed in stamping upon the body of English letters for three hundred years the seal of Protestantism?

It is of high interest to be able to answer that double question, for without such an answer we can but imperfectly understand the later story of England. But when a man must also be called not a man only but a poet, especially when he can but be called a great poet, and among the greatest of all poets—one of the rare immortals—it is not enough to say, "Such was the man"; it is not enough to present one coherent image, with the motives and character of a single nature. You must present the poet as well as the man—and the two are separate.

How towering verse comes to be written by mortals none have explained nor can, save by inspiration; which is as much as to say that something divine is revealed in the poetic speech, not through the poet's will but through some superior will using the poet for its purpose. It is the afflatus of the God.

Those who will not admit a spiritual element in things but make all nature One, deny the reality of all that the senses cannot appreciate and measure. It is the simplest and the basest solution, the most thoroughly inadequate and therefore the most popular with our contemporaries. It is called "materialist," and is the ruin of understanding. For such as cannot conceive the supernatural a piece of verse or of sculpture or of painting is explicable at once in terms of the body, and therefore, finally in terms of matter. The word "Beauty" loses its significance, as do the words "right and wrong" and "justice." "There are no gods, so what's the odds?" and under the influence of this drug the glory in things fades out to nothingness. For such as are soaked in materialism—and they increase rapidly—the highest verse can only be a function of the man who wrote it, and the man who wrote it a function of physical things. So do they judge; but it is to be remarked that not only is there never found among them a poet, even of the meanest breed, but that neither is there found among them a man to whom the sacred fire can be communicated as he reads. To put it bluntly, there is not one of these our modern materialists who so much as knows what poetry is.

But to return: you have, I say, these two distinct figures, the Man and the Poet.

The man you may describe so vividly and well, with such knowledge of his life in detail that he stands out living before the reader—yet if he be also a poet that picture is of no consequence. The fellow does not count; he would not have been heard of but for his verses; and his verses are not his own. It is through him that they reach us, his acceptation of the mysterious influence, his industry in fashioning it to the ear, his tenacity in following up its impulse—all these rightly give him fame, so that we say justly enough of him, "That glory is of Theocritus, this of Keats"; and our fathers in the remote beginnings of Europe testified to this when they gave its origin to the word "Poet"—which is the Greek for a maker. Yet must we never, when, for the sake of comprehension, we discuss the work of a great poet, chiefly consider the man himself, nor trace to the accidents about him (even of the most intimate kind) the seed of the heavenly flower. The seed of Poetry floats in from elsewhere. It is not of this world.

Therefore it behoves us, when we attempt to put before our fellows the poet as he was and is, to present mainly what he is—the still living thing which he was given to do—his verse. Only after that should we add what he was, the character and circumstance of a man now dead; and we only do it in order that we may the better understand the Word committed to him.

This double business is not easy, and indeed no man ever fully succeeded in giving to the study of a poet true unity.

He who describes the Poet and his verse may get a false unity by making the human being the author of all; making *him*, and not his Master, to be the God. It is the common way. The Muse in him makes the man's very body sacred. Because the head is crowned with laurel its features must be called sublime. But this is idolatry and idols do not live.

Or the teller may provoke laughter by nothing more serious than a contrast between the man and the holy thing with which he was entrusted. He whose hand held the creative pen, whose tongue used prophetic speech, was foolish in this, despicable in that, weak in the other; base in such and such a circumstance, ridiculous in such and such a quandary. He is grotesquely out of tune with the heavenly thing which it was granted him to set forth.

So we may, instead of Deifying the man, degrade the Poet; but this method also is false. Though there must always be contrast between fallen man and the Divine remainder in him, it is none the less true that a man thus used as an instrument of the God becomes conscious of the Divine, is made a companion of the power blowing through him. There is here (if such a metaphor may be used with respect) a sort of Incarnation, so that the name of a great poet, however lamentable he were in the things below his trade, is worthy of awe.

But if the Poet himself and his Poetry are thus so separate, how can a study of them be approached?

There is, I think, but one way of attempting the task: it is to speak first separately of the circumstance and character of the man, then of the poet; this done to follow his verse through his life, not as a commentary upon that life but as the chief business of it. For, of the man and his verse, his verse is still the greater of the two.

It is as though coming on a ragged piper crossing a heath at evening, and hearing his music, we were to take the wanderer in, to ask him whence he came, of what tribe he was and what adventures had befallen him by sea and land in all his minstrelsy. While he told us, and we honoured ourselves by his taking shelter with us for the night, our occupation would still be his music, and he would concern us mainly, or only, as the player thereof. When he had passed on his way at morning we should strongly remember the song and the singer, but only half remember those things in the singer's tale which were lesser than, or of no moment to, his song.

THE MAN

John Milton the man, elected to such high destiny, was one who—but for such election—would have been a somewhat solemn, self-absorbed scholar; too sensitive and therefore given to quarrel—that, and no more.

John Milton, living through an age free of conflict, would have acquired some repute from his vast reading and facility in various tongues; but such repute is neither exalted nor much enduring. Great learning—particularly in the dead languages—will give a man some name, but hardly a name deeply engraved upon the tablets of his people.

John Milton well mated, to a woman suitable, with humour to compensate his own lack thereof, a woman tender to his absurdities and ready to accept patiently his dreadful selfishness, would have been not only a scholar renowned, but (so far as that is possible to an isolated man) happy—and therefore negligible. As it was, John Milton, chosen to be the master poet of England, was thrown into a conflict more heated than any other in all the story of England. It compelled him to a long exile of eighteen years from the company of that which alone distinguishes him—his divine Muse.

This gap and halt came in the very midmost of his life. It might have destroyed him as a poet. We shall see that it did not; and why.

Again, so far from being well mated he fell upon a most grievous accident in marriage; he was ruined, and in the chief event of life. He found himself, too late, coupled with one wholly unsuited to him, ungracious and to him unwelcome. His timidity had known women too late, and this one (perhaps the first woman he knew) flouted him and rendered him ridiculous. The bitter experience wounded him with a wound that endured throughout life. After his thirty-fourth year he was a different man.

By the public political conflict wherein he was wholly caught up, by the disaster in his home, he was annealed. His metal received through suffering a certain temper such as comes in no other fashion than by the furnace first and then the shock of cold. But with all this he would still have remained little known, and John Milton the man—somewhat more significant through his ordeals, but never very significant—would have remained obscure. The common illusion by which we read into a man those things which he has been granted to do—and such things are greatest of all in the poets—has made everyone approaching a study of his life seek to find in it something of the magnificent. Such an element is not present in Milton the man. There is anger, there is tenacity, there is a special kind of courage, but not magnificence—save in verse. The Poetic Grace, to which he responded, was magnificent indeed.

So one may look upon a violin, tarnished and of a seemingly common kind—but there comes one who takes the bow and draws from that undistinguished thing the voice of Heaven; and after hearing that we do indeed revere the instrument laid back in its worn and dusty case, for it has been the medium whereby the soul of man, athirst for beatitude, received a momentary promise of refreshment—whereby man, the exile of the outer night, got a glimpse of light through a crevice in the door of home.

Milton the man was somewhat slight and short even by the standards of those days, when men (at least men of his social class) were smaller than they are in the England of our time. This figure, so short and slight, was well formed and remained well formed throughout the span of its years; in youth and central manhood not without vigour (making of him a fair fencer) and inhabited by a vital spirit which bore long vigils and surmounted with success all the obstacles of mental tedium and bodily fatigue.

The one grave physical defect which at last so cruelly matured, weakness in sight, he knew nothing of in all the earlier part of his closely packed life. The shadow of it menaced him before forty; it slowly grew. But even when full blindness fell upon him (and, alas, he was hardly forty-three) the restricted body was still vigorous, reasonably spare, suffering from no excess of flesh. He slept well till towards the end; only towards the end had he the infirmity of gout. As might be expected in one who so lived by reading, he would force on headaches, but, for the rest, the spirit was supported by a body saner than itself and better balanced. It was the saving of him in a temporal way, for such health lasting so long supported his confidence, forbade him remorse and—what was really a pity!—forbade him contrition also. It is often so with good health, that it draws a veil between a man and self-knowledge, and supports pride.

From quite early youth onwards the face was grave, not very pale, illuminated by grey eyes and framed in silky brown hair. Its expression was not without occasional smiles, it certainly was not without courtesy, but the smiles were rare though the courtesy was permanent: I mean, in his general conversation with men, for in public controversy his discourtesy was enormous. As might be expected of a soul steeped in the traditions of our culture and at the same time secretly too timid, he preferred an easy carriage with his fellows to the harshness of his violent conviction too much expressed. It was in his pamphleteering, not in his daily talk, that he exhibited the roughness of the recluse. All through his life he was for fellowship in a moderate way, and at the beginning of it he enjoyed what did not come to him again—a profound friendship with an equal, who died.

Two twin emotions governed the mind of Milton through all the quiet beginning of his life, before he was caught up in the storm. These were an indurated egoism, and what has been called "a high seriousness." Each was a defect, standing as they did uncorrected by humour and quite ignorant of what is the spiritual root of humour, humility. When the troubles came upon him, relieved at first by the excitement of combat, his lack of humour was somewhat corrected by the heat of battle, but his pride was only exaggerated and made worse.

This egoism of his was such that he could not conceive himself ever to have been mistaken or an opponent to be other than a villain, or any misfortune of his to be in part due to his own fault or other than a cruel imposition of Fate—say, rather, of God trying His elect and faithful servant. It led him into exaggerated vanities, which grew on him, as vices do with age, and was worst in his last years, when he solemnly affirmed that the Holy Ghost visited him by night.

And that gravity of his (it was really the worship of himself upon a pedestal) was not proof against criticism; let alone insult. Under attack he lost all dignity; yet through a life of nearly seventy years he still regarded himself as something chosen and set apart, and published that important fact at large to the world. When men debate whether he may be called Puritan let them be certain that this at least in him was Puritan; for one of the marks of the Puritan is boasting.

His virtues (or perhaps they should rather be called qualities) all proceeded from the intensity of his character and will. Of their fruits the greatest was industry. This, allied to tenacity, never left him; it appeared in the first few years of his too-solemn boyhood, and it worked furiously almost to the end. Never was such a mill! And it ground a vast heap of grist. He can be blamed for displaying his learning too much, but what a wealth he had to display! It was an age of learning, and his contemporary Burton in "The Anatomy of Melancholy"—that gold mine of a book—gave proof of such a mass of reading that many of the greatest scholars believed him to have invented texts which later research has identified, though to this day many still remain untraced. How the men of the seventeenth century acquired this particular kind of facility it is difficult for us moderns to understand; but there it was. Milton, before he was a man, could not only read his Greek and Latin as tongues of daily familiar use to him, but had "commenced Italian," helped thereto by that which was so strongly to affect his whole life, his friendship from boyhood with Charles Deodati. Yes, and Hebrew too, or "the Chaldee" as he will have it.

There was something about him which not only acquired through reading this vast accumulation and through a powerful memory the retention of it, but impelled him continually to produce; and—what is greatly to his honour—to produce upon a wide field, largely spending and dissipating his forces, which is the best proof a man can give of inexhaustible reserves. Had he never known what it was to rhyme or to construct blank verse, he would still astonish by his range of knowledge such few as might come across his work.

He pours out Latin verse in a spate year after year of his youth, he carries on a correspondence which, though we only know most of it by allusion and certain relics, seems endless; he acquaints himself further (and, as he himself thought, thoroughly) with the Tuscan Italian; he fights upon five fronts—political, critical, classic, theological and personal. He is for ever challenging first one, then another; throwing his spear now against the constitution of the Church of England, now against the Christian institution of marriage, and now against the Trinity itself. By way of relief from such enormous labours he undertakes a History of England, sketches a Latin grammar, composes a treatise on education, and peppers all he does with bouts of cursing and bellowing at those who dare to differ from him. He advises on every political matter, careless whether he is heard or not. He does all these things while still learning more and more, and during some years of his widest activity, working as Secretary to the Government. It is difficult to affirm, but I should not wonder, should one be at the pains of numbering all he did, his scholarship would turn out wider than any other man's, even in that age of tremendous scholarship. And this scholarship the tireless machine of his industry used and re-used perpetually.

John Milton was timid; but the word must be used in a special sense. His was not a general timidity but rather a shrinking from contact, which is only another name for sensibility and will be found in most artists. It was especially noticeable in Milton.

But the word "timid" in his case meant more than that. We must extend it to imply caution: the avoidance of ill consequences, and especially physical ill consequences, to himself. He was combative enough, but combative on paper—and if he was combative occasionally in defence of things which were not generally accepted yet the whole sweep of his polemical work was on the winning side. Nor was it accidental that he was on the winning side—Milton's cataract of tracts, when they are violent, is turned against those whom he felt to be inferior to him in ability and standing, or those who no longer hold political power.

A very good test and proof of this caution in him is the effect it had in making him see exactly where official power at each moment amid such rapid changes lay. We have the same thing to-day with people who like to join in public life without running too much risk. Thus not only Cromwell was worshipped by him—at the right moment—but even Vane. Fairfax is praised until he loses power, and then neglected. Not only does he adopt towards the prisoner King the attitude common to all that was official on the winning side at the end of 1648, but he even brings in a silly jeer at Charles for solacing himself with Shakespeare. That was quite inexcusable, for if there was one writer in England who had testified to the greatness of Shakespeare it was John Milton. He waits until the King's doom is assured before urging his death, and does not publish till after that death. He takes refuge more than once in anonymity. He did what he did because he was constrained to follow his tide. The only noticeable exception to all this was his attempt to stand against the reaction after Cromwell's death; but indeed that attempted stand of his was in itself a proof of timidity, from its lack of vigour and from the safeguards he set around it.

On what perhaps he cared for most—his growing Unitarian convictions in theology—he was cautious to the end, and so it was with his support of Polygamy and his limiting of God's omnipotence, his denial of the full creative power. He may have said that he desired to publish them—but he did not in fact publish them; and that has had a curious effect upon the national reputation of the man. All during that century and a half when his was the highest literary figure in the estimation of his fellow-countrymen he passed for an orthodox Protestant Christian of the Calvinist colour, like any other of his political group; and the late discovery of his formal defection from orthodoxy (which no one really discovered until the nineteenth century was well advanced) has not been able to change the tradition.

The chances are that if you ask any man of good average education even at this late day what Milton's religion was he would reply, "Why, the religion of the independents, Cromwell's religion"—which it was not. He had long before the grave begun the business of a fresh heresy. What then was his religion?

The characteristic of Milton's religion was a combination of two things which hardly anyone else at the time did combine. These two things were the Calvinist worship of a monstrous God, and the antique worship of beauty.

But of these two elements the second was original in him from the beginning; the young Milton, the Milton before

[41]

thirty, the lyric Milton, had not in him the unmistakable tang
of the Manichæan: he as yet worshipped no Moloch. The intimate experience of his own family, the influence of his father,
the official spirit of the time during which he grew into manhood (he was born just after the Gunpowder Plot) made him
of course anti-Catholic, but this anti-Catholicism in him did
not exclude Pagan antiquity at all, nor did it at first exclude
that living tradition by which Catholicism stands for the ancient
culture of Europe and is nourished by the classics.

The ode to the *Nativity* might have been written by a warm
Catholic from beginning to end—and happy would it have been
for the large but confused Catholic minority in the England of
Milton's day had they been able to boast a rhyme of half such
power and value!

The Petrine allusion in the *Lycidas,* late as it came in his
youth, brought in though it be against the corruption (as he
thought) of an Establishment becoming hateful through Episcopacy, is in the same tradition. All the *Allegro* and all the
Penseroso are filled with that tradition. It is not till he begins to
engage in controversy that the Calvinist side of him develops,
and not till he had suffered grievous misfortune, embittering
him, that it comes to equal or nearly to equal his delight in
beauty. It was solitary contemplation—for which his mind was
only too well fitted—it was the turning over, unaided one may
say, of the great problems, that thrust Milton (as it has thrust
many another man) out of balance through excess of awe. He
dwelt on the overwhelmingness of God till at last he was almost
sunk into the religion of terror, and certainly sunk into the
Calvinist conviction of Election—with himself, of course, very
high indeed among the Elect.

Increasingly, as he grew older, did his religion become an-
thropomorphic: he sees his Creator as an elderly person, majes-
tic but revengeful, possessed of dreadful strength dreadfully
used, but still an old gentleman who acts and talks like one.

And it is through this conception of a God so limited that he drifted before the middle of his life into his Arianism, denying the full divinity of Christ, and into his denial of God's full creative power.

For Milton possessed to an exceptional degree that prime English characteristic—vivid visual imagination. It was later enhanced by his blindness, and it was a function also of his energy. That same quality of his which permitted him an equal activity of brain at sixty-five as he had had in his twentieth year, informed his visions with life. All Milton's mental images move and are: they work at their most vital when the man himself is nearest death.

Next in our estimate of Milton the man, we must remember that he passed in his thirty-fourth year through a violent emotional revolution: a moral earthquake.

It must be laid down of all men that character is impressed by experience; it cannot be otherwise, though secluded and quiet lives sometimes seem to run much the same for forty years and more, and in their age to retain the simplicity of youth. But in Milton's case the stamp of experience was very deeply marked, for it was an experience of humiliation and rage—a disaster coming upon him in the very midst of his powers, and one from which his serenity never recovered.

This stroke was his young wife's desertion of him, immediately after their marriage, in 1642. Had John Milton been less tempered the blow would have broken him: as it was it threw him into a paroxysm; fever entered his blood and remained there. He was ever afterwards watching Fate, expecting to be made a victim once more. When he actually *was* made a victim by the breakdown of the Commonwealth and the return of the King, the change of circumstance did not strengthen that mood—for that mood could not be strengthened—but it confirmed it. After the year 1642 Milton was always inwardly calling himself (as much during his greatest triumphs as during his worst misfortunes) the Chosen of God, and after 1660 he was a martyr, suffering persecution at the hands of God's enemies.

This inward rage strengthened him. The injustice on which he brooded was a stimulus and a support. To such a mood we owe the final miracle whereby in blindness, impoverished and amid the ruins of his cause, he produced the *Samson Agonistes* and completed *Paradise Lost*. Thanks to that mood he stands before us in the very last years at his full measure and even his early triumphs seem less memorable than his end.

Such was the inner background constantly: but meanwhile, as I have said, he was a man of sociable daily converse.

He was not without acquaintance, even in his latter political disgrace, and his circle was widespread. Society pleased him, and his fellowmen; they found him, on that account, good company enough; the more so from his sting of scorn—for he did not use this against those present, and men will always relish its application to others than themselves. Such acrid comment was emphasised by the peculiarity of his clear voice, for he spoke with what we call to-day the French "r," the guttural you so often hear in men from Devon and almost everywhere in England north of the Tees. This burr was thought by some to be the signal of his acerbity in criticism, and it was certainly a vocal accompaniment which gave that acerbity a special edge.

In all the considerable body of men of whom some he admired, a few respected and to many was attached in moderate fashion, he never discovered more than one strong friendship— his friendship with Deodati. All that emotion in the *Lycidas* is an artificial emotion—or perhaps one should say the emotion of an imagined death. When the death of that one friend did come—Milton was already thirty—he wrote what he had to write in a long Latin poem, the *Epitaphium Damonis*, very different in texture from the *Lycidas:* too conscious, too laboured. So throughout his life we look in vain for that note of intense affection which in the greater part of poets is the thing by which we may know them. We look for it in vain save in the one exception of Deodati among all the men with whom he associated: and of that intense friendship which bound him to Deodati he left no sufficient monument.

For the affection of women (I mean for the receiving of it) Milton was very ill fitted, and for the giving of it not fitted at all.

His relation with women in youth is unmistakable: he was afraid of them. It was a subject of jest among his equals during his earlier years, and a jest which he resented. But the laughter was legitimate. He boasted of that reserve in a discreet fashion, but the boast was insincere—he could not have broken his reserve in this matter, even had he willed to do so. When at last, very late, he made up his mind for an affair (it was of course to be a marriage) he must take a girl little more than a child whom he could approach the more easily because her family was in his debt. Why she left him he never understood, nor did he feel she had made reparation when she consented to return.

As with his first wife so with his children, he was at odds with them all. There was but one woman for whom he felt something which may have been gratitude and may have been attraction towards an imaginary image, for when he came to possess her he was already blind, and she died in little more than a year. This was his second wife, to whose memory he raised the enduring monument of a sonnet: among the best of his unequal sonnets. The third wife was good to him, she gave him the food he liked, ordered his household, and made his old age the easier; but there is no record of strong affection here.

It is strange when we consider all this, and blindness added on top of it, that the mind of John Milton was not oppressed by loneliness: by darkness yes, by isolation yes, but not, properly speaking, by loneliness. He was ever in a throng of acquaintance, whether through conflict or through visions. And here also the intensity of his character came in to save him. It thrust outward against the void; and though he never knew what others were, but saw everything in the light of his own excellence and certitude and eminence and the rest of it, yet he was, spiritually speaking, in the company of others all his life.

If he was spared loneliness, he was also spared all trace of penitence. He was one of those very rare men (some think them fortunate) for whom self-blame, let alone remorse, is inconceivable. A defect so absolute diminishes the man, and however much an admirer may share Milton's own self-admiration, that defect cannot be denied.

But we must set against that defect a good quality sprung from the same source—inflexibility in the achievement of a task. We all know the emotion aroused in us by the sight of a fellow-being unbowed to fortune, challenging even time itself and riding the deficiencies of the body. That admiration which we feel, that homage which we spontaneously pay to those who so carry themselves in the battle, must be amply paid to John Milton. Never was in the history of letters such a resurrection as that of *Paradise Lost*, of the *Samson*—the glory of his end.

The man had lived his considerable life, he had served his political and religious cause with vehemence, he had attained an eminence which seemed to guarantee him an unbroken security in fame, when, almost suddenly, all his supports broke down. The republican structure on which he had risen and by which he was maintained collapsed; he was in danger of violent death, of imprisonment, he was condemned to hide and (what for a man of his temperament was hardest of all) to silence. And he was condemned to all this with age coming upon him, and what would be the chill of it had he been as other men are.

His life had been lived and—by 1660—was apparently concluded.

But Milton would have none of that; he chose the moment to complete the very large thing which gave him not only much the most of his renown, but that element of solidity and permanence in fame which seems to adhere to achievements not only in proportion to their quality but to their bulk. And having done this, and spread out for the gaze of his fellow-countrymen that mountain range called the *Paradise Lost,* he was not content until he had set up one more isolated monument, that tall and single peak the *Samson.*

Then indeed the work was done and the character accomplished. Milton under the name of Samson had triumphed over his enemies, but not until Milton under the name of God Almighty had triumphed over the rebel Angels, nor until, under the name of Satan, he had made a fine and lordly thing of his throne in Hell—and all the while Milton as Adam was in imagination managing a wife for some few years without catastrophe, and moving in high company, giving good food to Archangels.

His egoism had served him well, and of all his qualities had best helped him to correspond with the gift of poetry extended to him by that Power (once called Apollo) which does extend it—which uses a man for its own purposes and makes him, side by side with his limited, defective humanity, also a Poet.

THE POET

Three characters distinguish Milton the poet, and in their perfection raise him to the height we know, far excelling Milton the man. The first is rhythm, the second visual imagination, and the third form.

The first two he acquired as an Englishman through an endowment quite beyond the ordinary with faculties which are essentially English; but the third, form, he got by the steeping of his youth in the classics, and notably in those of the Imperial Roman tongue.

To these three characteristics many would add a fourth, his continuous effort at the sublime; but this seems to me a department of his visual imagination.

When we speak of Milton's "rhythm" we mean an unfailing appetite for effect upon the ear of modulated sound and an almost unfailing power to achieve it—but also something greatly more. Rhythm is an essential of poetry. It is that by which poetry exists; for poetry is song. But poetry is also magic, and magic reposes upon the mystic quality of words. Nor is it only the words that make a poem—it is the order of the words, that is, the harmony wherein they are arranged. For though the Word is the stuff of a poem, and though the occurrence of the very Word is marked at once by the joy of the reader, yet the Word is what it is, and produces its effect, only because it stands where it does—a figure in the pattern, a member of the scheme.

By what process words so chosen and so ordered in exact arrangement illumine their theme with a divine light, we know not. Mysteries are never fully revealed, and the indwelling spirit of poetry is the most mysterious of human affairs. But the medium whereby the influence reaches us is, and can only be, rhythm: that which moves the dance and that which

breathes in music: that also which pulses throughout all creation and testifies to the living Spirit of God.

These melodies in verse of which rhythm is the soul draw
their vitality from a rich diversity; multiplicity is life, and the
vigour as well as the piercing loveliness of Milton's highest
lyric are the direct fruit of this gift. His loom was manifold.
For in Milton's reaching out for and grasping rhythm in his
English verse, from the beginning of his effort in childhood up
to his end upon the edge of the tomb, he was granted in
abundance a wealth of multiplicity.

I say "in his lyric." It is necessarily in the lyric that this
quality of rhythm is most apparent; and, if one may say so,
least subtle. But there is another department, peculiar in modern vernaculars to English poetry, the department of blank
verse—and in this the subtler values of rhythm made Milton supreme. In a sense he created English blank verse, for he lifted
it from stage use to pure literature, from the spoken, acted and
emphasised thing, to the thing read alone.

It is the second duty of rhythm after first it has built up a
form of verse to guard that form from monotony; and it is because Milton was so vastly endowed with multiplicity of
rhythm that he could boldly set out into that ocean of blank
verse, adventure in which he himself established, and the ex-
ploration of which has proved so perilous to those who came
after him.

The metre of English blank verse, used for thousands upon
thousands of lines in *dramas* before Milton's day, is a metre of
ten syllables arranged in five feet, that is, feet of two syllables,
each foot consisting of an unstressed syllable followed by a
stressed syllable—the same which, in Greek and Latin where
it is a matter of length and not of stress, is called an Iambic.

Use this metre exactly and the monotony becomes, when
merely read, not acted, intolerable. The danger of such monot-

ony is always present. We can discover it frequently even in the *Paradise Lost;* we find it lamentably repeated in the *Paradise Regained.* But this metre is, in good hands, capable of almost infinite variation. It is patient of redundant syllables. It admits inversion of emphasis, of the trochaic (one unemphasised followed by one emphasised), of the anapæst (two unemphasised followed by one emphasised), of ceaseless play between lesser and greater and stress in changing portions of a line; and in that great mass of Milton's work which falls under the definition of "heroic iambic pentameters," the avoidance of repetition in stress, the glancing rhythm within the line is perpetual, and the play upon the variations almost infinite.

It is true that the English language lends itself to this avoidance of monotony in regular forms by the very great choice it presents in length and stress of words: of this natural advantage Milton made full use. He did not create it, but he exploited it thoroughly.

For English possesses in perhaps equal number—at any rate in a vast number of either kind—powerful monosyllables both extended and abrupt which check the run of the line as by a curb. The extended word "strength," for example, or the abrupt word "rang." English has also monosyllables of another kind on which the voice lingers more gently and which it prolongs, the word "mourn," the word "far," for example. It possesses polysyllables that carry on the breath and the sense together; long, significant words with which you may solder together two halves of a phrase on doom, or end a chosen line on storm with a gradually accumulating sweep and thunder, as of a breaker on a beach. For example, of joining:

> "But him the Inexorable still refused";

of a crescendo:

> "Hissed on the shrieking shore and Ponderous plunged."

English possesses also in its numerous enclitics, its idioms compounded of muted half-pronounced sounds that are hardly adverbs or prepositions, but rather small servants to the main words, an inexhaustible store for filling the crevices of the metre. English has within itself material for a multiple effect as great as any that a language can proclaim. And yet with this language, as with any other, only the masters of the first rank can achieve that consistent and living variety in unity for which the universe is our model.

The famous opening words of the second book in *Paradise Lost* may show what I mean. Note how the syllables contrast with, perfect, hold, and then hasten on one the other and how this group of five lines make up between them one organic whole:

> "High on a throne of royal state which far
> Outshone the wealth of Ormus and of Ind
> Or where the gorgeous East with richest hand
> Showers on her kings barbaric pearl and gold,
> Satan exalted sat. . . ."

See how the two long and stressed syllables of *"throne"* and *"royal"* support each other, yet without repetition: how the long *"far"* at the end of the emphasised line carries on the ear through the next sentence of unstressed words whose appeal is through the use of unexpected place-names (in which, as we shall see, Milton excels). Then, in the third line, with *"gorgeous,"* the stressed long syllable appears again, striking in the midst, till the sharp monosyllable at the end halts the reader to prepare him for the liquid motion of *"showers."* Mark how this fourth line runs like the gems and metal it speaks of, in a cascade concluding with the tinkle and ring of their fall. Then the three final words, simple, decisive, bind up the picture together and present it, apparent to the mind as though to the living eye.

All this in Milton (and the careful analyst could present a book full) was instinctive: but it was also conscious and worked. It was inspired, but guided; and when the inspiration failed the guidance was at fault. But had the guidance altogether failed, we should have had fragments or isolated fine lines instead of that great and almost united heritage which Milton bequeathed to his people.

Sometimes intending a variety, he attains it not. This is notable for instance in the latter part of the *Penseroso* where there comes once and again something dangerously near jog-trot, and I have mentioned his numerous dulnesses in blank verse. Sometimes in his determination on variety he oversteps the mark, like a dancer who, attempting a difficult movement of the foot, slips and falls short. At the very opening of the ode on the *Nativity*, for instance, you get that in the second line. But nineteen times out of twenty the attempt succeeds, and succeeds as though success were inevitable; three syllables for two, introduced never so frequently as to break the unity of the passage. Even (now and then) a new word or a strange one (though Milton himself has forbidden their use and blamed the use of them by others) is thrust into the lucidity of his expression—not in order to give pause but to emphasise.

Note this further thing about the divine gift of rhythm vouchsafed to this man—that he never falls into the common fault of excessive alliteration, that is, the easy trick of accented syllables wherein one consonant sound is repeated for the sake of a violent rhythmical effect. To over-use this element is, in English verse, a permanent temptation, and one of our moderns (great enough, God knows, at his best), Swinburne, flaunted it, not as an aid but as the very spirit of his manner. Milton uses it permanently, but with subtlety, never allowing it to be master, never allowing it to be an end, or even a chief means. Alliteration should be a seasoning, not a meat, and in this just restraint for the thing—even some contempt for it—

Milton inherited as always from the classics. He kept in perpetual recollection what is due, even in poetry, to reason.

The visual imagination which was Milton's second strength I have called, like his sense of rhythms, national.

The exceptional power of visual imagination in the English explains much more than English verse, it explains English fiction and, in great measure, English history. The peculiar strength of this faculty in the English is to be seen in many another department of their activities—in the liveliness of their historical myths, in their succession of landscape painters, even in the taste of their populace for elaborate pageantry and ritual. It is seen also in those recurrent moments of intense emotion upon occasions often trivial and always far removed from the direct experience of the excited crowds. They will show a violent, though often brief, enthusiasm of hate, pity, or glory for things which are only names, the fall or the relief of a small post in the Antipodes, the misfortunes of some far distant figure, the virtues of one long dead supposedly heroic: Mafeking, Dreyfus, Drake.

Well, this character of intense imagination, of vivid pictures in the mind, fills Milton's poetry. Milton's whole verse is a series (in lyric as in epic) of strongly-lit visions—strongly-lit and clearly outlined too. The rout of the Old Gods in the ode to the *Nativity;* the mixture of some Italian mountain painting he must have seen and of English summer fields in the *Allegro,* a lighted window high up in its tower in the *Penseroso* —even the sudden words "thrice-great Hermes." It is all pictures; and the place to be given to this genius is of the sort we give to certain of the ancients, who can in a stroke of three words evoke a landscape as though they had created it before our eyes. So Virgil, "amica silentia Lunæ," in which a man can see the fleet, hardly heeling before a warm breeze by night, over the Mediterranean seas. So Milton, "apparent Queen unveiled." A man can see the moon veiled in cloud, and thence

[53]

emerging into full brilliance against the English sky upon a summer darkness. And is there not the very brushwork of the Renaissance Italians before you (and that of the contemporary Flemings) in "The mountains on whose barren breast," etc.?

This preoccupation, or rather this possession, of the man by the vision of earth and sky and sea ousted his sense of personality in the imaginary beings of his recital. None are very living, not even Charles Deodati as Damon. Edward King hardly appears in *Lycidas:* he is a shade; and of the crowds in *Paradise Lost* Satan alone has some substance.

It need not have been so; landscape and personality are not mutually exclusive; in Shakespeare the two go together. But for both to be present there needs ample room. With Milton persons and their contrasts were vague, or for the most part non-existent; contrariwise, he was intoxicated by landscape, and there again he was national.

It may be debated whether the landscape of Southern England moulded the English literary mind, or whether it was something in the national spirit (a fantastic suggestion—but then we are dealing with fantasy!) which, by preserving and moulding, created that natural beauty of the English habitation and external world. Englishmen could not have made the English skies, but they had much to do with what you see when you look down the vale of Severn from Bredon Hill. There is landscape in the largest sense, the landscape of earth and sky and the palaces whereby man has ennobled his habitation; there are ceaseless visions of such external things urging Milton, so that, when with his pen he wrote, as when in his blindness he dictated, in a facile stream, it is still great landscape which appears and reappears.

The picturings of this mighty artist, we may repeat, are affected by a determination on the sublime. That determination was in Milton a little too determined; it was a little too much of a task, closely connected with his private looking-glass as well: the mirror in which he saw himself as the mouth-piece of his Creator, as the privileged revealer of awful things, as not only a seer but a prophet. But where a mere biographer of Milton could, if he cared, make all this pride seem silly enough as a part of character, as an element in his verse it was of the highest value.

It is on this account, this fixed effort at the sublime, that Milton falls sometimes into the ridiculous and more often into the dull, yet has a strange power of making us forget these lapses and remains in our minds, after a long and full reading of him, the mighty figure that tradition accepts.

That tradition is just. The general reverence for Milton's name was no convention with our fathers; it proceeded from a lively sense of his exalted achievement, which sense, if our sons shall lose it, they will be the poorer.

Yet how frequent are these lapses and, in his later work, how astonishingly prolonged! In the second half of *Paradise Lost*, indeed everywhere after the first four books, one comes upon them as the traveller through a luxuriant hill country comes on a barren patch of sterile rock and sand. Take, for example, the intolerable three whole pages and more of Old Testament Précis in Book XII! There may be pleaded for it that it contains for our delight one of the worst lines in the English language:

"Egypt, divided by the River Nile."

For that gift we may be grateful; but it does not suffice.

He seems to have gone—especially in his last years—upon the principle that his election as the mouthpiece of God the Father permitted him everything. He could spout what he chose. It would all be divine in origin, and if some did not appreciate it the fault was theirs. In earlier youth it was not wholly thus with him, and we have his own record to show that one composition at least he laid aside incompleted and never resumed, having discovered his own failure. Query: Had his blindness something to do with this insensibility of his to his own defective effort in age? Perhaps it did add something to a native self-satisfaction. For the sight of the printed word aids criticism and many will admit that they can with difficulty judge verse in manuscript, and with more difficulty if it be only recited.

It has been said that the poetic gift excludes humour, but that saying is imperfect; it is not the poetic gift which excludes humour but rather the conviction of a mission which *tends* to weaken the critical sense, and therefore the quick distinction between what should be food for laughter and what not. The power of criticising one's own verse and selecting what shall survive, excluding what shall not, appears in varying degrees not according to the greatness of a poet's inspiration, but capriciously—now strong in a man who has only written verse of a secondary sort, and now so weak in a man who has written certain imperishable passages that one can get more enjoyment out of exposing his masses of rubbish than out of tasting his few successes. Intense appreciation of the ridiculous has actually made men poets, and with such the comic or grotesque or merely laughable stands in their work side by side with the liveliest lyric verse. So it was with Aristophanes and so it was with La Fontaine.

In Milton humour was so lacking that when he attempted attack in this form he is himself the object of our ridicule, and not the opponent whom he would have made our laughing-stock. We shall see this clearly enough when we come to the most absurd of his sonnets. And indeed all through Milton's work this incapacity for laughter appears. When Milton attempts humour it is as though some great ecclesiastic, devoted to high ceremony, were to stand upon his head before the altar. But when he attempts the sublime, there he triumphs: he triumphs in the very space, the very vastness of the scale upon which he can successfully work; he triumphs in the suggestion of unscaleable heights, of depth upon depth, of light supernal and of majesty.

I fear the present generation may think me ridiculous when I say that Martin seems to me the best illustrator of Milton. Well, so it is. The mezzotints and even the paintings of Martin render, I think, to the eye something near to what Milton saw within himself. They are not great art, but they correspond to their subject.

Then, lastly, we have *Form:* and in his worship of form we touch not only the very core of Milton's poetic nature, but the chief effect his work has had upon English letters. It was by this that he so nearly restored to us the classic sense, so nearly gave us for all the future a permanent vehicle which we have missed.

When a commentator in the generation succeeding Milton said of him that he was "An Antient born 2,000 years too late," this was what he meant; and the appreciation was just. He felt to his marrow the creative force of restraint, proportion, unity —and that is the classic. All the antique world lived by such a spirit. Not only our own direct ancestry of Greece and Rome, but the Assyrian and the Egyptian also. All was done within a Norm, whether the work were in marble or in song. Lyric and epic, history and the records of great lives, temples and market places and their statuary and their tablets were the monuments of this moulding force, this active simplicity. Rule and its authority invigorated the powers of man as pruning will a tree, as levees a pouring river. Diversity without extravagance, movement which could be rhythmic because it knew boundaries and measure, permanence through order, these were, and may again be, the inestimable fruits of the classical spirit. A common culture was heard in all verse and prose, seen in all building, so that a person, one soul—as it were, one God— breathed life into the whole.

Fools say that English is refractory to such high influence, and even boast that something in our nature forbids obedience to those trustees of beauty, to those warranters and guardians of great work which are called the classic laws. They have so debauched themselves with emotion sought to an extreme, have become so dependent on violent stimulus that they are drugged insensible to harmony; this evil having come upon them they excuse it by calling it inevitable and native to their blood.

It is not and cannot be so with any member of a commonwealth rooted in the great past of Christendom. It cannot be so with any that may still recover the half-forgotten tradition of Europe.

Those who so speak are like a man who, coming in on the glory of a Dodonian face, on such a revelation as the bended head from Albania lately given to Diocletian's baths in Rome, complains that it is cold, being without motion and of stone. If he will stand in contemplation before it and alone he will observe a mysterious life within and all that should communicate with the very inmost of his heart. Perfection breathes there; the divine awakes; the statue descends and lives.

Part Three

Lyric

Lyric

ORIGINS

MILTON was born in December 1608, in the full blaze of English verse at its noon. Spenser was but lately dead; Shakespeare had more than seven years to live. *Othello, Hamlet, Antony and Cleopatra* had just appeared. The sonnets, long known, were immediately to be printed and universal. All Milton's first years to his seventeenth were a preparation for the lyric.

From his childhood, from his first acquaintance with letters, he had been steered by circumstance to song; but song was for him introduced through the severe doors of scholarship and controversy. It is as a lyrical voice attempting flight that we approach his youth, but that youth was stamped with certain characters which were to determine all his strained career.

Two things powerfully affecting Milton's life were prepared for him long before his birth and are closely mixed with these first lyrical years. These two things are the deep religious cleavage within the Milton family, and the sources of the poet's material prosperity—that is, the money dealings and money-lending of his father.

At the end of the sixteenth and the very beginning of the seventeenth century, in the last years of Elizabeth's reign, the victory in the great religious quarrel of the past had been won: that victory had already been apparent after the failure of the Spanish Armada in 1588: it was clinched by the effect of the Gunpowder Plot in 1605-6.

The old religion was no longer, as Milton grew into boyhood, united or led. Those who regretted it were more and more divided between civil and religious loyalties. They were still at least half the country in numbers, but they had no programme; they had had no serious candidate for the English throne since the killing of Mary, Queen of Scots, in early 1587. Their opponents had enjoyed the support of all the organised forces in the State for forty years—that is, for all the active lifetime of a man. The pressure had been increasingly severe under the guidance of William Cecil's unique genius; this had been applied in just that crescendo and use of opportunity which gave to the Protestant victory a stamp of something irrevocable, and fated to succeed.

Nevertheless, though the victory was won, the fruit of that victory had not been garnered, nor was it certain what form the results would take. There was still this very large number—half England—who in varying degrees clung to the national tradition, the age-long Catholicism of the English people. It was inevitable that it should be so, for men do not lightly abandon the habits of a thousand years.

But the wide, confused host of those who still felt thus during Milton's childhood were of very varied emotions—emotions varied as much in quality as in intensity. Catholicism had been slowly identified with foreigners; the growing national feeling, the growing "religion of patriotism" was associated with the other camp.

It had been impossible since 1560 for all save a very few to practise the old religion, so that, for the masses who retained a strong attachment to it, that religion slowly became a tradition and a memory rather than an experience. In the last phase of this long process Cecil and those whom he had trained to govern conceived a policy which could not have been pursued in the earlier years, but which it was possible, half a lifetime before Milton's birth, to put into practice. It had long been treason to harbour a priest, treasonable to follow the ancient worship, and the last turn of the screw was to cripple the Conservatives of the governing classes by subjecting one who absented himself from the official Protestant worship at his parish church upon a Sunday to a fine the modern equivalent of which would be from £35 to £40 each time.

There had already been a vast turn-over in wealth following upon the religious change; the ruin of those among the gentry who adhered loyally to their ancient faith and the transfer of their property to those who had abandoned it. This last pressure would hasten the process, if indeed that pressure could be fully applied. But in the nature of things it could not be fully applied; only very rich men could pay such a fine regularly. It was demanded fitfully and sporadically; it was much more a threat than a regular levy, save in the case of some few whose fervour was known and whose fortune marked them out as obvious victims for those by whom the fines were collected at a profit. Yet here and there you would get some man, even of the less wealthy, who in his exasperation and enthusiasm would occasionally sacrifice the great sum demanded. He could not keep it up if he were of the middle class; a single payment would be but a "gesture"—and a fearfully expensive one. But (and this is the point) when that gesture was made it was a proof of the utmost intensity in conviction; it was next door to martyrdom. And here it is that we get the connection of all this with the Milton family.

The ancestors of John Milton the poet had been farmers, large and small, in the district lying immediately to the east of Oxford city and University. Most of them seem to have been small freeholders, whether in fee-farm * or wholly independent: some very well-to-do.

The one who was contemporary with Queen Elizabeth, Richard Milton, was of the latter kind. He was a yeoman; that is, a man possessed of land of his own, substantial, though not upon a scale that warranted gentility. He had presumably what we should call to-day from his rents and other sources to be mentioned in a moment the equivalent of some few hundreds a year. How much exactly we do not know, but if we were to say five or six hundred pounds a year, the income of a prosperous farmer, we probably should not be putting it too high—more likely too low.

This Richard Milton, already an old man in the last years before 1600, was also a local official: "Under-Ranger," if we are to trust tradition, in the Forest of Shotover—that is, the waste and partially wooded land lying on the heights near Oxford, which still bear the name of Shotover, though they have long ceased to be public property. A "forest" had meant for centuries not a district necessarily wooded, but a district outside the feudal system: not divided into Manors nor producing rents for the landed class, but under the direct government of the National Government, the King. The forests of England, wofully diminished in the past by encroachment of the wealthy, and of royal sale and gift to them, still formed a substantial fraction of the national soil in 1600; and those who administered them were civil servants under the Crown. Of such it seems was Richard Milton, adding his salary to the revenue of his land.

Now this man was among the most intense adherents of the old religion; and it is on record that he twice, for a period of

---

* We have already touched on this important matter of the English "Fee Farm." A homestead held of the lord of the manor *"in fee-farm"* was a full possession, heritable from father to son: a freehold. But it paid a small annual quit rent, or fixed due. Most English yeomen between, say, 1550 and 1650, were of this status. Later, after the Civil Wars, the great landlords destroyed and ate them up by the law they passed in their House of Commons, amusingly called "The Statute of Frauds."

half a year, went to the extreme of paying the fine (quite out of proportion to his means) which could legally be demanded of those who refused to be present at the parish church of a Sunday. He, out of that middle-class income or property of his (whatever it may have been), paid twice, at the end of two successive quarters in one year, the (to him) very large sum of well over £400 in modern money.

The effort cannot have been kept up long; it must have crippled him even to have made this once or twice as a protest, but it suffices to show how violent and tenacious was his attachment to his creed, and his corresponding hatred of its new official and persecuting enemies.

Now this old Richard Milton who thus suffered for the Faith had a son John, born probably at much the same time as Shakespeare; coming to London like Shakespeare as a young man, probably round about 1585. And the reason that he came to London was that his father had cast him out for throwing in his lot with the new official religion of the day.

What the young fellow's motives were—whether the common one that there would be no chances in life for those who remained attached to the defeated side—or from personal conviction, which did affect by this time a considerable number of the younger generation, at any rate so it was. He had gone over to what the old man regarded as the enemy, and the old man broke with him.

This young John Milton who so went forth to seek his fortune in London after the quarrel (still aided perhaps somewhat by his father, or it may be quite cut off and dependent on his new friends) was the father of the poet. The bitter quarrel was not a thing of once and for all, in spite of the cleavage between the old man Richard and his disinherited son John. It continued to affect the Milton family for years—indeed for the better part of a century. When John Milton had prospered, becoming a wealthy Scrivener,* three children survived of the many born to him; first a daughter, then some years later a younger child John, the poet; another boy, seven years younger than John, called Christopher.

Now Christopher as he grew up seems to have hankered after the ancestral Catholic tradition. Nothing is commoner, where there has been a bad family quarrel, than this division in the second and even the third generation, brothers and cousins taking opposite sides. So strong was this in Christopher that when he was in his turn prospering at the Bar he continued an open adherence to Catholicism, grave as the handicap was. It was only when James II made his great (but doomed) attempt at toleration that the man got his chance, and was raised to the Bench as a Judge. His eminence was sufficient to preserve him his pension even when, after the Revolution of 1688, he had been deprived of his Judgeship on account of his religion.

Such bitter and exasperated antagonisms were common in myriads of English families during that century of furious debate under the Stuarts before England settled down to social unity and to the accepted Protestantism of the succeeding hundred years. But in the particular case of the Milton family the quarrel has proved of national importance, for this reason: that it moved the poet from youth onwards to an increasing repulsion against the old religion and so lent the force of high verse to the growing Protestant Movement. This hatred of Catholicism appears perpetually in his writing; it is intense; it is only saved from wild excess by that respect for proportion which never left John Milton save when his vanity was offended.

* A Scrivener was one who drew up formal legal documents, looked after the affairs of those who bought and sold and mortgaged lands under such documents, and thereupon had opportunities for investing the money of others, often at his own discretion; or, in fashion more or less temporary, using the same to his own advantage, much as a modern solicitor does.

Now why was this family exasperation of John Milton against Catholicism of such great importance in the history of England? Because a nation is made great by its writers, and because it is *they* who form the national mind.

All official England from the early seventeenth century onwards was anti-Catholic, no one more so than Charles I and Laud in 1630-40; no one more so than the High Church members of the long Restoration Parliament after 1660. But even among the official leaders there was a faction which remembered, and half loved, though they were incapable of joining, the Catholic side of the battle. Had a chief literary figure, a powerful poet, been with the Catholics in this debate, or even indifferent, it would have made a great difference to the future. As it was, his exasperation against the Roman communion weighed the scales down heavily upon the other side.

The voice of Milton, growing to be in the long run the voice of England, was to be heard as a Protestant voice, filling the national air with its eloquence and pronouncement. It is true that if John Milton had (like his brother) harked back to the old family tradition and fallen in with Catholicism, he would never have become the national poet; yet would he have had great influence. Even had he been neutral, things would not have been the same; but being what he was from the beginning—anti-Catholic and increasingly so—he was particularly to affect the mind and character of the English people. It was only one unit: but it was a powerful unit added to the winning side.

So much for the first and main point of the two: Milton's religion. The second, the nature of the Miltonian fortune, though of high moment to the poet's life and the understanding of his character and its development, is not of the same major consequence.

That Milton was born in a well-to-do household and a household increasing its wealth was fortunate indeed for English

letters. Very great poets have been trained in anxious poverty
and perhaps in part inspired by it; but they could not live
serene, and the high dominance of Milton depends upon his
serenity. Never to have felt material anxiety, always to have
been well provided, gave him that warm balance, that sort of
eager repose which marked him for the classic temper. This
restraint, in his poetry at least (for no man was less restrained
in controversy), that worship which he paid throughout his life
to due measure in the use of words, has somewhat diminished
him for the moderns. Such diminishment is but a passing phase,
for Form endures, and Milton worked in granite.

Had this considerable family income proceeded from rents
in land or some other impersonal source connoting gentility,
the tale of Milton's life would have been other; but the source
of that income was of a very different kind—it was money-
dealing and money-lending. When John Milton the elder (the
poet's father) had come up to seek his fortune in London
(being backed by someone whose name we know not, but presumably of the new religion) he must have been advised to try
his hand at advancing money as a business—the door to which
trade the profession of Scrivener would open to him.

The Scrivener, as I have already mentioned in a note, was
ancestor to the solicitor of our day—perhaps it would be truer
to say one of the ancestors. His original function (before the
trade was thought important enough to have a Charter) was the
drawing up of documents essential to valid conveyance of real
estate by sale or bequest.

At first a Scrivener's chief quality for success was mere cal-
ligraphy—hence his name, "a writer." But it also meant an acquaintance with legal phrases and with the forms that leases
and sales and bonds and all the rest of it should take. In any
important matter of negotiation the Scrivener was necessary;
from knowing all about legal forms it was but a step to being
consulted on such things—and from that but another step to

giving advice for purchase, exchange and investment; from that but another step to what has been from that day to this the mark of the trade—money-dealing.

Clients would entrust funds to their chosen Scrivener, these clients would be content if they received the interest, leaving to him the trouble of investment and without following it too closely. There was opportunity, as there is to-day, for honest gains by commission and by fixed fees for special work done; but there was also opportunity for the sort of thing which lies at the origin of banking—that is, the use of another man's money without letting him know too much what you are doing with it. There was opportunity—at the worst—for embezzlement. It is noteworthy that John Milton the elder had in old age to suffer an action for the recovery of money which had been entrusted to his firm and which that firm was accused of misappropriating.

But for the moment we are not concerned with that—rather with the function of the Scrivener as a money-lender. John Milton the elder lent money at interest as part of his business, and among others he lent a sum (a considerable sum) to a certain man of gentle birth (or at any rate a gentleman by marriage) called Powell, living in the great house of one of those Shotover villages whence the Miltons themselves had sprung, the manor house of Forest Hill.

The deed was one of disguised usury—the common form of those days—whereby a smaller sum of money was lent upon the promise to repay a larger one at a later date. The deed in this case was one for £500, the equivalent of well over £3,000 to-day. And what is interesting, it was written down in the name of the younger John Milton, the poet, while he was yet but a lad at the University. In other words, his father took this form of providing the boy with certain maturing property.

Now the consequences of that piece of money-lending we shall find to be considerable. We shall find it at the root of that

[69]

which had so great an effect upon Milton's character and spiritual fortunes—his unfortunate first marriage with the daughter of his embarrassed debtor. For Milton's first wife, Mary Powell, was the child of the Lord of the Manor of Forest Hill, part of Shotover outside Oxford, the place whence the less well-born but more prosperous Miltons arose.

Remembering these two essential circumstances in the forming of the young poet's mind, his father's prosperity through money-lending and the vivid religious quarrel which so nearly touched that house, let us turn to his growth.

To explain a man as thoroughly as may be (to explain him fully, even in so simple a case as Milton's, is impossible), a first necessity is to know his childhood. The effect of early experience upon later character has not the all-importance which a modern fad gives it, but it is very important. The cleric who said—some three hundred years ago, I think—that the first seven years determine life, exaggerated; but to neglect them is to exaggerate much more: moreover one must carry on the age to fifteen or sixteen in judging a character largely formed, as Milton's was, by reading.

Now we can rarely know the early years of a man long dead; they are not the years in which contemporaries remark him. The best evidence (when you can get it sincere) is that afforded by the memories of the man himself, especially if he records those accidents, chance influences, which seem to have little importance, but which are of such profound effect—for instance, the childish dream of St. Anselm when he found himself, in sleep, upon the snows of the Gran Paradiso.

Now in the matter of Milton, though the man was overfond of describing himself, we have very little of this kind. He gives us a few phrases upon his early studiousness and there is a word or two of Aubrey's (transmitted after many years) upon his youthful scribbling. Most of our evidence here is external. We know the circumstances which surrounded him and something of his physical condition. He lived his childhood in the good City house of his birth, at the sign of the Spread Eagle, which was in Bread Street, out of Cheapside to the south, in the heart of London. He lived there from when he was coming to notice the world around him through boyhood and adolescence. These were the years in which the religious revolution—confirmed by William Cecil a lifetime before and very gradually making its way through the English people—had turned the corner and was firmly established. He was a little boy of four when Robert Cecil died, having accomplished his father's work and seen to it that the England of the future should be Protestant.

His great contemporary, the Catholic Ben Jonson, was thirty-three years his senior. He had all around him in childhood and youth the impression of that divided England where what had been an official faction in his father's day was becoming the majority of the nation. A very large body of Englishmen were still attached to the ancient religious traditions of the country, and among them a considerable proportion openly declared their sympathy with the Catholic past, while a much smaller number felt so intensely as to sacrifice their fortunes in opposing the new religion.

The household of the money-dealer and lawyer in Bread Street was naturally on the extreme of the official side. It was not only Protestant, it was also, in tendency, already Puritan. But only in tendency: open Puritanism, as early as 1608-20, was the badge of an as yet small though rapidly growing body, to which the Scrivener would have no very good reason to adhere. He had every reason to be official, but the Official Religion, the established church, was opposed to all extravagances and enthusiasms. The Court, during these central years of James I (who had come to England as King five years before John Milton's birth and did not die till the lad had passed sixteen), was gay and coarse. The wealthy who guided society disliked

[71]

any criticism of their pleasures. The best literature—and men of letters counted for much in that older England—was devoted to Beauty and contemptuous of her enemies: but the hatred of Beauty as of Joy was the very mark of the Puritan.

England still hated Puritanism; the burgesses of the City of London were less fixed in their opposition to the new Puritan zeal than the rest of the country: also the proportion of Catholic-minded people among them was less than elsewhere. Anyhow, for a man with the character of John Milton the elder, bent on business advantage, the position was clear. There could be no advancement in affairs save through the Established and Official Church. To its anti-Catholicism he heartily subscribed and in this his eldest son, John Milton the younger, was trained.

Apart from the obvious professional advantage of such a position there was the strong family reason for it—the original quarrel of this Scrivener with his father (the poet's grandfather) in the matter of religion. There was the ever-present peril of some new family trouble, because the natural desire to return to Catholicism reappeared in the Scrivener's younger son, and indeed the danger of a general Catholic recovery still appeared as a menace—though a dwindling menace—to all that was now Protestant in the nation.

The child John Milton, then, lived those first years in the atmosphere of the now well-rooted governmental Protestantism, within the framework of which emotional appeal would later be to what may be called a vaguely Calvinist, or diluted Calvinist, tone of thought.

Apart from this moral atmosphere there were certain social conditions affecting the child and his future. In the first place there was that material ease, that sufficiency of money, for leisure and for the amenities of his rank in life, which Milton enjoyed right on until the troubles of his later middle age. One effect of this was to give Milton a class feeling which increased as his life developed, until he came to despise and hate the populace. He had side by side with his power of vision the contempt which the burgess feels for the artisan; and at the same time the gulf which the burgess feels between himself and the great world above him. He had planted in him a middle-class contempt for the masses, which comes out continually in his controversies and increases with age, until he has persuaded himself at the end of his life that they are of a different spiritual stuff from himself.

To this material ease we may ascribe, in part at least, the lack of adventure in Milton's character. In youth he isolated himself because, being well-to-do, he was able to do so without discomfort; but it did not prove to his advantage, especially in his relations with women. At any rate he had never known poverty or even strain, and all his earliest recollections were those of sufficient wealth.

The next point, also making for isolation, was a difference in years between himself and his only immediate companions. He had properly speaking no playmates. His only sister was several years older than himself, his only brother seven years younger. At school he made only one friend, but a very close one: such a devotion as the isolated feel.

A fruit rather than a cause of his isolation was that passion for methodical study which began to possess him from the very beginning of life. His father encouraged it, and it was clearly an appetite in him, a desire, for it grew stronger with every year that passed. Such industry left him possessed, when at last his sight failed after his fortieth year, with an astonishing mass of full, not sporadic, instruction; the whole of it classified, at his fingers' ends. His childhood being full of the beginnings of scholarship and widespread learning these flourished and increased in him like a vigorous tree. They nourished and filled him, but they had one evil effect in that they gave him a sense of his own value inordinately swollen. There was certainly food for pride in such erudition, but, in his spiritual loneliness, Milton's pride grew out of all bounds.

Yet another influence surrounding that childhood was music; on account of his father's devotion to that art (or entertainment) we are certain that the very first artistic impressions to reach the child were those of music. The household was a resort of those who felt as it did in such things; and the importance of music was impressed upon this child by all the conversation around him. But the connection between music and the poetic art must here make us pause and consider exactly what its effect on Milton as a poet may have been.

To begin with, we must admit that the influence of music upon the life of Milton was very great—but did it affect his verse? I think not. How much he cherished music we discover from some of the best and some of the worst of his verses; from the superb line on "Heaven's great organ" or the sufficient "on hearing a solemn music" to the dry and awkward sonnet in praise of Lawes. When something in a writer's life is spoken of by him not only in the best of his work but in the worst, then may you be certain that that thing is a constant concern.

But does a constant concern with music affect a man's style in verse, let alone advance it? The conclusion would be facile that the poetic gift and an attachment to music were connected, and even identical, but such a conclusion would be false. Very few of the poets, great or small, have been affected by music beyond their fellow men. To many of the best (Baudelaire, for instance), music has seemed "a disagreeable noise." At the best we may say that the poet is inclined to *song*, and it is true that all the verse worth calling verse is a kind of song; it is also true that when the writer attempting verse fails to give it a kind of songfulness he falls off the poet's throne and is on the ground: or (more often) has never ascended that throne. The poets are many who having written songs have had tunes in their head for them, and there are some few who have composed the airs as well as the words. There are others to whom an air has suggested his words, and of these Shelley is perhaps the most famous and that tune which inspired him with "I rise from dreams of thee" is as lovely as its verbal fruit; the marriage between speech and song can be perfect.

Yet is there no true connection between the excellence of verse and the musical art, especially when that art suffers the complexity of harmonics. Poetry is essentially simple; it is one voice expressing itself in one succession to which there can be no accompaniment. There is no counterpoint about Poetry. If we narrowly observe those who, in their modern multitude, are most easily inebriated by the emotions of complicated music, we shall find them as a rule the worst critics of verse.

Certainly in his father's case a passion for music was very hostile to the understanding of what poetry should be. John Milton senior was guilty of some of the very worst lines ever penned—it is to the fame of his son alone that we indirectly owe their preservation.

I write that phrase unhappily, for it would seem only right that the very worst verse should have a shrine of its own, and should be remembered for ever. There is something great about such depths of badness.

These two things in Milton, his love of music, his poetic art, must, then, be kept separate; the one does not explain the other, and Milton's love of music, his inheritance in music, his comprehension of music, belong to Milton the man not Milton the poet. For Milton the poet they might be a theme, a subject; they were in no way a creative force. Indeed there is far less actual presence even of song in Milton's verse than in that of most poets; less than in his model, Spenser; less than in that mighty senior in whom his youth had so much delighted, Shakespeare.

I do not allude in this to Shakespeare's conventional tribute to music; I mean the lilt of his Lyrics, which do certainly sing themselves, and which, since most of them presumably enshrine something, or much, of popular traditional lines, were no doubt also composed with some popular airs in mind. "Sweetheart mine, where art thou roaming?" can hardly be presented without notes, nor can "When that I was a little tiny boy": and these are like hundreds of their peers—for instance Du Bellay's exquisite *Hymn to the Winds*. But Milton hardly ever has such dances.

   .   .   .   .

The chief thing to remark in Milton's school life at St. Paul's, near his father's city home, was that unique friendship of which so much mention has already been made. From boyhood he was linked closely with Charles Deodati (whom the English also called "Deodat").

This lad, who was much of Milton's own age, a few weeks younger, was at St. Paul's with him, and there grew up between them an affection which illuminates the poet's life until his thirtieth year.

This boy, Charles Deodati, was only half Italian in blood. His name and part of his family tradition were Italian and he may have had something of the Italian spirit which bent his friend's mind continually towards Italy; but neither the blood nor the culture of young Charles Deodati was in the main Italian.

The story of his father's presence in England is what one might expect; the grandfather had been one of those numerous Italian Protestants (numerous at least among the intellectuals) who dot the later Renaissance; those of whom Giordano Bruno had been the most powerful and the most repulsive. But this grandfather Deodati had not been of Giordano Bruno's pantheist school; he inclined more to what may be called the "straightforward" Protestant movement, the new Churches, and of course, in particular the Genevan Calvinist. He left Italy for Geneva; one of his sons became famous there as a theologian;

another, fairly well known in medicine, came over to England, married wealth and settled down as a physician in this country. This was the father of Charles, young Milton's friend.

Very much of the little we know on Milton's youth was the result of that friendship. The two corresponded in Latin, each stimulating the other to the composition of Latin verses— wherein young Milton was to excel. It was doubtful at one moment of his youth whether Latin would not be Milton's chief medium of expression; it was by deliberate choice that he determined, somewhat later, to practise in his native language. It is a choice for which we may be grateful; reminding one of Gibbon's similar determination, but not in his case spontaneous. For Gibbon acted on the advice of a friend. He was persuaded to write his "Decline and Fall" in English rather than French on being assured that the expansion of the Transatlantic colonies would ensure him an audience with posterity.

Verse, be it remarked, was in these early years of Milton's a habit, a task; an occupation second only in the time he gave to it to his devouring studies, and coming before his studies in the importance he attached to it. He had begun versifying when he was still a little boy of ten, if we are to accept (as I think we ought to do) the traditional account of him current in the next generation. It is a common enough failing or pastime in childhood, it continues with many into early manhood: but here with Milton it became something more. He saw himself from the very beginning as a dedicated Poet: a *Vates:* a priest of the Muses: a creature superior through inspiration to the ruck of mankind. He was writing as early as his fifteenth year verse which he thought worth keeping. It was religious verse, of course, for religion was the preoccupation of the scholastic world in which he lived.

Those early verses were imitative, but they are on that very account valuable to us because we thus discover the sources on which he had worked. I say "on which he had worked" rather than "which inspired him," for that is a next point in all that Milton did. Let those who do not understand the nature of poetry remember that this very great poet wrote in order that he might produce exercises in verse; all that he did was of set purpose, hammered out, polished craftsmanship from beginning to end. Without the Muse such diligence and such detachment would have destroyed the poetic value of the output; but with the Muse that value was enhanced by industry.

These two early fragments (adaptations of Psalms) have the further advantage to us that they disclose what is essential in Milton as a writer of verse—his incapacity to avoid occasional true poetry in all he wrote under the poetic form. Save in a few exceptions which will be later remarked, he never wrote so badly or so dully but that there would thrust out in the midst of it a memorable shoot of genius, even if it be only one word, such as the famous "tawny kings." Another before him had used the word "tawny" once at least, of Africans, as he did; but I think he found it; I doubt his copying it. The word was suggested to both men by the lion, and it is good.

Deodati left St. Paul's School for the University, for Oxford, at fifteen; Milton for Cambridge two years later, in the Lent term of 1625, some few weeks before the death of James I and accession of King Charles. He was entering his seventeenth year. He was there to spend at Cambridge the next seven years of his life and to fulfil the complete ritual which ended in those days with a Mastership of Arts.

CAMBRIDGE

Those days were the second or middle phase of the two ancient English Universities, when they were being transformed through the general transformation of England which had begun with the great revolution in religion of 1560-1600.

The later mediæval University had been a place where endowed scholars of all classes, but mainly of the less wealthy, were able through the charity of the founders to acquire the Humanities. The Universities were wholly clerical; and the lads who had been under the discipline and tuition of those austere but decayed colleges passed, for the most part, into the clergy. Their seniors who taught them were of the same kind and had been undergraduates of the same kind in their time.

The modern University, as we had it in England during the eighteenth and nineteenth centuries, was, in the main, a playground for the younger men of the wealthier classes; but it was also a testing place in which the members of those then governing classes could be watched and judged. The University preserved, of course, even on into the nineteenth century, a certain proportion of learners from the less fortunate English families, though never, or hardly ever, from the masses of the people, the human material which had originally supplied it in the earlier Middle Ages.

The seventeenth century in this as in everything else was a transition between the old popular Catholic England and the new aristocratic England that was to come. Increasing numbers of undergraduates were coming to the colleges of Oxford and Cambridge from the wealthier land-owning families and with them the sons of the great merchants and prosperous lawyers. The social centre of gravity at Oxford and Cambridge had shifted by the time the young John Milton, but lately passed

[79]

his sixteenth birthday, entered at Christ's on the 12th of February 1625.

The mark of the change in the University system was that an increasing number of lads were paid for by their parents and enjoyed privileges giving them a higher social position in the College than living upon the old endowments would have done. It is remarkable how high that payment has already become. Although the young boys had no luxury (they slept two or four in a room) John Milton's father had to find much what a modern parent would have to find to put his son in the same position, that is to say, rather more than £300 a year. On such a sum the sons of well-to-do families would enter as "lesser pensioners": only a few of the very wealthy counted as "greater pensioners" and sat with the Fellows of the College at the High Table. The old equality of the earlier Middle Ages had been long forgotten.

Christ's, of which the boy thus became a member, was a College of some importance. It had a total membership on its books, Dons, graduates and undergraduates in residence or gone down, of close on three hundred; and in so considerable a body the new arrival was lost and undistinguished.

He remained of no especial prominence during all those seven years, though his scholarship was precocious and remarkable and though his Latin verses (which he wrote in profusion) were excellent, though his industry and accumulation of learning were noted. He left, at the end of his course, a young man in his twenty-fourth year, with a name retained by some few among them but, as might be expected, with his genius little known and himself not yet conspicuous.

Of those seven years during which John Milton passed through his adolescence and matured, two things must be remembered.

The first is that he, thus obscure, produced in the very middle of the time, unnoticed, one of the high masterpieces of English lyrical verse. Christ's had possessed without knowing it a captain among the poets of the English. That masterpiece was the Christmas Ode which he composed on coming of age.

The other, less memorable, point concerns Milton the man rather than Milton the poet; but it had a deep effect upon his life. He was refused his Fellowship.

It will be best to deal with this second point first, and we must begin by appreciating what a Fellowship meant in those days. It meant as it means now security, an established academic position and a sufficient income (though not on the modern scale). It hall-marked a man as it does now; for a College was not supposed to elect a Fellow incompetent to teach or profess the kind of learning in which he had graduated. It generally connoted the taking of Holy Orders in the official State Church and, when the man should marry, the provision of a living for him in one of the parishes of which his College had the patronage. A Fellowship was already, also, something of a small social honour.

Now Milton had no need to demand economic security of his College as a reward for his remarkable scholarship. He was the son of a substantial lawyer and money-lender who had only two other children—a daughter already married off and one younger boy. Nor was the refusal of a scholarship what it is to-day, a sort of blame attaching to any conspicuous name among the younger gown.

To-day if a senior scholar who has proved himself in the schools and is among the first of his kind is candidate for a Fellowship, to refuse it him is to send him into the world disgraced. It is as though the Fellows of the College had said, "You may be brilliant, but your learning is not solid"; or "You may have an academic standing, but your character leaves much to be desired." In Milton's day the disgrace was not so deep. Still, to be refused a Fellowship when one had attained a certain academic position and clearly desired election was a disagreeable incident and could be used against a man in later life. It was so used against John Milton. It was, indeed, only so used by his enemies and they talked very exaggeratedly about it; they said that the University had "spew'd him out"—and that was much too strong. But it is true that Cambridge saw fit not to give Milton its academic hall-mark. Cambridge said, as it were, "We understand that you are of some promise; we think you above the average in your studies, you are most proficient in the dead languages and something more. But you are not altogether desirable and we do not regard you as being quite up to our level."

He had not impressed the authorities of the College by any reputation for power in the writing of English verse—from what we know of the English verse written by some of those Dons they were hardly capable of judging, and anyhow excellence in English verse is no ground for a Fellowship.

Why did the Dons of Christ's (and no doubt the same would have been true of the Dons of any other College) thus reject him? It was because there was something not amenable in the lad as he grew up; a power of sarcasm emphasised by that roll of the letter "r" in his gullet, "a sure sign" said a contemporary, "of a sarcastic temper."

John Milton had good manners, he had charm, he could get on well with people whom he desired to please; but the young man could not conceal his sense of superiority and his corresponding contempt for those whom he felt—rightly enough—to be his inferiors. That was against him: Dons are uneasy in the presence of Genius.

It may also be that another thing against him was an obsession appearing early enough in his life, in embryo at least—perhaps not long after his twentieth year: a reaction against religious authority.

He, long after, explaining why he had not taken Holy Orders as his family desired him to do—it would have been the natural sequel to a successful University career unless he chose to follow his father's trade—said that he had been "outed" by the Bishops.

Like most of Milton's pronouncements on his own grievances the thing was an afterthought to explain something which he did not define and was perhaps not fully conscious of at the time. When he graduated, just after coming of age, he subscribed to the regular formula of the State religion, the supremacy of the King in all things spiritual and ecclesiastical, and (a critical point in the debates of the day) that "the order of Bishops is not against the word of God." There is no document remaining to show that he had as yet any objection to the organisation of the national Church under a hierarchy: and after all he was very young.

Nor—in what he wrote at least—had the strongly Protestant feeling in this matter yet appeared; it was not widespread in families such as his. For though Calvinist Archbishop Abbot was losing power and Laud was rising there is no sign of Milton's feeling at the time one way or the other. Plenty of young men in the low church party were being ordained, and Laud himself and the right wing of the Established Church were Protestant enough. Nor were the authorities of his College hostile to the rising feelings which were—much later—to make Milton a protagonist against Episcopacy.

Rather was it Milton's intensity that lost him his Fellowship. The same thing that made the lad quarrel violently with his tutor (and he seems to have been sent down for a short time after his matriculation as the result of that quarrel), compelling the authorities of the College to find him a new one, may have impelled him to unwise jibes in the matter of ecclesiastical organisation.

At any rate the thing stands and it is significant; John Milton, a young man of outstanding scholarship, much more learned than the bulk of his fellows and sufficiently distinguished among them to merit promotion, as a matter of course was refused his Fellowship.

It is sometimes said that the disgrace was due not to any illwill on the part of the Dons (who thus made fools of themselves before posterity) but to the intervention of the new young King of England in favour of another. That excuse will not hold water, nor avail the Fellows of Christ's. It is true that their first election to a Fellowship at a time when they might have chosen Milton fell upon a certain Edward King, and that this candidate was chosen because, though four years younger than Milton and two years junior to him in College standing, they had received a command from the King, Charles I, to give the young fellow this job.

Edward King was a blameless young man with much influential backing, the son of a father who had spent his life in the Public Service, connected with the government of Ireland under Elizabeth, under James I, and still now under Charles. That father was not very wealthy—Edward King himself was entered as a junior pensioner like John Milton—and no doubt the revenue of the Fellowship was a thing worth having for him. At any rate, the Royal command could not be passed over. But that *won't* excuse the Dons, for there were two later vacancies to which Milton might have been elected and from which he was also excluded.

So much for that. The incident is not enormous; it did not leave any violent resentment in Milton's own mind; he could get on without a Fellowship, and we may repeat that the honour did not mean quite what it means now; but it is significant of his standing and of certain difficulties which had already appeared in his dealings with others, though certainly his temper was not yet in any way soured.

The other matter of those seven years, the very great matter in the story of English letters, was young Milton's Ode on the Nativity of Our Lord.

He produced this, as we have seen, in the first weeks after his twenty-first birthday, just after the Christmas Day of 1629, in the opening of 1630; it was already known in manuscript when, in the latter part of that same year, Edward King was elected a Fellow of Christ's. It may be presumed that none of the Dons had an idea of what had appeared—that a new and very bright star had arisen and was to shine permanently splendid in the heaven of English lyric verse. The poem was not to be printed for some years, and they may be excused on that account, as also when we remember that the academic atmosphere is not one in which great verse is recognised until it has passed into text-books and anthologies.

The Ode on the Nativity came after a considerable production of verse on Milton's part; it was to be immediately succeeded by further and inferior work. It is likely enough (we might almost say, certain) that he did not himself know how great was the thing he had done. Yet one would have thought that only to read it, especially to read it to oneself half aloud, should convince any man who knows what poetry is.

Listen to this; hackneyed though it be, it is only hackneyed because it is part of the current wealth of mankind:

> "But peaceful was the night
>   Wherein the Prince of Light
> His reign of peace upon the earth began.
>   The winds, with wonder whist,
>   Smoothly the waters kissed,
> Whispering new joys to the mild Ocean,
>   Who now hath quite forgot to rave,
>   While birds of calm sit brooding on the Charmèd wave."

And to this:

> "Ring out, ye crystal spheres!
>   Once bless our human ears,
> If ye have power to touch our senses so;

> And let your silver chime
> Move in melodious time;
> And let the bass of heaven's deep organ blow;"

Repeat that line which the young man was privileged to write by the inspiring powers, "And let the bass of heaven's deep organ blow."

One might quote for ever, but it would be treason not to print here the concluding vision:

> "And all about the courtly stable
> Bright-harnessed Angels sit in order serviceable."

That second line is a consolation to carry with one throughout life: and yet it is not the summit of the splendid thing. The summit is in the last lines of the penultimate stanza:

> "And the yellow-skirted fays
> Fly after the night-steeds, leaving their moon-loved maze."

There you have the English lyric in all the wealth of its glory. After he had written that there was no more doubt that this pen was guided by the Gods.

Yet in what he had hitherto written in verse (and we have seen that he had scribbled away from childhood) there was nothing on the same level. The poet had pierced here and there in the lines he wrote upon the death of his little baby niece when he was only seventeen, especially in the Spenserian description (and it was Spenser whom the young Milton had most devoutly read) of the car of winter,

> "Icy-pearled,
> Through middle empire of the freezing air."

He had suffered, as youth being imitative must always suffer, from the poetic vice of his time, the "conceit," that is, the quaint and forced comparison. There is something of this even in the Christmas Ode here and there; in the opening especially, where he pictures the earth clothing herself in snow in order to look pure.

In his Latin verses, written the year before to commemorate the Gunpowder Plot, there is already that strong visual imagination, those "pictures in the mind" which later mark all he did; the vision of Satan hovering over the world (the same as later inspired George Meredith's sonnet), and the white rim of breakers making a frame round Britain; but there is nothing to foreshadow the swift emergence to the very climax of the English lyric which those twenty-seven Christmas stanzas are. These are separate and apart. They are like some piece of storied enamel, from which here and there flakes have chipped off, showing the rusty metal below; but the whole glorious with colour and flashing, here and there, with peculiar encrusted gems.

Those who would understand the fate of Milton, what happened to him during his nearly seventy years of life, most of them passed in conflict and in trial, should especially note this about the triumph of the Christmas Ode, that it is in the older religious traditions of England.

This young man who had just come of age stood, as we know, on the further Protestant wing of that society; but the old religion was in his immediate background, and the Ode to the *Nativity* is as much a part of the European tradition in Divine things as any Italian picture of the Mother and the Child. The man who, after the tragedy which fell upon him a dozen years later, was to question more and more the central doctrines of the Christian religion, was still unquestioning. The man who before he died was to argue exhaustively against the Godhead of Our Lord, introduced his first masterpiece with the words, "the Infant God."

The whole of the great Ode is soaked in that Catholicism which has been called by modern men (more unbelieving than Milton himself in old age) "the great romance of Europe." If

[87]

while we read Milton's later secret attack on religion, the *De Doctrina,* we lay down the book for a moment and murmur to ourselves some passage from the Christmas Ode, there comes upon us some such feeling as comes also upon a man who, in the fatigue and disappointment of age, recalls, in a sudden vision, the radiance of his youth.

This triumph is emphasised—framed as it were—by the weakness of the earlier efforts and the insufficiency, and occasional real badness, of what immediately followed. For what immediately followed the Ode was an abortive effort on Our Lord's Passion, and the memorial lines on Lady Winchester.

The effort on *The Passion* John Milton had the grace to abandon after the eighth stanza. He was right. It fails altogether. It reads as though he had tired of it almost before he began. He gave it up deliberately, and it is the only example (so far as we know) in all his career of sufficient self-criticism. He was not a man to admit his own failures easily, and he was lacking (as so many very great poets have been) in a critical faculty for judging his own performance severely enough to sacrifice it. It is this lack of critical power which allowed him to publish mighty poor stuff in the sonnets, with good stuff, and stuff of the very first quality, side by side with the bad.

But there are two fragments, one of which we know to belong to the months immediately succeeding the Ode to the *Nativity*—and written therefore much at the same time as *The Passion*. They are the fragment *On Shakespeare*, the date of which is fixed by the figures 1630 attached to it in the first printed collection, presumably at the author's authority—and the *May Morning*.

The first was not printed until it appeared in company with other eulogies as a sort of introduction to the Second Folio, in 1632, two years later. It was therefore, we may presume, spontaneous, written for no set occasion, and certainly it reads as though it were unpremeditated and immediate.

It is the most naïf, the least worked, the most exuberant piece of rhyme John Milton ever wrote down. It runs all of a piece, immediately, from the source, and it is enthusiastic as he very rarely was, later on, about anything other than himself and his visions. It is young, is this "Epitaph on the Admirable Dramatick Poet W. Shakespeare."

It starts from scratch at the top speed of a hundred yards' sprint:

"What needs my Shakespeare, for his honoured bones."

It remembers Spenser in the phrase "Star-y-pointing." It condenses very finely (as to sound) a conceit too involved as to sense ("Dear son of Memory, great heir of fame" wants unravelling and checks the flow: thousands quote it who could not tell you what it means). It ends in a much too elaborate conceit with another irrational phrase ("our fancy of itself bereaving")—but it is *alive*.

The second fragment is the ten lines *On May Morning*, the date of which can only be guessed; but it is easy to believe that they belong to an earlier rather than to a later year, for there is a suddenness about them and a simplicity which Milton, while he increased in power, did not recover.

It is in truth a song—one of his few. It is song in the exact sense of a restricted composition suggested by a tune or suggesting a tune, requiring the human voice as one reads it. *That* was not native to Milton save in one or two examples written for the *Comus*. And these were much more done to the order of Lawes's music than produced at Milton's will alone. No, he was not a writer of songs; and sometimes, when he is compelled to adopt such a form, he breaks down; witness the choruses in *Samson Agonistes*. Nor is he here very successful, though the fourth line, bad as horticulture, is charming as sound. Here it is, that the reader may judge:

"Now the bright Morning Star, Day's harbinger
Comes dancing from the East, and brings with her
The flowery May, who from her green lap throws
The yellow cowslip and the pale primrose.
Hail bounteous May that dost inspire
Mirth, and Youth, and warm desire!
Woods and groves are of thy dressing;
    Hill and dale doth boast thy blessing.
Thus we salute thee with our early song,
    And welcome thee, and wish thee long."

Before he left the University he failed again, by trying his hand at the comic in two short pieces; couplets upon the old University carrier, Hobson, whose death at the beginning of 1631 moved many rhymsters to some exercise of the kind. Milton would have done better to have kept out of that crowd. His efforts at laughter were never successful, and here he actually divagates into punning—for which he was not made.

In the next year he did produce, without suppressing it, a dirge upon the death of Lady Winchester, which is again far below the standard we associate with his great name. He was in his twenty-third year when he wrote it, some time after April, which was the month of that lady's death in 1631.

This new Winchester title was a very wealthy one; the young couple were therefore socially famous, and the death in childbirth of the bride became, for not a few, a chosen theme. But to that theme John Milton did not rise. Here was immense wealth, considerable inheritance in blood, close connection with the men who had made the great religious revolution and established the new England; for this John Paulet, the fifth Marquis of Winchester, was a great-grandson of William Cecil, as well as heir to a huge legal fortune.

The bad verses here and there (as perpetually happens in Milton's failures) flash out into a piece of indubitable poetry. After such mere dust as:

"The honoured wife of Winchester,
A Viscount's daughter, an Earl's heir,
Beside what her virtues fair
Added to her noble birth
More than she could own from earth
Summers three times eight save one
She had told, alas too soon," etc.

you get a couplet which is the real thing. It is in the passage
upon Hymen, the God,

"And in his garland as he stood
You might discern a cyprus bud"

and again, thirty lines further down the long composition,

"Here be tears of perfect moan
Wept for thee in Helicon."

This is not superlative, though it has the ring. But it does not
save the thing, for all the rest is on a much lower level, and the
end is a bathos: He sees the unfortunate young wife in Heaven:

"With thee there, clad in radiant sheen,
No Marchioness, but now a Queen."

—which is deplorable.

All this must be said if we are to understand the surprising
adventures of Milton's first affair with his Muse, how, woman
that she is, she befriends him and turns against him alternately.

The truth is (I think) that it was part of his immaturity, of
his very slow development, of his imperfect introduction to the
fulness of life—which in due time was to produce the tragedy
of his first marriage.

He was still hesitant in these last days at Cambridge. He was
not sure of his standards. When he was fully used by the Inspiring Power his youth uplifted him, and the innocence and
zest of early years produced admirable things—but the lack of

experience and uncritical weakness of youth also persuaded him to retain what he should have destroyed.

There is to be found in this mediocre poem on Lady Winchester a point of great interest, the contrast between Milton's serene youth and the Civil Wars of his troubled middle age. For consider who Lady Winchester's husband was. John Paulet, the man for whose consolation in his great loss these and the other threnodies upon the young dead wife had been written, was that same Winchester whose palace with all its treasures was to be so savagely destroyed in the Civil Wars at the hands of that Cromwell who was to be Milton's employer and whom Milton was to belaud later as the chief of men. This same Winchester, whose family it was agreed to belaud and around whose greatness the sheaf of verses was laid, was strongly Catholic. Milton had written, in 1631, as had the others, under the shadow of Basing House and its splendour: he was not angered at its Catholicism *then*. Remember what Basing House was to mean in 1645! The charred ruin, the massacre without quarter and the horrid loot of the man whom other men called "loyalty."

And that baby, for whom this woman, his mother, gave her life, grew up to be a renegade, a traitor, a typical Whig debauchee, betraying his religion, his family and his King.

On that very unsatisfactory note the Cambridge youth of Milton ends. He is in his twenty-fourth year, in that July of 1632, and there was to come next in his life a sort of pastoral episode wherein, fostered by seclusion and repose, the final lyrical work of John Milton flowered. They were the six years (or nearly six years) which produced *L'Allegro* and *Il Penseroso*, the *Comus* and the crowning achievement of the *Lycidas*. It was in this same year (1632) that Milton the elder, John Milton the successful Scrivener, determined to retire. His younger partner Bower had now completed his term and was a full member of the Scriveners' guild; he could be entrusted with the management of the business. The senior partner left his London office and the Sign of the Spread Eagle in Bower's hands and bought a house at Horton, a Buckinghamshire village in the angle between Thames and Colne, hard against Windsor and Eton, a day's ride from the capital.

He was well on in the sixties; he desired to end in peace; and the place was peaceful enough for the making of a soul and the completion of a man's days. It was to Horton therefore that his son also came to live in that security and seclusion to which he was drawn by a strong desire, a sort of instinct, not wholly of the man but rather of the poet; an instinct that might be called the instinct for self-preservation not in the man so much as in the higher powers who had set aside the man for their purpose. The Muse of Milton had made up her mind, and she was all for his withdrawing awhile from the world.

Therefore it was that her votary proposed to his father something that must have seemed perhaps at first shocking to the old man. He would take no profession; he would live for his scholarship and his verse alone.

We saw how it had been intended that this University career

of the son should end in a clergyman's living. Since he had been refused his Fellowship it was the natural thing that one of his attainments should take Orders in the new national Church—and all the young man's temperament would have seemed, to what is always the insufficient judgment of elders, to be suited for that. It would have been perhaps even more to the father's taste if his elder son should have taken on the business and increased the already substantial wealth of the family. This also he refused; his younger brother Christopher was to be the lawyer, but he, John Milton, would be neither lawyer nor parson. The much later pretence he made that he had been virtually refused a clerical career by his distaste for Bishops, already described, played no part in either determination. No; the poet who had so well proved himself a poet in at least one great stroke would build a hermitage for his soul, and therein devote himself only to his high calling.

He had already, before he went down, written that sonnet on his twenty-third year which will be dealt with in its place among the other sonnets; and therein, as we shall see, he regrets the lack of fruit, the tardiness of his life (as though the Christmas Ode were not a sufficient fruit!); but his conception of activity was not an external one. He knew well enough what a poor thing a mere scholar is; and there is a letter of his extant in which he admits clearly enough the peril of falling into nothingness through abandonment of outward activity.

But his purpose to stand apart without profession or uniform —only to write—was steadfast and so remained. Its monument is the touching and occasionally beautiful Latin verses which he entitled *To my Father*, the plea which he made to that authority for following up his strange but fixed purpose.

Here he was, a young man of twenty-four, who having been denied his fellowship at the University, yet had come down from it not only full of learning and power of expression, but already with a certain reputation for these things: here he was, the eldest son and heir of a prosperous money-dealer, one whose substance he would naturally use and increase till it might have turned into one of those considerable fortunes which were in the later seventeenth century the forerunners of modern banking.

There lay before John Milton junior a prospect such as founded in that day a score of great fortunes. He would have none of it. He would not be a Scrivener, nor consider the future increment of that to which he owed his leisure and present freedom. He would continue to enjoy that leisure and that freedom, but it was sufficient for him. He desired no increase.

Now contentment with an ample livelihood is common enough, indeed the man who is eager to increase an income already sufficient is an exception; but the *second* decision which the young Milton took was remarkable. Not only does he refuse to be a Scrivener or a money-dealer, he refuses to be anything else—at least he refuses to be anything else of a recognised sort; for good writing is not a profession: no man lives by the Muses. The natural course and the one which his father would have been proud to see him follow would have been the taking of Holy Orders. He refused to do so.

We have seen that his belated religious explanation of this action, years after, is insufficient: Milton was not yet a Puritan; his prelatic excuse is a false one. His true motive he gives at the time in his Latin verses to his father; he desired complete independence of any professional tie in order that he might write and only write; and this because he already obscurely felt within himself those powers of which later he was to boast continuously—but not unduly. He guessed himself on the way to a wealth of fame.

But it was fame to be acquired by a special sort of industry, tenacious, unceasing, almost fierce, taking out of a man all there was in him: the greatest effort in the world, the creative effort of the poet who is not content to be spontaneous, but who builds and perfects.

Further, Milton was not afraid of "what men call idleness." The energy in him was of that kind which is supplied to the spirit through the body. It was such that his natural spirits never failed and this creative man was driven by his blood to all manner of creative work unceasingly. He knew that this urgency was in him, this motive force. Very rare indeed are the examples of literary leisure and energy combined: they were combined here.

In earlier times when great repute led to patronage, your considerable artist with the pen or the brush found industry worth while and could make his talent his trade. Later, in the nineteenth century, a man might hope for a competence earned through his reputation as a writer; he might even hope for a modest revenue to be earned by popularity as a writer of verses; and though such popularity is not of its nature closely connected with excellence in verse, yet Victor Hugo, the greatest of the modern poets, enjoyed it—and Tennyson, who may, of the later names, be perhaps reckoned next to Hugo, enjoyed it also. There is something ridiculous in this connection between great verse and good money, and the coincidence will hardly recur. Still, that coincidence did exist after Milton's time by a wide public and before Milton's time by patronage—but in Milton's time it did not exist.

It is to be remarked how slow he was to admit authorship: to sign and to publish. *Lycidas* appears almost anonymously under initials. The Ode to the *Nativity* comes out as an undergraduate exercise, not published for years. The sonnets are kept in manuscript year after year, some of them, even, not given to the world until after the writer's death.

This reticence in youth in so great a genius—and one moreover who himself affirms that love of fame which he certainly felt—I should ascribe to three causes combined; first to what is often forgotten about such men, sensitiveness to criticism; secondly, to the appetite for amendment, and thirdly to an odd certainty of fame, a security for the future, which makes those writers who possess it indifferent enough to the verdict of their contemporaries. They are indifferent, that is, not in the sense that they do not resent blame—they will extravagantly react against any belittlement of their achievements—but in the sense that they do not feel praise in their own day to be necessary to their final position. That position will be established in any case; and since no literary fame is worth having that is not posthumous, they are in no haste: can wait a generation, a lifetime, or a century. They are already in possession.

Milton's sensitiveness to criticism was not greatly exercised in the matter of his verse; it was rather in the matter of politics and doctrine that he felt it, as in the first example of all his explosions, when he so furiously struck at the man who had blamed him for his heresy on the question of divorce. Therefore this first motive for the keeping back of his authorship of poems is the least; the second, a desire to test his verse, is the strongest.

There is always in the poet who knows his business best a sense of having failed to reach his goal; a feeling that something must yet be changed before he can be content with his handiwork. This feeling undoubtedly halted Milton. It halted him the more because he was an extreme example of the poet who fashions as well as creates, who carves and puts together his lines; who rides, controls and manages that afflatus upon which another kind of poet depends.

Against such a view it may be urged that Milton's manuscripts do not show, as Byron's do, for example, a mass of revision; and that later imprints passed by him rarely differ materially from the earliest version, as they commonly do with other and especially later poets. I do not see the two things as contradictory. A man may be filled with the sense of incompletion and yet not complete the thing which disappointed him. He can be uneasy all his life over phrases for which he cannot find a substitute, and though uneasy, after long hesitation still leave them standing because no alternatives come to him. This passion for amendment was, as I say, the strongest force at work; but the third must be remembered—Milton's prevision of immortality.

All the great writers of verse—or nearly all—have felt it; most have boasted of it; so also have much lesser men who had no right to feel it, for the reliance of the greatest even may be misplaced. Ronsard had led the way in this; Shakespeare had followed him. They each had said, of casual praises in rhyme, directed presumably not even to a beloved object but only designed as part of an exercise in verse, "Because I wrote it, you shall be immortal." That also is what Horace said of the little spring of water which he found so delightful; it would be exalted, *"nobilis"* among the fountains of Italian hills—and so indeed it has been for two thousand years.

See Milton, then remote in little Horton, in the paradise of South England, preparing to build up permanent things.

The first fruits of Horton were those twin exercises in verse, *L'Allegro* and *Il Penseroso*. It is possible that the sonnet *To the Nightingale* was also written at Horton, though in the collected pieces it has been placed first, before the sonnet on his twenty-third year. But at any rate the *Allegro* and *Penseroso* are the main results of his early and planned seclusion.

They should be called, I say, exercises in verse: not to belittle them, God knows, but because they are manifestly of deliberate and intended construction, written as a pair and a contrasting pair, like twin ornaments of the Renaissance; twin pendants, carefully designed and executed with the utmost fineness.

It is the special mark of those two imperishable monuments of Milton's craftsmanship that the vigour of sheer poetry runs through them, casting forth passage after passage, phrase after phrase of the unmistakable thing: Beauty stamped and rendered unchangeable:

"Where brooding darkness spreads her jealous wings
And the night raven sings."

When he could write that couplet in the first lines he knew that he was sure; and thenceforward there runs through the whole length of the *Allegro's* hundred and fifty lines that multiplicity of rhythm, that ease and mastery in the handling of the English octosyllabic couplet on four beats which has not been and will not be surpassed. It may be compared variously to the run of a fleet of boats under sail, lifting to the little seas; or to a mountain stream carrying itself on joyously in perpetual self-expression, never repetitive, yet always one. It is the English landscape from morning to evening, and on the background of it those great pictures from the south which he must have seen, and which gave him those other two lines,

"Mountains on whose barren breast
The labouring clouds do often rest."

It is impossible to choose in the troop of loveliness; but in those two lines perhaps one may find the most complete effect of realised imagination: Milton proclaiming the beauty of this world.

It is the mark of a constructed poem—and all poems should be constructed: long poems, to be of any endurance, *must* be so—that their conclusion fitly rounds them off, ending the newly created thing upon a note of perfection. So it is with the *Allegro:*

"That Orpheus' self may heave his head
From golden slumbers on a bed
Of heaped Elysian flowers, and hear
Such strains as would have won the ear

> Of Pluto, to have quite set free
> His half-regained Eurydice."

To read that is enough.

The *Penseroso*, as it was certainly written second, so also is
just touched with fatigue. Nor do the opening lines show the security which those of the *Allegro* have. Indeed the poem does
not truly open till its eleventh line:

> "But hail, thou Goddess sage and holy,
> Hail, thou divinest Melancholy,
> Whose saintly visage is too bright
> To hit the sense of human sight."

Yet does the verse take some little time to get into its stride,
and what is best comes interwoven with what has less succeeded. But how much and how continually it succeeds! If
after such a success as:

> "I hear the far-off curfew sound
> Over some white-watered shore
> Swinging slow with sullen roar;"

he sinks to what is perilously near prose, as:

> "Or if the air will not permit;"

he then rises again at once to a picture that fills the minds of
all of us in the dusk of our winter evenings:

> "Where glowing embers through the room
> Teach light to counterfeit a gloom"

and the visual imagination comes in conspicuous:—

> "Let my lamp at midnight hour
> Be seen from some high lonely tower
> Where I may oft outwatch the Bear
> With thrice-great Hermes, and unsphere

The spirit of Plato to unfold
What worlds or what vast Regions hold
The immortal mind that has forsook
Her mansion in this fleshly nook."

How much he must have worried about those two "uns," tried to replace them, and then given them up in despair! They could not but offend him; yet if he told himself that the run of that passage was enough to float such clumsiness, he was right.

The *Penseroso* is both a trifle too long, and not so strong on the wing as the *Allegro:* but at its best it touches the mark of the best in the *Allegro*. Moreover, its ending does not entirely justify the occasional half-tediums and unworthy lines that come before. But no one else could have done it, and it must have confirmed the writer in his growing certitude of himself.

Of Milton's poems written during this lyrical phase of his youth at Horton, *Comus* is that one which had most effect upon his life, and has become perhaps the most familiar to our own time.

It was not always called *Comus*. Milton did not give it that name. When he collected his verse in print for the first time more than ten years after the play had been given he only calls it "A Masque," adding that it was given at Ludlow, setting down the year and the name of Lord Bridgewater. It came to be called *Comus* because some short name had to be given it, and Comus was the principal character—the harmless Godlet of Revels turned under the writer's prejudice into a sort of maleficent demon.

It is a pity that the *Comus* should have become thus famous, for it warps the popular conception of Milton's genius. It is overlong; it was clearly written under difficulties which the writer could not surmount; it is of a form wherein he did not excel. There are exquisite single lines and not a few good groups of lines in the composition; there are memorable brief songs;

but as a whole it fails to reach his highest. The blank verse which takes up the bulk of it lacks that marvellous variation wherewith he later learned to play upon this medium, and lacking which the English unrhymed decasyllabic becomes monotonous beyond all other metres.

This false fame enjoyed by the *Comus* has two causes; first the poet's own attachment to it; next—that which is the curse of all effort at judgment in letters—adventitious sentiment: that is, a motive for liking or disliking a work of art through a like or dislike of the subject rather than its matter and manner—by which alone (save in extreme cases) it should be judged.

Milton was evidently impressed by the surroundings in which the *Comus* appeared. It was his first important introduction to the world. For the first time he received praise from men whose opinion counted. Now with a young poet (and he was only twenty-five) this matter of praise from elders who are also in the public eye is of great moment, even to one as wrapt up in himself as Milton was, and as worshipful of himself. In youth that sort of official appreciation tells heavily. He had already had a trial run in what he later called the *Arcades*, when the first hint of these things appeared; but the occasion of the *Comus* was grander and of more permanent effect upon him.

He owed the opportunity to a friend of his family and of himself, Lawes, a musician; and therefore indirectly to his father's taste for music, which that old fellow so amusingly combined with the drawing up of deeds and the advancing of money at interest.

Henry Lawes was a man who played a much larger part in Milton's life than Milton's vanity would perhaps have admitted. For an unknown and very young man, however determined on fame, to be taken up by an artist so well known as to be almost a national figure always creates a strong bond between the two, and the junior of the pair always feels a certain awe of his senior. Later, when the younger man has become more famous than the elder he may be a little ashamed of the early patronage, and even inclined himself to patronise in turn the man who began by patronising him and giving him a lift.

It depends upon the nature of the poet. One man will feel permanent gratitude; another will become an enemy through feeling himself under an obligation and humbled by the recollection of the time when he was insignificant. With Milton these emotions took no extravagant form either way; he repaid Lawes by writing a sonnet to him, and he kept up the friendship.

When he wrote that sonnet Milton had in his own turn become a great public figure, and much greater than the man he was praising. It is only just to remember, moreover, that the thirteen years' difference between them counted much more when Milton was twenty-five than when he was in his later thirties. To the Milton of *Comus* Lawes was venerable—approaching forty—a man born eight years before Queen Elizabeth's death; one who almost dated from an earlier world; whereas when the sonnet was written the one man was approaching middle age and the other was elderly.

I will deal with that sonnet in its place. It is not very good. We know its date accurately, for of the two copies written out by Milton himself (both in the Cambridge Manuscript) one was dated February the 9th, 1645, with the initials "J. M." It was not printed until three years afterwards, coming into a sort of preface to a body of verses written in praise of Lawes by various people, belauding the music which he and his brother had written for a number of Psalms. The sonnet dates therefore, as to the writing of it, to the year in which Lawes was fifty and Milton thirty-seven; and it did not appear until Milton was just on forty and Lawes fifty-three. Lawes was indeed so much the more important man of the two at the period of the

[103]

Comus that when he had that Masque printed (1637) he did not even put Milton's name on it, but only his own; and it must be remembered in his excuse (if he needs excuse for such action) that he was in the heart of the great world.

A Wiltshire man, born at Dinton, up the Nadder Valley above Wilton on the Wincanton Road, he had become, when he was just over thirty a member of the King's Music; and in the year before the *Comus* came out, and even before the *Arcades*, he had written music for another Masque of Bridgewater's, which was given in Whitehall. He altered the order of the verses at will. He even thought himself free to change at least one of Milton's lines for the sake of his own music; he took the last line of the "Sweet Echo" song, and changed "give resounding grace" to "hold a counterpoint," so that the line no longer read "and give resounding grace to all Heaven's harmonies," but the technical conceit, "and hold a counterpoint to all Heaven's harmonies." It has been argued that the change was not made by Lawes, but by Milton himself —but the theory can with difficulty be defended.

Lawes being an important figure socially as well as the leader of his profession became, through his knowledge of music, his teaching of it and his production of it an intimate in the houses of a whole group of wealthy people. Notably was Lawes devoted to the Egertons—the legal family which became so rich in the last years of Queen Elizabeth and the reign of James. He was particularly a friend to the widow of that first Egerton who had been Chancellor, under the title of Ellesmere.

This old lady (for she was old in the years of Milton's early boyhood) was known (from her first marriage) as the Dowager Lady Derby. Her son by her second husband was made the first Lord Bridgewater. It is in connection with these two people that Lawes comes on to the scene in Milton's life.

This important old lady, patroness and crony of Lawes, had

a pageant got up in her honour by the younger members of her family, to be played at her house, Harefield, near Uxbridge; and Lawes was of course to be the musician thereof, to write the tunes and arrange the whole affair. He needed a libretto, and called in young Milton—that young Milton who was just home from the University and of whom men sometimes remembered vaguely that he had written verses. He could be depended upon to turn out lines fitted to the airs. He did so; and the few songs of the *Arcades* are the result.

They are not on a high level, and the blank verse which separates them is no more remarkable. Also they are absurdly sycophantic, making out old Lady Derby to be "a sudden blaze of majesty," and again, "too divine to be mistook," "seated like a Goddess bright, in the centre of her light"; and just at the end of the first song there is a line so startlingly bad that it lingers in the memory and will not out. It is written to rhyme with "gods" and it runs "Juno dares not give her odds." Lady Derby had to start at scratch.

The chief interest to us of these three short songs and fifty odd lines of blank verse called the *Arcades*, is the appearance in them of themes and actual phrases which Milton was to use again and again. Here are the River Alpheus, and here is Arethusa; here is the perfume of an early English summer morning, ". . . early, e'er the odorous breath of Morn." Here is the music of the spheres; here are the shears which cut off the lives of men; here is the condemnation of that grossness which forbids man to hear heavenly harmony—and all the rest of the Miltonic luggage.

It is impossible that such a poet should write even a bare hundred and nine lines without something of his magic piercing through; the last song has the charming two lines,

> "Nymphs and shepherds dance no more.
> Trip no more in twilight ranks."

But it is not just to consider the *Arcades* as anything save an introduction, both in the social and the literary sense: they are but the foretaste of *Comus*. Anyhow, they satisfied Lawes; and that is why the *Comus* came into existence.

Lawes being commissioned to produce a Masque for old Lady Derby's son, Lord Bridgewater, on his taking up the office of Governor in the Welsh Marches, now turns as a matter of course to young Milton for the libretto—it was the year after the *Arcades*, 1634.

He did but a half-service to English letters by so doing. Milton untrammelled would have given us far better things, as we realise when we consider that the *Comus* comes in between the *Allegro* and *Penseroso*, its forerunners, and the *Lycidas*, its successor. Milton was never made to cut his cloth to another man's measure. Lawes was the arranger of the Masque. It must be of a certain length to fit a certain space of time; the actors must be few, and therefore the speeches long; and of these few actors two must be children and one a quite young lad—all taking their parts for no better reason than that they were the young people of the house. Local features must be brought in, such as the river Severn, in the shape of a goddess; possibly a sort of vague plot had to be worked to—though it is more probable that, in its main features, the action was of Milton's own design. We may be fairly certain that Lawes had written his music before Milton was commissioned to find words for it. Under all these handicaps was the *Comus* written, and the reader feels them weighing on him as he reads. Thus such lines as these:

> "I came not here to pursue the stealth,
> Of pilfering wolf; not all the fleecy wealth
> That doth enrich those downs is worth a thought,
> To this my errand and the care it brought."

And Milton is troubled otherwise in *Comus*. Now and then his sense of metre fails him in the *Comus*. The line "If you let slip time, like a neglected rose" is much too redundant. It is very well to have the twinkle of added syllables, and no one grew to be a greater master at that than Milton, but this example is too much of a good thing—you cannot pronounce the line at all unless you emphasise the word "time" and slur over all the four words before it.

Yet are there in these thousand lines whole passages of well-minted Milton; metal of the authentic stamp: most memorable groups of lines.

For example:

> ". . . the gilded car of day
> His glowing axle doth allay
> In the steep Atlantic stream.
> And the slope sun his upward beam
> Shoots against the Dusky Pole."

Look how "Steep" gives the whole landscape: the god dropping down the very wall of heaven into the waters, and the shaft of his last glory striking upwards to the roof of the skies—as such beams from under a cloud used to do in our English air at sunset.

Or again:—

> "Braid your locks with rosy twine,
> Dropping odours, dropping wine . . ."

The beginning of each song is on the same level. Hear this (speaking of the human voice in song, a sound which always moved John Milton to an ecstasy). Comus is speaking of the lost lady's singing, which he has overheard in the recesses of the wood, the notes of her. This is what he says:—

> "How sweetly did they float upon the wings
> Of silence, through the empty-vaulted night,

With every fall smoothing the raven down
Of darkness till it smiled."

It is admirable—and that last conceit is one of the rare examples where this sort of trick is at once natural and alive.

Or listen again to this, from the invocation to Sabrina, Goddess of the Severn river.

"Listen where thou art sitting
Under the glassy, cool, translucent wave,
In twisted braids of lilies knitting
The loose train of thy amber dropping hair;"

"*Under the glassy, cool, translucent wave.*" That line is itself clear water. It could not be surpassed.

Milton had much of Shakespeare in his mind when he was writing the *Comus*, though certainly his blank verse in it falls terribly short of the Master's best. But he was no longer in his first boyish enthusiasm for Shakespeare. By the time that he was writing the *Allegro* (being then between twenty-four and thirty) Shakespeare was no longer something surpassing Kings. He was very good, no doubt, although his verse went anyhow, without construction, like a bird's song—and much later we shall find Milton using King Charles's devotion to Shakespeare as a reproach against him. He has here and there in *Comus* a line which is pure Shakespeare, such as "doing abhorred rites to Hecate." And again, "live like nature's bastards, not her sons"—which is Shakespeare's "Then am I Brutus' harlot, not his wife."

Another of the best passages cannot be denied Shakespearean parentage, it might be Ariel himself speaking. It is the opening of the Guardian Spirit's last passage:—

"To the ocean now I fly,
And those happy climes that lie
Where day never shuts his eye,
Up, in the broad fields of the sky."

Not only is it a reminiscence of Ariel, but it is worthy of Ariel—which is surely saying much. But just before the end comes in a piece of pure Milton:—

> "And from thence come soar as soon
> To the corners of the Moon."

Yes, if any other man of that time had written it, the *Comus* would have been marvellous enough, for the scattered loveliness interspersed among its monotony. But being Milton's and coming between the *Nativity* and *Lycidas* one wishes it perfect.

Yet I repeat the *Comus* is over-rated, because Milton himself felt it as a date in his life. The important people surrounding the Egertons heard it, and talked of it as they would not have talked of the fragmentary *Arcades;* and they were the people who made opinion. Lawes himself was delighted, not only from hearing such praise from the very rich, but on his own judgment of the thing. He was at the pains to write it out with his own hand more than once, and to send it round; so the name of John Milton pierced. Many now knew that he was a poet, some were saying that he was indeed a poet; and he himself, hitherto so hesitant and desiring delay, was willing to come forward.

Remember, it was the midmost of those happy years—the happiest years that England was to know for many a long day after—when King Charles I in his thirties was fully exercising his vigorous and equitable rule. A prolonged peace was over all. Trade was mounting rapidly and wealth with it. A general prosperity nourished England. The factions which were to end it all had not yet grown formidable—even in Scotland.

Three years after the performance of the Masque, in 1637, Lawes was at the pains of publishing the *Comus;* and the printed copies were circulated. Milton, now no longer very young, nearly twenty-nine, found himself a public author. A year later, before he started for Italy, he had the courage to send an example of the *Comus* to Wotton, his neighbour, the Provost of Eton and a retired Ambassador. He received in return praise not only warm but judicious. It was thus that Milton was, by *Comus*, "made"—as we to-day use the word "made."

But in truth a poet is made more slowly and more thoroughly than thus.

Turn next to the second and worse reason for the false position of the *Comus*—its adventitious interest. That fungus and pest of all poetry takes many forms; to-day it is at its worst in the form of patriotism, for that noble emotion now carries on its back verse of the very worst, and lifts to the first class of reputation verse which properly belongs to the second or the third—or the tenth. This adventitious interest in the case of the *Comus* is the Manichæan taint: the essential of what we have called in this country, since the late sixteenth century, the Puritan spirit. In Milton's day it was the obsession of a faction only; to-day, largely diluted, it runs through the whole of our society.

The root of that spirit is the nervous terror bred by excess of sensual enjoyment. An excess of sensual enjoyment breaks down the nerves even more surely than the partial and insufficient repression thereof. On this emotion is founded the conception of natural things as evil and in particular the horror of sex; in a lesser degree of wine.

Not only does the whole argument of Milton's *Comus* turn upon that theme, but the ill savour of it touches the verse.

In Milton's fresh youth there had been no trace of such a savour. He was Biblical, as all around him were; he was anti-papal for all around him were so. But he had as yet showed no dread of the flesh: now his celibacy is beginning to tell on him; he is developing a twist. He was already too much cut off from "the other half of humanity." That separation was to deepen until it led to the howling error of his too-tardy marriage and thence to his grotesque dread—and therefore assumed contempt —of woman.

Hence the false morals of the *Comus*. "Go an inch too far and you will turn into a beast, perhaps a vampire!" The *Comus* might have been called "Oh! my Brethren! Beware!" The writer sermonises repeatedly—*Comus* carries the air of sermonising as does a tin chapel. The central aim of the Masque is that.

The story told therein is typical of the new plant which was now growing in Milton's mind and was to mix so strangely with his love of loveliness. A young virgin gets lost in a wood; the evil enchanter Comus lurks there, keeping state with a rout of horrible companions, men and women retaining human form save for their heads, which have gone bestial into the likeness of wolves and swine. Comus would debauch and destroy her, to render her like these his companions; she conquers through the power of chastity.

Sound morals. But what is unsound about them is the emphasis, and the turning of that Comus of whom Ben Jonson had made a sort of more energetic Silenus, an honest emblem of jollity and feasting, into something from the Pit. Anyone suffering the Manichæan taint and desiring to spread it to others may quote passage after passage from the *Comus* in argument; it has been so quoted perpetually.

Nor let anyone imagine that Milton's *Comus* will lose in the future from our modern gloomy excesses towards what is, apparently, the other extreme. The modern welter of obscenity is not the opposite of Puritanism, but its twin. It is as Manichæan as was the old dread of the best and simplest pleasures. It is founded, as was Puritanism, in a perverted hatred of joy. But the Puritan did at least look forward to beatitude. He was "elect." His modern counterpart is still the enemy of laughter, but, in the place of lecturing and boasting, he snarls and despairs.

I must not leave the *Comus* before touching on the three brief things which would seem to belong to the few months between it and the *Arcades*. They are of curious interest because they so well exemplify the unevenness of the pen which strove uninterruptedly to maintain its highest pitch. These are three short pieces of iambic verse, each of little more than twenty lines in length.

The first, to put them in Milton's own order, was provoked by the memory of a concert—a piece of what is to-day called "sacred music," or was so called until yesterday. The third and last is a second effort to carry on the theme which had so gloriously succeeded in the *Nativity*. He now tries the Circumcision, possibly just after the first of January, 1634 (to use our modern calendar); and fails, though not as disastrously as he failed in his effort at *The Passion*.

The first piece on music has much success about it, but it is not of the best. It boasts at least one first-rate couplet:

> "Where the bright Seraphim in burning row
> Their loud uplifted angel trumpets blow,"

but it also admits such a phrase as:

> "Harps of golden wires,"

and the perfectly damnable line (damnable as verse, admirable as sacramental philosophy):

> "Dead things with inbreath'd sense able to pierce."

Here is a line so rocky that you can hardly read it as iambics at all—or indeed as anything else.

But the middle piece, the piece *On Time*, rises high above this; and that anyone may judge, let it (as it is so short) be repeated here in full, over-familiar though it be.

> "Fly, envious Time, till thou run out thy race
> Call on the lazy leaden stepping hours,

Whose speed is but the heavy plummet's pace;
And glut thyself with what thy womb devours,
Which is no more than what is false and vain,
And merely mortal dross;
So little is our loss,
So little is thy gain.
For when, as each thing bad thou hast entomb'd
And last of all thy greedy self consum'd,
Then long Eternity shall greet our bliss
With an individual kiss;
And joy shall overtake us as a flood,
When everything that is sincerely good
And perfectly divine,
With truth, and peace, and love shall ever shine
About the supreme throne
Of Him, t' whose happy-making sight alone
When once our heav'nly-guided soul shall clime,
Then all this earthly grossness quit,
Attired with stars we shall for ever sit,
   Triumphing over Death, and Chance, and thee, O Time."

How perfect is the twelfth line, "with an individual kiss," and what a complete winding up of the whole—a line to be always remembered, "Triumphing over Death, and Chance, and thee, O Time!"

It was not intended that Milton's plan of seclusion should be fulfilled. The *Allegro* and the *Penseroso* were perhaps completed, the *Comus* and its difficulties had certainly been surmounted, when within four years of his having come down from the University, in his twenty-eighth year, there fell upon his old father something out of the past such as does fall on people who make their money doubtfully.

While John Milton the elder was still busy in London drawing up deeds and placing his own money and larger sums entrusted to him, before he retired to Horton upon his accumulation, there had come to his office of the Spread Eagle one John

Cotton, who had put into the hands of the firm (Milton and Bower, as they would now be called, for Thomas Bower had been the elder Milton's apprentice and was about to become a Scrivener in his turn) the considerable sum of £3,600—well over £20,000 of capital in our modern values.

As many a man does with his solicitors to-day, John Cotton trusted Messrs. Milton and Bower to find him borrowers who might take the money at usury on good security at the rate of the day, which was 8%. The firm placed out the money at interest among various borrowers, most of them of good social position, and presumably provided with security. It was among the last of the transactions at that office which the man whom we may call "the senior partner" can have been engaged in; for it was just after this sum had been entrusted to John Milton and Thomas Bower that the elder man (he was probably seventy) had given up his active attention to the business, leaving this care to his junior while he himself retired to Horton.

It was in 1636 and in the month of May, while the poet's mother was falling into her last illness and the quiet household was already disturbed in anxiety thereby, that it received the shock.

Old Cotton being dead, his nephew and executor, Sir Thomas, a Huntingdon Baronet, had brought an action against old Milton for the recovery of £1,600.

The accusation of the plaintiff was that towards the end of his uncle's life (he was well over eighty) the payment of the interest on the money entrusted to Messrs. Milton and Bower had grown irregular and was lessening. It was lessening (said the plaintiff) through the deliberate fraud of the defendants, who were keeping it back in order to frighten old Cotton into a bad bargain. Old Cotton had as a fact been frightened, and did make a very bad bargain. This bargain was suggested to him by Milton and Bower in company with an attorney of the name of Holcher. Milton and Bower and the attorney had bribed the man who was then looking after Cotton, giving him more than a thousand pounds of our money, to persuade his senile charge that the debtors could no longer pay properly and that it would be better to take cash down, at a loss, for his chances of recovering the sum he had originally entrusted. Old Cotton was so persuaded, and took £2,000 of money down, for the £3,600 he had originally parted with.

The balance of £1,600—something like £10,000 in our money—remained with Milton and Bower after the criminal bribe given to old Cotton's factotum had been recouped. In other words, Mr. Milton senior and his partner Bower were accused of embezzling money to the tune of some £10,000.

Such things are not uncommon in relations of this kind; there is nothing unlikely about the account of the plaintiff— who also, by the way, says that he offered to repay the £2,000 on condition that the original £3,600 should be handed back to him—which restoration of their ill-gotten gains Milton and Bower had refused.

The process was served at the beginning of the next year, 1637. It was served upon the Milton household but probably not at Horton, more likely at the offices of the firm in Bread Street. It is significant that Mr. Milton senior at first preferred not to meet the charge, and his partner Bower, in London, acted in the same fashion. The Court fined old Mr. Milton £12 or so, in the guise of costs for contempt, and sent Bower to prison until he should consent to reply to the charge.

Before the end of March the Court had yielded to the plea that Milton was too old to travel and that it was not his fault that he had not appeared. And at the beginning of the next month his younger son Christopher (who was just of age but not yet called to the Bar) testified on oath to his father's inability to make the journey. John Milton senior was allowed to depose in his own house at Horton.

In the middle of all that worry poor old Mrs. Milton died.

She was buried in Horton Church: and the law went rumbling on.

A belated defence was attempted. It amounts, when you have ploughed through the legal jargon, to a statement that the plaintiff had been a willing party to the whole affair, a denial of bribing old Cotton's factotum—and all the rest. That was Bower's plea: he had been let out of prison to make it.

As for Mr. John Milton senior's deposition, it throws the blame on Bower, and asserts that he himself, John Milton senior, though he was offered the purchase money by old Cotton in his panic, had refused to accept it, telling the creditor that there was ample security and that he had nothing to be frightened of. Later he had heard (he said) that the poor old boy went back to Bower without his (old Milton's) knowing anything about it, and that Bower had played on Cotton's fears, had offered the insufficient payment, had had it accepted—and was in general, the villain of the piece.

In the upshot the Court accepted old Milton's plea (a man who was certainly about to be, if not already, his son-in-law, Agar, who had witnessed the deposition, himself belonged to the Chancery Office). So that was the end of *that*. John Milton senior was not condemned; his partner Bower was out of gaol, but left with a very unpleasant story attached to him—and in general the Milton family had been through a bad quarter of an hour. And that is why I say that John Milton junior must have been glad when, after April 1637, the business was over, that he at least had refused to be a Scrivener.

Meanwhile the displeasing episode had borne one solid fruit —it had caused the poet to go out of his way to give a certificate of honesty to his parent, whom he calls in plain Latin a man of the utmost integrity.

The reader will I think agree with me that the most astonishing thing about all this business is the absence of a document. No one seems to have produced a receipt in connection with any of this money; the whole thing was verbal and everything depended upon the memory and credibility of the witnesses. Happily for Milton's peace of mind, the Court having accepted his father's story rather than Bower's, John Milton the younger, relieved of these anxieties, turned again to what he hoped would be the sole occupation of his life. An opportunity was afforded him at that very moment for his genius to express itself upon its highest level.

He wrote *Lycidas*.

> "Yet once more, O ye laurels, and once more,
> Ye myrtles brown, with ivy never sere,
> I come to pluck your berries harsh and crude,
> And with forced fingers rude
> Shatter your leaves before the mellowing year:
> Bitter constraint and sad occasion dear
> Compels me to disturb your season due;
> For Lycidas is dead, dead ere his prime,
> Young Lycidas, and hath not left his peer.
> Who would not sing for Lycidas? he knew
> Himself to sing, and build the lofty rhyme.
> He must not float upon his watery bier
> Unwept, and welter to the parching wind,
> Without the meed of some melodious tear."

Great structures are known by their beginnings and their ends. It is with such music that *Lycidas* triumphantly enters the world.

It was on the morrow of the earthquake in the Milton household—the death of the old mother, the exposure of the old man in the Cotton business, followed by that visitation of the plague in the summer which accounted for one-third of the mortality in the little parish—in the autumn after all these things, November 1637, that John Milton in his twenty-ninth year produced one of the master poems of English: for it was in this month that he completed the *Lycidas*.

Were there not one other peak in the early lyric achievement of Milton—had he not written when just entering manhood the ode on the *Nativity*—the *Lycidas* would be called not only a summit of English verse but the summit of all Milton's creative affair. Milton the poet establishes himself there for ever.

No praise of the thing is extravagant, no dwelling upon it excessive. A man coming on it first, as did I who write this, in boyhood, is struck at once spell-bound. A man returning to it in age, as I do now, discovers its splendour to have survived undimmed. Of how many things outside the ancients can that be said? The long and crowded business of human life and the weariness of repetition have no more affected the *Lycidas* than passage of the years affects a diamond. "The soul's long dues of hardening and decay," which—on this side of death—render it callous even to beauty at last, spare the *Lycidas*.

It is a delight to remember that this perfect thing was designed. It was made of set purpose: it is architectural and willed. Of the proof that this is always so with Milton no better example can be chosen. We have direct evidence of this in a passage which Masson carefully analysed in his monograph—the passage in which all the flowers are summoned for the adornment of the drowned man's hearse.

> "Bring the rathe primrose that forsaken dies,
> The tufted crow-toe, and pale jessamine,
> The white pink, and the pansy freaked with jet,
> The glowing violet,
> The musk-rose, and the well-attired woodbine,
> With cowslips wan that hang the pensive head,
> And every flower that sad embroidery wears;
> Bid amaranthus all his beauty shed,
> And daffadillies fill their cups with tears."

These nine lines with the exquisite catch of the half line in the midst, "glowing violet," were deliberately added on a blank space opposite in the manuscript, and then, having been added, were varied again—worked in together like a woven pattern. Often does this kind of labour undergone result in high verse; and secure of his talent is the man who so labours.

There is no reason to think that Milton felt strongly about the subject of his threnody. King had been preferred to him for a Fellowship; the two men knew each other; but they moved in different worlds outside the University, and within the University they were divided by what at that age separates young men of the same college—two years' seniority—and on the top of that four years' difference in age. When King had come into College he had been a boy of fourteen; Milton was completing his eighteenth year. Nor was there anything in King to attract the intelligence and taste of John Milton. He was of rather better birth than the poet, with very much stronger social backing (to which, as we know, he had owed his Fellowship) and his exaggerated reputation was of that academic kind which is invariably false. We can judge of this, for his Latin verses have been preserved.

The occasion which gave English letters such a possession was the drowning of this personage on his way to a visit in Ireland, where he had been born. He had sailed from Chester in the August of that year (1637), and the boat in which he sailed made shipwreck in the Estuary of the Dee; some were saved, but not King. Whereupon his fellow Dons, to whom he seemed so important, collected memorial offerings to his memory.

These were twelve pieces of verse in English, twenty in Latin, thirteen in Greek—all bad. I can find only two lines in the whole lot that are even so execrably bad as to be worthy of remark—the badness of the rest is common badness. But these two superlatively bad lines I will quote, as adding pungency to the bugle-call of *Lycidas* which follows them:

"The early Matins which you daily said,
And Vespers, when you dwelt next door St. Chad."

[119]

I hope that these lines will not (as the phrase goes) "easily be let die." They are from a fellow cleric, senior to him, the Reverend Henry King, a Canon of Lichfield, of St. Chad's Cathedral.*

The last, the thirteenth of the English pieces, is the *Lycidas*. How came it to be there? It is a fair conjecture (from what one knows happens in these cases) that some Don remembered how young Milton had written verse when he was up at Cambridge and thought he might be worth approaching to add his little contribution to that of the more regular University poets. His College may not have thought much of him, but a man who is known to be practised in rhyming is always useful on these occasions. What they got for their pains was that verse the clarions of which ring out unchanged in fresh glory after three hundred years.

What is the topmost of this achievement, what is the crown of it? Surely the line, "Smooth sliding Mincius, crowned with vocal reeds"; which on a man's first hearing of it, takes root in his mind for ever. How well it is emphasised, that line, how well framed and introduced by the calculated irregularity of what precedes it! "Smooth sliding Mincius, crowned with vocal reeds" is the very sound as well as the picture of a river moving all in one, full to its banks and silent. But that introducing line before it is in direct contrast:

"Oh, fountain Arethuse! and thou honoured flood."

It may be that some would rather choose, "Flames in the forehead of the morning sky" as the summit-line. It is more commonly repeated because it comes nearer to rhetoric.

---

* While I am on this matter I cannot bear to leave out something that would have delighted Swift, who would have seized upon it for his Scriblerian essay on *Bathos*. Here it is, unfortunately anonymous, the only unsigned piece of the batch:—

"When Phœbus shines within our hemisphere
There are no stars; or at least, none appear."

One high critic has preferred:

> "Aye me! Whilst thee the shores and sounding seas
> Wash far away . . ."

but for me that passage is a little spoilt by the conclusion of
the second line, which is unworthy of the rest, for it ends
"where'er thy bones are hurled." Now that last word is introduced awkwardly enough to rhyme with "world" three lines
on. Indeed the necessity and difficulty of rhyming to "world"
is the pitfall of English verse. Also we find in this same passage
the first example, I think, of Milton's masterly use of place
names:

> "Where the great Vision of the guarded mount
> Looks towards Namancos and Bayona's hold."

Having discovered this artifice, Milton secretly takes it away
and hides it, to be his own. It has become peculiarly his, and
none after him attempting to recover what seems so facile a
method of securing effect has been able to rival or even approach him. The artifice grows upon him with the years; and
in the resurrection of him in his old age, in his mighty vindica-
tion of himself through *Paradise Lost* and *Samson Agonistes* he
strikes that cymbal of the place name again and again.

Such is the mastery of the *Lycidas* that I know not how to
write of it without reciting it in full. This I cannot here do;
this study does not permit the space for full quotation—and,
anyhow, what petty stuff must be any appreciation of a master
at his highest. Yet I will quote the end, though all men know
it by heart, for the end and the beginning determine such things
as *Lycidas*.

> "Thus sang the uncouth swain to the oaks and rills,
> While the still morn went out with sandals grey;
> He touched the tender stops of various quills,
> With eager thought warbling his Doric lay:

And now the sun had stretched out all the hills,
And now was dropt into the western bay.
At last he rose, and twitched his mantle blue:
To-morrow to fresh woods, and pastures new."

Milton despised obscurity. What is remarkable in one who nourished his verse with perpetual allusions, he hardly ever consciously allowed obscurity even in these. He hardly ever alludes to what a cultured reader might not be expected to know, nor, when he makes some dark parallel, does he make it too dark for immediate grasping. Yet here, in *Lycidas*, comes the first (and famous) exception; the two lines put into the mouth of St. Peter where he threatens vengeance against the kind of English Churchmen whom Milton did not like. He almost certainly, in this year 1637, had active little Laud in his mind's eye:

"But that two-handed engine at the door
Stands ready to smite once and smite no more,"

wrote John Milton; and from the day he wrote it to this no one has been quite sure what he meant.

Tom, Dick and Harry have each tried his hand at interpretation. Tom says it is the axe, Dick says it is the House of Commons coupled with the House of Lords—and Harry that he cannot for the life of him tell what it means. Harry is wise. But the very fact that the allusion cannot be settled does but the more emphasise the strength of the verse, and indeed those who apologise for obscurity in general—as for instance the unintelligible Mallarmé—use that very plea. "So and so would not have attained his full verbal effect unless he had enhanced the magic of verse by the use of obscurity."

In English the best-known example of this excuse is the plea advanced for Browning; though Browning himself protested that his obscurity was not wanton; that he racked his brains to achieve lucidity. Well, if he did, he did not succeed.

LYRIC

I have heard the same plea put forward with regard to Pindar, whom Greek scholars assure me is natively obscure. I cannot here speak for myself, but the only two men I ever knew who read Pindar as they might read their own native Browning or their own native Mallarmé, and who delighted in him, Jean Jaurès and the late Professor Phillimore, both assured me that this was true. Each of those great scholars equally assured me that in losing his obscurity Pindar would lose half his value. It may be so: but for my part I cannot but believe that, though lucidity is not in verse as in prose the very soul of the matter, a sufficient degree of it is due to the reader; and for that matter to the Muse.

So much for *Lycidas*. It has but one rival, the *Adonais* of Shelley. *Lycidas* and *Adonais* look on one another like twin columns of beauty on either side of a gulf—a gulf of five generations. *Adonais* is the more poignant, *Lycidas* will prove the more enduring; for it remains within the due limits of fancy and of men's reason, and its outlines are of clear proportions. It has also this superiority over the other, that it was written while still the strength of the Christian religion remained. The seventeenth century was of lasting stuff through discipline and doctrine.

The painter Turner (I have been told) desired that a certain picture of his which he held to be his masterpiece should hang side by side in public with one by Claude Lorraine. "For," said he, "posterity will thus discover me to be the greater." He was wrong, it is Claude who has shown himself immutably serene and radiant for 300 years, while the other blurs. For men must not exceed.

After *Lycidas* nothing more: no more song. He played with less than half a hundred lines in Italian, but no one has called them poetry, not even himself—still less the Italians. He produced one noble Latin exercise; but of English Lyric verse— his supreme employ—nothing.

There is a famous foreign phrase saying that in every man there is a poet who died young. This animal seemed to have expired in Milton when he was twenty-nine. We have all known it happen earlier, and the history of literature is full of warnings against trying to keep it alive too late. John Milton was not the man to force verse, though he was the man to work hard at it: and now he ceased.

The failure of his English Muse turned out to be not death but an eclipse; yet this much is true, that the *happy* lyric never returned to him even in the rare short outbreaks of passion in his later epic verse: the *happy* lyric note is no more heard.

It is often found that men who have exercised the poetic faculty, when their failing inspiration no longer permits them a long flight, do occasionally, as though regretting their loss, set down things upon a shorter model: *these*, they feel, these at least, they can accomplish. Many have been contented, under such an inhibition, with the epigram. John Milton fell back now and then upon the sonnet during his years of poetic silence, and loudly expressed prose.

Those few sonnets were, for the most part, not inspired. That two or three should have shone out in such a waste of mere controversy is striking enough—but of all that later. For the moment the main thing we have to remember is that after Milton the man passes the age of twenty-nine Milton the poet halts. The activity of his mind was elsewhere, and remains elsewhere during all those middle years which for most men of letters are the period of capital production.

It seems a strange thing to have happened; not only because the inspiration had been so strong but because there was an equally strong power of concentration to sustain it, and a still stronger ambition. In some degree the blame lies at the door of external things—political circumstance, the great quarrel between the Kings and the Squires, the Civil Wars—but only in some degree.

The outward revolution which was just beginning did call the man away from beauty, because it bereft him of mental repose: already, in the *Lycidas* itself, protest against the Laudian government of the Church had appeared, and that remarkable forecast of a coming vengeance; but the power of song might yet have been restored to him but for another inward revolution—the failure of his marriage—so much more important to Milton the poet even than the national revolution was to Milton the man.

However, it is important to keep in mind, even when one is concerned only or chiefly with the writer, that public affairs were at this very moment, after his writing the *Lycidas*, falling into turmoil. Englishmen had not yet grasped, perhaps, what the growing discontent in Scotland would lead to; but the verdict in Hampden's Ship Money case was delivered in those years and there was violent discussion on it long before Milton's Italian journey.

That journey may also account in some degree for the absence of lyrical composition in 1638-39. Anyhow, the silence had begun, though the turning point had not yet come; and that is why these months between the completion of the *Lycidas* and the marriage which was to change everything should, I think, be called an Interlude.

It has been said that, had Milton died in his thirtieth year, getting off young from the burden of this world, undelivered of his two Epics of *Samson* and of the greatest of his sonnets, he would be remembered only as an important minor poet.

That conclusion is quite false. A man does not write four such things as the Christmas Ode, the *Allegro*, the *Penseroso* and the *Lycidas* without achieving what is called immortality. He does not write them without becoming a prime possession in the treasury of his country.

It was, indeed, the extraordinary resurrection of his last years, the epic achievement, which gave Milton the full place he holds; but still, the early lyric would have been enough, and what he did before as yet he knew the great and necessary misfortunes of human life, makes him a sufficient monument.

He went off next travelling to Italy, in full comfort, with a servant attending him. He was there received and flattered by the greatest, nurtured by their conversation, imitating their verse in their own language (not too successfully, the Italians say). It was not Italy, thus visited, which, though it greatly pleased him, taught him Italian; he had already had Italy within him through his long close friendship with Charles Deodati, he had already used the Italian names and followed the Petrarchian model in the sonnet. He set forth upon his leisurely return. He later described it as flying back to his distressed country on hearing the news of the troubles beginning, but this, like nearly every other flourish of fine motive in Milton's life, was an after-thought.

He was in no kind of hurry. Even if he had been sufficiently interested in the rising political troubles of his country—which as yet he was not—he could not have foreseen any more than could others to what grave dangers the situation as it stood at that moment was to lead. Two more years were to pass before he should even set pen to paper about them and produce the first of his pamphlets—the attack on Episcopacy.

The Italian journey left no deep impress upon the man and still less upon the poet. He found it interesting and amusing, he drew from it some few allusions discoverable in his later work, but it was for him nothing of that revelation which it has been to scores of other Northerners of his own trade.

There is no need to wonder that the Italian voyage should have made so little effect upon Milton's style, imagination, product and life. He was a man so much turned inwards that not even Italian fields and mountains instructed him, let alone the crowd of beauty in architecture and painting. Another way of putting it is to say that he noted it, but already had it within him before his travel began.

A first journey abroad was not, of course, in 1638, the novelty it is to-day. Christendom was far more united then than it is now. The disruptive effects of the Reformation were only beginning to tell. All the older generation of Englishmen still thought of Europe as one thing, and of England as a province of that thing. The new religion was not yet firmly established even in its own places; our civilisation had not yet fallen into the two opposing camps which were to divide it for good after the end of the Thirty Years' War. Milton belonged, it is true, to the younger generation who had been brought up to worship the nation; but then so had all his contemporaries, and nearly every one of them who travelled "reacted" to travel far more strongly than ever he did.

He came back chiefly remembering the flattery he had received from his Italian hosts, the courage he had shown in attacking the religion of those hosts, their appreciation of his good looks and still suave manners—for the spoiling of these by lacerated pride and wounded honour was to come later. And he was always ready to allude to his having met Galileo—because Galileo had come to loggerheads with the Pope.

For the rest he had already soaked himself in Italy through the classics; his youth had already received the Ausonian vision fully, and there is more of the Italian air and soul and hills in the poems written before ever he left England than in the *Para-*

dise Lost, because he had nourished himself upon the *Eclogues* and had seen, as vividly as with the living eye, the landscapes of Virgil.

On getting back to England in August 1639 he learned that, in his absence, Charles Deodati had died. He commemorated him in the fine Latin Pastoral called "The Epitaph of Damon" (*Epitaphium Damonis*). Would it not have been a great thing for English if he had written that Ode in his native language— would it not then have surpassed the *Lycidas?* It is not probable. The Epitaph was called forth by a violent personal emotion such as Milton had never felt for that anodyne acquaintance Edward King: the whole of his youth was buried in the same tomb with Deodati, and he never made a friend again: but it does not follow that this threnody would have corresponded to those deep feelings.

It must be remembered that the greatest verse does not proceed immediately from the strongest feeling. The greatest verse calls up the strongest emotion in the reader, but in the writer it is a distillation, not a cry. One may question whether it would be feasible at all to surpass the *Lycidas*—and the *Lycidas* was written upon an artificial theme, set as it were for a composition; it concerned a man with whom Milton had little connection and for whom he felt no special attachment: yet all this in no way weakens it.

The greatest sonnets of Ronsard were (I am told) written down (and written to no one in particular), when the Queen, finding them upon his desk, read one or two and said that they ought to be dedicated to a Maid of Honour of hers, a certain Helen, who would be proud to see her name attached to them. Ronsard was as willing to have that name as any other, and the famous stuff has made famous that same name of Helen. They have been called these hundreds of years, "Sonnets to Helen," yet Helen had nothing to do with them—and that is how great verse is written.

[128]

Milton having thus returned to England did not go back to Horton. The political struggle had begun, he was by nature attached to it, and he proposed to remain where its development could be watched. He lodged first with one Russell near the City end of Fleet Street; but that was only while he was waiting to move into a fairly large and convenient house in Aldersgate, outside the City walls and on the road that goes north, near the gate itself. This was a house with a garden, and to have a garden to his house was a necessity with Milton to the end: it lay back in a sort of alley from the main road, it was quiet, and all that he desired. He took there his two little nephews, the Phillips boys, his sister's sons, to whom he had promised to teach the humanities; and there he wrote the first four of those pamphlets which were to come out so rapidly from his pen year after year from the summer of 1641 when the first of them appeared (on the nature of Church Government) to the last two, immediately before the Restoration in 1660, when he still pleaded for a solution which had become impossible.

There were nineteen years of it; and it is tempting to close the first phase of Milton at this point, when there appeared the first of those many controversial tracts which he issued during this middle part of his life, between his thirty-third and his fifty-second year which is barren of verse save for a few sonnets.

It is tempting to start a new chapter with these first prose attacks against Prelacy—that is, against the Government of the Church of England by Bishops—in the summer of 1641, and to say that with these the polemic—that is, the fighting and angry—Milton begins.

But such a distinction would be superficial. It is true that these first four pamphlets, appearing in 1641 during the manœuvring for position which was to end in the Civil War, have nothing in them of lyric; but they do not open a new chapter in the man's development, in his inner and essential character. *That* was to come after the breakdown of his marriage in the following year, 1642. It was the woful business of his wife's desertion, of his humiliation, that changed Milton altogether and made him (who had proved himself already so great in verse and might have continued to be great in controversial prose) something more than controversial—a creature with teeth and claws, a man rabid in attack as in defence—a man provoked to paroxysm by opposition; a man enraged.

These four Anti-Prelatic tracts are pretty dull, save where they are sometimes exuberant; but they nowhere rave or curse; the man's temper is not yet soured. The last of them (the answer to the Remonstrance) is lively and often amusing; it is the writing of a man who fences hard and well, not that of a man wounded. But when the true polemic phase begins you find the change—and it begins with his pamphlets on Divorce. Henceforward he is burning. Henceforward, the moment he deals with anyone whom he regards as an enemy he pours out torrent upon torrent of personal and offensive abuse. We shall see later what new kind of man it is who writes the *Colasterion*, the attack on Salmasius, the virulent *Defensio Secunda*.

One thing these first four early tracts of his do clearly show. He was not the stylist he has been called. He had fine flights of rhetoric and good, concise, brief summaries. He discovered striking phrases and metaphors. His powerful brain was always lively and his fancy vigorous. But he did not control his pen in prose as he did in verse. He, the most economic of men in the Lyric, was the most diffuse in the treatise. Even when he starts clearly he soon falls to muddlement, like a man who should take a good path across a moor at night, but, losing the glimmer of its whiteness, goes off into a boggy patch at the side.

For one example out of dozens to show how easily he slipped out of lucidity into what may be called haggis prose—a mass of ill-ordered mixture—read his first lines. He is setting out to write—it is the first of his pamphlets at the beginning of the troubles before the outbreak of the Civil War—*Of REFOR-MATION touching Church Discipline in ENGLAND and the cawses that hitherto have hindered it*. He opens with his views on that happy event, the Reformation at large, and this is how he does it:—

"Amidst those deep and retired thoughts, which with every man fully instructed, ought to be most frequent, of GOD, of his miraculous *Ways* and *Works* amongst men, and of our *religion* and *worship* to be performed to Him; after the story of Our Saviour CHRIST, suffering to the lowest bent of weakness in the flesh, and presently triumphing in the highest pitch of glory in the Spirit, which drew up his body also, till we in both be united to him in the revelation of his kingdome; I do not know of anything more worthy to take up the whole passion and pitty on the one side, and joy on the other, than to consider, first, the foule . . . corruptions, and then after many a tedious age the long desired but much more happy reformation of the Church in these later days."

There you have it before you, that style which we have been told—in all the blind conviction of hero-worship—is a model for all writers of English. See how one thing in this passage suggests another at random, how whatever leaps up in his mind is thrown in pell-mell until the whole is a perfect labyrinth of verbiage. And it is not the worst example; we shall come to others more amusing later on: but it is sufficient.

It may be urged that all great writers of prose thus suffer at times from confusion through fatigue; but Milton falls into it so often that it is actually characteristic of him, and the clear passages—let alone the noble ones—are exceptions, and rare exceptions at that. In this very place, for instance, a little further on, the reader is delighted to find the ancient Church Universal there vividly called "the old red dragon" (where "red" is the operative word). And wretched little Edward VI appears as "that Godly and Royal child."

If he had always or even commonly lashed out like that in these tracts it would be a pleasure to read them; as it is, the task of reading them is a burden.

It may be objected to me that the greatest master of all in the department of English prose (I mean Cranmer) was capable of worse. Cranmer's letter to Henry VIII in the matter of Anne Boleyn (I think the longest rigmarole without a pause that I know) is worse. It makes a whole page of close print in which the pen runs away at random, stumbling over itself like a panicky man flying for his life over rough ground at night. But then with Cranmer that is quite exceptional and the occasion excuses him. He *was* in a panic, scribbling away for dear life—with the image of that coarse bloated figure, King Henry VIII, only a quarter of a mile away in the Palace over the water; the cruel little green eyes, the scant red hairs on the large pasty face, and the loose mouth which could and did speak sudden death, were close before him. And Cranmer, when he took his time over it and wrote delicately and lovingly like a miniature painter the words of that idiom which he enshrined for ever in the Collects and the Litany, proved himself supreme, in prose, after a fashion that Milton never did nor could.

All Milton's prose faults are present in these first political efforts, and they got worse later on; the virtues of his prose, which are chiefly to be found in the oratorical passages and especially in the passages of abuse, developed with time also. His rhetoric, in which he is most lucid and readable, gets more eloquent as the years proceed; his vituperation coarser and more violent—and coarseness and violence are virtues in vituperation.

Here are present also of course all the original parts of his religious position; his growing Protestantism, his inclination for the independence of congregations, or at any rate of opinion, and the unfettered right to lay ecclesiastical assembly. But it is noteworthy that the heresies in him do not yet appear in these days of 1641, before his marriage. On the contrary, there are open affirmations of orthodoxy, and actual blame of that Unitarian conviction which he himself later adopted.

To begin with we have of course the long and turgid sentences from which he never escaped except when he was moved to eloquence or to slanging. The first sentence opening the ball is characteristic of a thousand others which were to be written during the next score years.

Milton's defect in this has been excused on the plea of fashion. All men of his time, it has been said, wrote sentences of that kind; and one critic has even gone so far as to tell us that it is we who are to blame for not being able to follow them. But the plea is false. To begin with, those of Milton's contemporaries who wrote best did not suffer from this defect, but more important is the fact that Milton's long sentences were not co-ordinated. There was no consecutive order in them, and, what was worse, no proper subordination of the subsidiary to the principal. It was Ciceronian Latin which made him write long sentences, but he could not transform Ciceronian sentences into English. The eighteenth century could do that. Milton, to whom the eighteenth century looked back as to a God, on account of his poetry, was not the model of their prose.

Consider for instance this passage, in which he is laboriously excusing himself from a charge of too much criticising the Fathers of the Church and the Martyrs:—

"And herewithall I invoke the IMMORTALL DEITIE Reveler and Judge of secrets, That wherever I have in this booke plainely and roundly (though worthily and truly) laid open the faults and blemishes of FATHERS and MARTYRS and Christian EMPERORS; or have otherwise inveighed against Error and Superstition with vehement expressions, I have done it, neither out of malice, nor List to speak evill, nor any vaineglory; but of mere necessity, to vindicate the truth

from an ignominious bondage, whose native worth is now become such a low esteeme that shee is like to finde small credit
with us for what she can say, unless shee can bring a ticket from
'Cranmer,' 'Latimer' and 'Ridley'; or prove herself a retainer
to 'Constantine' and wear his badge."

Observe how clumsily he handles a relative, "whose native
worth is now," etc.—properly that word "whose" should apply
to "bondage." He means of course that it shall apply to "truth"
five words earlier.

Then again, he cannot ravel up the sentence at the right
place; he goes stumbling on past the natural ending because a
new idea occurs to him, he does not stop at "she can say" and
begin a new sentence; he jots down, shoves in, a further modification which had occurred to him—and then adds to that yet
another in order to bring in Constantine.

His sentences are not long through too much repetition
(which at least makes for clarity) nor long through adjectival
clauses, which also argue lucidity—but through too many ideas
striking him at once in the midst of his writing, and his introducing them all in a heap, undigested. Having mentioned
Truth, for instance, he must suddenly go off on a side-track
about his misfortunes. In Milton's mind, perhaps on account
of his being so steeped in Hebrew writing, there is a tendency
to proceed from word to word rather than from idea to idea.
It is the same alien thing as confuses the reader in the Epistles
of St. Paul.

You find also in this first pamphlet of his that worship of
England, that new intense patriotism, which I have called a
prime part of his religion.

It had already of course appeared in his verse, it was the
mood inherited from the great constructive work of William
Cecil, who planned to ally patriotism with the religious revolution over which he presided. This worship of England appears
almost at the beginning of the first pamphlet, before he has

written much more than a thousand words. Pleading as he is for an extension of the Protestant spirit in the English Church, he brings in that most unhistorical idea which has since his time been repeated unceasingly—the idea that England was the originator of heretical attacks against the unity of Catholic Europe. It is the idea which engendered the description of Wyclif as "the morning star of the Reformation."

Milton was wrong in this, as people usually are when they write nationalist history. Since he was fond of Latin tags, I beg his shade to excuse here the most threadbare of all tags: *vixere fortes.*

It applies here very thoroughly: there were plenty of attacks on the Church before Wyclif. Not only was a great part of Christendom turned away from unity by the Mohammedan heresy, several centuries earlier, but the Catharist heresy all but broke up the civilisation of the West, half-way between the Mohammedan attack and that of the Reformation. Mohammed also was moved by the craving for simplicity, he also reacted against sacraments and images and a priesthood, and all the rest of it. His followers also, by the way, reacted against wine. And the Catharists set up a Church of their own, but for that matter heresy must necessarily be as old as orthodoxy—the one provokes the other.

You find also in this first pamphlet of Milton's what you are to find throughout his polemical work, the habit of close argument, point by point. It was to grow to a maximum in the *De Doctrina.* And you find as well the appearance of that incomparable erudition which was for Milton, as a man, his principal glory. Hardly has he begun to argue that the early Bishops were chosen by the people and worked with their presbyters as equals than he comes out with a citation from St. Ignatius, followed by three from St. Cyprian—and all within a space of fifteen lines.

There also appears now, 1641, in embryo that talent for vituperation in which Milton was to excel. "The people of God redeem'd and wash'd with Christ's blood are now no better reputed than impure Ethnicks and lay dogs; the table of communion upon the brow of the choir fortified with bulwark and barracado to keep off the profane touch of the laiks, while the obscene and surfeited priest scruples not to paw and mammock the sacramental bread as familiarly as his tavern bisket." Then, after that, we get, "what a plump endowment to the many-benefice-gaping-mouth of a prelate, what a relish it would give to his canary-sucking and swan-eating palate."

On the other hand, this first of the string of pamphlets nowhere abandons what I suppose may be called Protestant orthodoxy—that is, the accepted main doctrines retained by the Reformers of the Church of England. The godhead of Christ, for instance: so far from showing Arianism Milton in these early pamphlets is still strong on the other side; blaming the leanings towards Arianism of Constantine, and speaking in so many words of the "Tri-Personal Godhead"—which he was later to make it his special business to deny. It is in the eloquent invocation to God that he may preserve the English Church from the monstrous Bishops that we get this, right at the very end of the tract:

"Thou therefore that sit'st in light and glory unapproachable, Parent of Angels and Men! Next thee I implore, Omnipotent King, Redeemer of that last remnant whose nature thou didst assume, Ineffable and everlasting Love! And Thou the third subsistance of Divine Infinitude, Illumining Spirit, the joy and solace of created things! One Tri-Personall Godhead!"

There it is, in all its plainness. "Tri-Personal Godhead." Men of Milton's kind are commonly white-hot in defence of their own consistency, and rave against any who point out to them a change in their opinion. He was, perhaps, later, when he wrote the *De Doctrina*, forgetful of what he had been only a few years earlier, when he wrote *Of Reformation in England;* but certain it is that in 1641 before the first great blow had fallen on him he held what those around him held in the prime matter of the Incarnation.

He followed up that first pamphlet which I have taken for an example with two others in the same vein, each following hot upon the heels of the other; indeed the third may have been published contemporaneously with the second, for he had been moved to it by another attack while the second was in the press.

The third of the Anti-Prelatic pamphlets, the *Animadversions*, have many an amusing phrase; and, forgotten though they are, and deserve to be, one very notable passage in which Milton declaims against the conception of a national Church is worth retaining. If the Church (he says) is to be called, as St. Paul called Her, a Common Mother, it must be a Church which comprehends all the European Protestants of his time. Such a Church Milton will admit by a vague metaphor to be a Mother, but:

"Let all genealogy tell us if it can what we must call the Church of *England*, unless we shall make every English Protestant a kind of Bacchus, to have two mothers."

He asks whether "we, who by God's special grace have shaken off the servitude of the Pope, should sink under the slavery of a familiar notion, the cloudy conception of a demi-island Mother," and genially adds that anyone who does this becomes "a Bastard" and "a Centaur."

The Anti-Prelatic pamphlets run their course: they make Milton a protagonist in the conflict just begun. They land him into what were shortly to become the Civil Wars. But they mean little in the story of Milton's pen, still less in the story of his life. It is not the four pamphlets opening in 1641 that impress the watcher of Milton. It is what followed in 1642. For that year, his thirty-fourth, was to determine his life and fate.

Part Four

Polemic

Polemic

THE DISASTER

IT was the spring of 1642. The Governor of Hull had defied the King.

The preparations for civil war had begun to fill London with rumour. They had brought John Milton himself to continue with curiosity those readings in the military science which he had always pursued and which he makes part of his system of education.

There was even some idea of giving him a command; the thing was talked of later and there is no smoke without fire: but a command was never given him. It was as well. He was absurdly unfitted for such a task. Imagine John Milton in a brass-hat!

There was something conspicuous about Milton's abstention from arms, for he was physically well fitted to serve. He was, by his own account, a good swordsman. He was only thirty-three. He might at least have accompanied the rebel armies or helped to recruit them in London. Rather in those eager days, when Captain Oliver Cromwell was beginning to train his double troop, and when Milton's political friends in favour of rebellion were getting back to their own counties to raise men, did his mind turn to something very different. He would marry —at long last.

It was late indeed for him to come to such a decision and the delay proved fatal to him, for he was—to put it simply and I hope decently—inexperienced.

He was not only inexperienced, but evidently doubtful of his gambit: he must marry, but whom?

He bethought himself of a possible approach, of a plan: he shrank from anything more hazardous, but one avenue towards wedlock lay open to him which he thought acceptable and possible. His fear of women had been laughed at, as we know; and we must not be too hard on him for having made a virtue out of it: such men usually do, and that without hypocrisy. But he did know that it was not a good preparation for what he was about to do. His moonlit simulacra of petty love were no proper foundation for the more serious business. That he had noticed a face here and there, that he had even addressed verses in a distant country to one woman would be of no avail now. There is nothing really of love in his early poems—not a glint of it in all their beauty. And his own arguments, as he set them down later, show that he had not felt his celibacy to be a strain —at any rate until lately, in his last twenties. *Sera Venus.* But he ought also to have remembered what he himself had said, that a belated approach to this kind of thing following on many years of shrinking from it, is perilous.

It was at Whitsuntide (and Whitsun fell that year at the very end of May) that he started out from London riding alone, telling no one the object of his journey. What he had in mind was the household of the Powells at Forest Hill outside Oxford. There he had a claim, for that household lay in debt to himself; and a girl whose father owed him money could not frighten him so much as another. He could appear with least awkwardness before such and even feeling some superiority: a financial superiority, which would counterbalance a certain social difference counting the other way. For the embarrassed Powells were of the landed gentry, and John Milton was not.

Richard Powell, the squire of Forest Hill, was indeed embarrassed, and had been pottering from debt to accumulating debt for at least sixteen years; borrowing from one man to stave off the claims of another, speculating in the hope of retrieving his position, getting deeper and deeper—but still a Justice of the Peace for his county of Oxfordshire and still, of course, a gentleman.

From what we know of his debts—there may have been any amount more, but I speak of actual record remaining to us—the list is significant. Apart from the original unpaid £500 (call it over £3,000 in modern money) wherein he was bound to John Milton, he had borrowed, eleven years before, £400 (call it £2,400 at least to-day) on his properties in Wheatley, the village near his home; then, nine years later, to pay off a pressing £2,000 and others (I give the terms in modern value) he raised £6,000 from a wealthy man, a neighbour within a day's ride—one Pye of Woodstock, later a pillar of the Rebellion in the Long Parliament. To raise that £6,000 he mortgaged his interest in his home itself, the manor house of Forest Hill. Then again the next year (1641), just before this momentous visit of his earliest creditor John Milton, he had raised yet another £2,000 from someone of the same name, Powell, who may have been a relative, pledging what remained of his Wheatley land.

He still floated, but precariously; for the credit of a man in his position could be stretched some way without breaking. His wife had brought him long ago a jointure of more than £20,000, and it had not yet all gone. Meanwhile he had bred some ten children, and of these the third, the eldest daughter, was a few months past her sixteenth birthday in those spring days of 1642 when John Milton rode out alone and silent from London upon his quest.

The ride was in no way perilous, the roads were still open; the first acts of war had taken place, the King had mustered his troops and the Parliament theirs, but as yet there had been no battle—when he appeared at Forest Hill and dismounted to carry out his plan.

By calculation all seemed suitable. The bride was so very young—he was twice her age—and the family under that long-standing obligation to him; the acquaintance was of equally long standing. He turned back for London a married man, bringing with him this very young bride, Mary Powell, and the promise of a £6,000 dowry; the promise only, for Richard Powell promised easily. With his wife he brought certain of her relatives to Aldersgate as well—who in their circumstances were not unwilling to enjoy a little hospitality.

There was unusual merriment in the Aldersgate house for some days, and then Mary Powell, now Mary Milton, was left alone there with her not discourteous but solemn and most uncongenial spouse. She found that he had for his companions his books, for occupation the teaching of his two little nephews (and it is said that one of her grievances was his harshness to these children); but it is also related by later gossip that the tedium of his academic bent, his "philosophy," was her chief burden. At any rate, she had enjoyed this situation a month or a little more, when she required a holiday. Might she not go back and visit her people at Forest Hill? It would only be for a few weeks of the summer; they were already in or near the beginning of August, and she would return at Michaelmas.

Michaelmas came, and she did not return; the exact John Milton protested in consequence. His letters remained unanswered. He still protested, and was still met by silence. He was at the expense of sending a special messenger on foot to travel the fifty odd miles (it must have taken him the better part of a week) but the servant was met at Forest Hill with repulse and insult and he came back with no comfort for his master. The thing was getting known, and would soon be a scandal. How it affected Milton's pride we shall see—the reaction took a strange form.

Meanwhile the Civil War was well alight; Edgehill had been fought, Charles had marched on London. The town was too large for him to take; the half-trained militia in their very great numbers, the earthworks that had been cast up, saved the capital and the cause of the Rebellion. But there had been a moment of great alarm—for the more peaceable burgesses very near panic—and it was in this crisis, in the middle of November 1642, that Milton wrote and affixed to his door that sonnet which shall be dealt with in its right place.

Here it is enough to say that the piece of verse is a vivid example of what distinction can be made between the poet and the man. For some seven weeks he had been brooding on his wrath, he had perhaps already prepared the first notes of what was to be in the coming year his public protest against the indignity to which he had been submitted; yet there comes out in the midst of such a violent but sordid domestic strain a pure piece of English poetry, wholly separate, like a jewel picked up in muddy ground. It was the first of those rare pieces of verse, each a sonnet, which were to appear during his years of violence and conflict in prose; and it was one of the best.

And now as the fighting season of 1643 developed, in the height of the summer when Waller and his army of the Rebellion were overwhelmed in the west, when Hampden died, when Newcastle conquered the North and Scottish aid for the Rebellion was being desperately demanded, the fruit of his accumulated anger appeared.

Henceforward Milton's change of character was set: he was a man with a burning grievance. It never left him. It coloured all he did. His mind turned upon it as upon a central pivot.

It was a grievance of a special kind; not against an individual, nor even exactly against the scheme of things, but rather a grievance against the unsuspected bitterness of the world as

[145]

revealed through the atrocious nature of woman, in the first place; but in the second place and in a larger manner in that fact that he—John Milton—had actually suffered, had been made a victim and (though he would never admit it) a laughingstock. From that winter of 1642-3 he is to be found occupied on the theme that woman brings evil into the lives of men, that woman is inferior, that woman is treasonable. He was further and more greatly occupied with the theme that even his own exalted self must for some mysterious reason suffer. It half bewildered him, but he remembers what he owes to his character of prophet. He was not a mouthpiece of the Divine for nothing; if he suffered he must suffer greatly. He is always in the back of his mind Milton Prometheus as well as Milton-everything-else.

And he has a new particular quarrel, which he carries on unceasingly, against marriage. He calls it a quarrel against incongruous marriage; but since the whole conception of marriage turns upon a bond, since a bond will always somewhere at some time chafe, and since all bonds especially chafed this particular man (so that it was humorously said that he could not bear his own garters!) to pretend that he favoured marriage when it was exactly perfect is as much as to say that he did not favour marriage at all. What he favoured was the complete happiness of John Milton through the sympathy and subservience of others—notably whoever might be closest to him.

In this matter he discovers the initiative, and that is a point well worth remarking, for with the rest of his activities it was not so.

In all else that John Milton did he followed, he did not lead; he waited until he saw the winning side; he waited until others had taken the plunge. He published no pamphlet against the Bishops until the big battle had been won in the Commons, until Laud was safe under lock and key and Strafford done to death. He praised not Cromwell until Cromwell had become a master. He did not defend the right of an imaginary Commonwealth to destroy the King of England until it was patent to all that the King of England's life was forfeit.

So it was throughout his career—in every matter except the matter of woman and marriage. There all that was most vital in him was stung to an agonised life. His vanity and his pride had both been cast down, he had planned and his plan had failed. A monstrous thing had happened—he, the chosen of his Creator, had been flouted. Therefore whenever he remembered the central tragedy of his life or was reminded of it by circumstances, he flies out upon his own account and waits for no man to blaze the path. He leads, he does not follow, and he leads pertinaciously.

He insists and re-insists and counter-insists upon divorce, the destruction of Christian marriage, as a thing odious to the freedom and dignity of man. He lashes out against it with furious invective, as though against an individual person who had insulted and wounded him to the core. Any criticism he attacks with an equal violence, he goes at it again and again, returning in one pamphlet after another. Because the censorship would be opposed to such license he attacks the censorship, pleading for freedom of publication with all the fire and the lack of definition which have marked such pleas in every generation.

He goes further, he pleads for polygamy. It is true that he did not dare to publish that plea. His initiative, however strong in this department, could not carry him as far as that. But he unburdened his soul by a very thorough examination of all that could be said in favour of multiplicity of wives as a thoroughly Christian idea. And in his secret researches on this matter he did not envisage successive wives, tandem, as is our modern fashion, but four-in-hand—after the fashion of the Mohammedans, certain savages, and the Old Testament heroes, splendidly led by Solomon.

Further disasters all nourished that emotion of grievance.

[147]

Did he go blind?—it was a cosmic injustice. Did the Republican cause to which he had devoted himself crash in a universal shout of popular contempt and laughter?—it was a direct insult to John Milton, as well as a danger which filled him with lively panic. Had he to live on, somewhat impoverished, somewhat lonely, seeing all whom he had attacked triumphant and the power which he had defended beaten down?—it was another series of blows delivered by the universe (one might almost say by the Creator) against John Milton. That was for him the meaning of all that happened.

From this towering absorption in self he drew the courage which has made him so deservedly glorious. This was the source of his unconquerable resistance and of his carrying the war into Africa, by triumphing—suddenly and in the midst of his dereliction—with the trumpet blasts of *Paradise Lost* and the organ roll of *Samson Agonistes*.

Having brooded all winter and spring over his humiliation, re-calling that first miserable marriage experiment, its ambiguous ending—neither one thing nor the other—the refusal of his wife to rejoin him, the insults and the ignominy; he broke out at last into his famous first pamphlet on Divorce.

He dared not sign it; although he could not contain his anger he dreaded the consequences of that anger; and the little tract of forty-eight pages came out anonymously, in the last days of July 1643.*

He had been nursing his anger ten months, since he had be-gun to feel certain of Mary Powell's determination to abandon him and make him ridiculous.

But his habitual caution availed him not. His style betrayed him, and Milton was soon quoted by name as the champion of an enormous and scandalous innovation, so shocking to all the air around that, even in the midst of the wars, the reverberations of that blow, though it was struck in a matter wholly discon-nected with the great issues of the time, were heard all around.

The noise grew and broadened, till Milton took the only course possible and defended himself by a counter offensive. He prepared a second edition of the tract, to which he was ready to put his initials at least, and to accept the challenge. It was nearly the double of the first in length, arranged in two books separated into chapters, and was proclaimed to the world with this resounding trumpet-blast of a title:

"The Doctrine and Discipline of *Divorce:* Restor'd to the good of both SEXES from the bondage of the Canon Law and other

---

* The tract was acquired by Thomason (who bought up every public writing he could as it appeared, and whose collection has therefore proved invaluable to history) on the 1st of August. It is marked with that date by him or by his orders.

mistakes, to the true meaning of the Scripture, in the Law and Gospels compar'd.

"Wherein are set down the bad consequences of abolishing or condemning of Sin, that which the Law of God allowes, and Christ abolish't not.

"Address'd to the Parliament of England, with the Assembly."

This word "Assembly" refers to a body of Divines and Parliamentarians who had been summoned by the rebels to advise and assist in matters of Religion. It had met in Henry VII's chapel, in July 1642, while Milton and his wife were still together in Aldersgate Street. One hundred and forty-nine members—ten Lords, twenty Commons, and the rest Divines. They were intended to replace the authority of the Bishops. They were not given true authority, such as the Bishops had had, but it was theirs to draw up reports and make suggestions upon which the rebellious section of the Parliament should act. Hence Milton's appeal to them *as well as* to the Houses.

There is so much of the tragic in the breakdown of any marriage that a man may be blamed for dwelling too much upon the comic of it; but really if one will go through the drudgery of reading the involved matter it is glorious fun!

This tract on Divorce was absurdly crude of language in too many places, but its touch of obscenity did not proceed from that modern indecent exposure of the soul which inspires novels written to-day, only to shock and to sell. What is extraordinary about it is the oblivion of pride. His pride blinded Milton to the fact that he was making a fool of himself. "I am John Milton; I speak, and you lesser men must hear me." He could not conceive that the lesser men would laugh at him, or that, if they did, it would matter. Yet when they laughed, or even only criticised, he saw red and screamed.

John Milton had no idea what a figure he made of himself, coming out thus with a sudden revolutionary demand for a change in all Christian society on the strength of his own ignominious private experience. Yet it was John Milton all over. It came from the certitude that John Milton was much the chief thing in the landscape; almost the only thing. John Milton's troubles are necessarily of a cosmic sort concerning God deeply and all his creatures. He could not dream that there might be legitimate laughter at the suffering of a divine seer, even when that suffering proceeded from such a farcical source. The pamphlet is also most Miltonic in its erudition, in its deliberate and laboured display of scholarship. He multiplies therein citations, deductions, parallels; he ponderously examines what may be said against his theme, and turns text after text upside down to make it say the opposite of what it does say. He drives home now and then with a really strong phrase; then he rambles, divagates and wanders.

But the gist of the whole thing is of interest to the modern world, for Milton's thesis is the thesis that has won the victory to-day in the modern decline of religion. Men do not excuse divorce to-day on a groundwork of texts; they do not brief themselves from the Bible, nor even from the codes of the early Christian Emperors as Milton did; but men's inward motive for affirming that divorce is rational and just, as men to-day outside the Catholic body do universally affirm, derives from the same moral attitude as that which Milton adopts. Marriage, to be a true marriage, must be a perfect companionship. A man being soul and mind as well as body, and the soul and mind taking precedence of the body, there must be a companionship of souls—or it is no marriage.

How can that condition be a sacrament (and the now thoroughly Protestant Milton lapses into calling marriage a sacrament for the purposes of his argument) which is a condition of misery? And what misery is greater than constant, hourly, uncongenial companionship?

The kernel of the affair will be found in the thirteenth chapter of this unique tract of 30,000 words. It is his "ninth reason"

—for here as always he tabulates carefully, setting out all his arguments in a row.

"All human society must proceed," he writes, "from the mind rather than the body, else it would be but a kind of annimal and bestial meeting; if the mind therefore cannot have that due company by mariage" (he spells it in the French fashion, "mariage," for the English word is of French origin, coming from the days when all the cultivated classes in England were of French speech) "that it may reasonably and humanly desire, that mariage can be no human society, but a certain formality; or guilding over, and little better than a brutish congress, and so in very wisdom and pureness to be dissolved."

As always, he bangs about him with the Scriptures like a flail. No man knew better than Milton that you could prove what you will from Holy Writ. He did also often sincerely use the texts of Scripture which had convinced him and which he thought should convince others, but here he simply brings them in to support a conclusion already arrived at through unhappy experience. It was experience which called forth this cry, long before he had rationalised the instinctive protest. He glories in exposing the inconsistency of the Puritan, who professes to base all on Scripture and yet will not listen to Scripture when it goes against him. And here he is on strong ground; for the Puritan can with difficulty explain (save through tradition, which he rejects) the shifting of the Sabbath to a Sunday—or for that matter the eating of black puddings and jugged hare.

Yet here amid the texts he has of course his troubles. He has to get over "whom God hath joined," etc., but he ambles through that happily enough. "Oh, yes, what God *has joined* must remain joined! Certainly! But then that word 'join' must be interpreted in the light of private judgment. It means not 'join' in the common use of that word, but is understood (though unhappily not actually stated in the Gospel) to mean 'in a real mutual suitability.' Where such suitability is present, *that* indeed is God's work. But it cannot be present through a mere writ or a mere piece of liturgy."

It is pathetic to remark, as we read, how he has to bring in, even in this connection, the new Messianic ideas that haunted him—the inspiration of all the winning side from William Cecil's Establishment onwards; the worship of oneself as a member of one's own people; the idea that one's nation must be the chosen nation. "Look," says he, to the fragment of the Lords and the revolutionary half of the House of Commons (he calls them "the Parliament of England") "look how this reform, if you will adopt it, will make England a pioneer, as she always should be, of right!"

It is exactly what we are to get later in the *Areopagitica*, where we are told that if England will only abolish the licensing of printed matter by authority she will lead all mankind with the torch of liberty. It was England that produced Constantine, says he (he was thinking either of the legend of St. Helen or the historical truth that the liberator of the Church set out from Britain). It was the English Druids who taught the Gauls their religion, and so now from England true doctrine can come again.

He ends with a passage of rhetoric, which is clear as his rhetoric always is—a point in which (as I have repeated) it differs greatly from his prose.

The passage is clear, I say, but hardly sublime, though he intended it to be sublime. But Milton, who reached the sublime in verse frequently and one might say almost as a habit, who made of the sublime in verse a sort of normal standard for himself, did not often reach it in any other medium. Some would say he never reached it in any other medium: certainly not in his Latin or English prose, and hardly even in his best rhetoric.

That he intended the sublime here is manifest enough, for he

[153]

leads up to it like a man trotting up to take a jump, and he is on his metal to give a striking picture of the national glory that shall succeed on the passage of this necessary measure, on the application of this life-giving law—that a man may get rid of his wife when she no longer suits him; and for that matter let us hope—though he won't say so—a woman of her husband. If only the rebel fragment of the Commons now in session at Westminster and their pendant, the Assembly of Divines close at hand, will allow freedom from the old constraints of Christian marriage, what vast good will follow! Here is his picture of it.

"Many helpless Christians will they" (i.e., the Parliamentarians and Assembly-men) "raise from the depths of sadness and distress, utterly unfitted as they are to serve God or man; many they shall reclaim from obscure and giddy sects, many regain from dissolute and brutish license, many from desperate hardness. They shall set free many daughters of Israel" (Israel of course is England here as usual; in the north of the island, however, Israel is Scotland) "now weltering in their sad plight; whom Satan had bound eighteen years. Man they shall restore to his just dignity, preferring the soul's free peace before the promiscuous draining of a carnall rage. Marriage from a perilous hasard and a snare they shall reduce to be a more certain Hav'n and retirement of happy society."

All that because poor little Mary Powell had found him altogether too difficult! Yet she had not betrayed him, as she well might have done. One who reads this inflamed stuff cannot but notice how the writer of it lacks grip: plenty of sound but no clear principle.

Indeed a sort of negative vagueness runs through all Milton's revolutionary work, even where he is most precise in his drawing up of arguments and discussion of pleas into "firstly," "secondly," "thirdly," it is always a set of reasons *against* some existing thing—never, or hardly ever, a definite proposal of policy.

[154]

How is anyone to distinguish in these new marriage laws what the sufficient cause for Divorce may be? When may a man, and when may he not, get rid of his wife? Milton gives no answer.

He quotes the old Byzantine Imperial laws permitting a new marriage after desertion, and in case of madness. He quotes of course, and was to quote again, pretty well everything that the Reformers had said, in all their variety, against Christian marriage (as against every other institution of European society); but he does not tell you which he approves among all those very different revolts; he is occupied only in showing how strong the case for divorce at large may be.

Since he will have it that there can be no true marriage without a satisfactory feeling of spiritual companionship he leaves the law-giver without any guide whatsoever: there is no test that can be applied, there is no definition.

Well, that is John Milton all over. We know what has happened to those who are of his mind; they have, as a rule, dispensed with marriage altogether. Their number to-day increases very rapidly; they will probably in the near future set the standard, or lack of standard, for all societies in which organised religion has gone to pieces.

Now in that attitude (which used to be called "free love") our modern practicers of promiscuous adultery are consistent and rational; they conform to their own principles. But Milton himself was not rational in the matter: he wanted a certain result which is unobtainable without the destruction of marriage and therefore of divorce itself; and yet he seems to have wanted it without disturbing the conception of the Christian family— for no one was more vehement than he was upon the authoritative bond between parent and child.

It was at Candlemas, the 2d of February 1644, that this second edition of the tract on Divorce had appeared; and thenceforward Milton might be gratified at least in this—that his name was now before the public after a fashion that he had not hitherto enjoyed—or suffered.

For we must appreciate, in order to understand the man apart from his poetic gift, that he was divided within himself in the matter of publicity. It is a common complication; especially with writers of the finer kind. On the one hand he loved fame, and had a sort of thirst for public acclamation; but he shrank from being the target of abuse and the recipient of moral blows. He was glad enough to be talked about widely so it be also quietly, and with mere laudation. Now this he could not be. He had taken the field in a highly unpopular and novel cause, and there was about him such a vigour of expression, in spite of the twisted and confused periods through which that expression was conveyed, that he called down upon himself the same violence which he used against others.

This sudden, hugely swollen notoriety cannot but have come as a surprise to him. In writing anonymously against Christian marriage Milton had sought rather to relieve a tension of temper within him which demanded satisfaction. He had indeed pleaded for a violent innovation, but it might have passed half-unnoticed among the very many revolutionary proposals in doctrine and morals the anarchy of the times had thrown up. Yet here he was, in spite of himself, the butt of dangerous and continued attack, and apparently unsupported.

His temper was none the better for having to live thus unwillingly celibate. He had attempted to soothe himself by a little mild philandering, the product of which we have in two of his least successful sonnets; but he was in a passion all the time. He had been wounded after such a fashion that the wound would not heal; it gangrened, and the whole of his inner self was and remained poisoned.

Such was the story of Milton's disaster and its first consequences. Thenceforward you have to deal with a new man, a man of far greater effect than had been the lyric poet and the pamphleteer against the Bishops—but warped, and carrying with him to the grave an angry sense of inevitable, unceasing conflict. Henceforward you have Milton polemic, battling.

Great as were the issues being decided all around him in this year 1644 (the year of Marston Moor, the year in which—though contemporaries did not see it—the fate of the English monarchy was decided), that year and the beginning of the next meant for Milton not the Civil Wars but Divorce—the doctrine of Divorce and the propaganda of that doctrine.

His whole energy went into it, and it absorbed him. His instinct that his own safety lay in the continuation of a vigorous counter-attack was sound, and inspired him throughout. He was preached at in a sermon before the Assembly itself, and that sermon had a repercussion almost as great as had followed the publication of the second edition of the tract itself. It was in the month of Marston Moor, July, but some days after the battle, that this sermon by Palmer was delivered; and Milton found another form of attack developing—the proposal for a stricter censorship—largely directed against himself.

In the first turmoil of the Civil Wars men had often ignored that censorship which in England, as in all other Christian countries, supervised the morals of the Press. Indeed no community can do without some such instrument, whether it be called a censorship or whether it be in effect exercised by magistrates judging each particular case. But the legitimate and constitutional authority of the King—the foundation of all order and law in England—having been defied, there had broken out during those first months of the Civil War a sort of anarchy in men's minds—especially in the minds of Londoners; for the commercial magnates of London and their wealth were the heart of the rebellion. Milton therefore in ignoring the censorship when he published the first edition of his tract was only acting as many others had done; and when the Stationers Company woke up to the fact that their monopoly was imperilled, the attack on Milton himself had matured.

Meanwhile he was vigorously keeping up the battle; and in that same month of July when the assault on him was at its worst he produced yet another tract in support of the first.

This second Divorce tract was a compilation of the arguments in favour of Divorce advanced by one of the original Reformers, Martin Bucer. Martin Bucer was one of those foreigners whom the little clique concerned with promoting religious revolution in England after Henry VIII's death had brought into the country.

The State was then (it will be remembered) nominally under the government of a little boy; a rickety child doomed to an early death and crowned under the title of Edward VI. The real masters of England at that moment were the Council and in particular the child's uncle, Somerset, and his gang—who with their successors were occupied mainly in loot. Bucer (Butzer is perhaps the original name) was Luther's younger contemporary, an Alsatian by birth and in religion a Dominican. Like Luther he married a nun, and plunged into all the Reformation controversy. He was in the forefront of the Protestant movement; and that was why he was called over to England just at the moment when the new religion was about to be imposed by force. In the name of the little boy-King the masters of England thrust this foreigner upon the University of Cambridge as Regius Professor of Divinity; and there at Cambridge some few months later he died.

Now it was a Godsend for Milton when he discovered how strongly Bucer had argued for freedom of Divorce; and he further discovered (or republished) an important historical argument which men had long ago forgotten and which was that during the attempted abortive religious revolution under the Council in 1549-53 a project for great freedom in divorce had all but become the permanent law of England.

[158]

Milton was at pains to translate Bucer's arguments, to support them with commentary of his own—and it shows his skill in controversy that he so immediately appreciated the importance of the weapon he had grasped. For Bucer's name now stood very high among Protestants in England, he came next perhaps after Luther and Melanchthon in the list of Protestant champions; and though he had been dead nearly a century, this republication of his convictions on divorce and his strong advocacy of it were of singular support to the campaign. It was a wise move, was this blow delivered by Milton a fortnight after Marston Moor.

He followed it up by a flank attack in the autumn upon the side issue of licensing, publishing the *Areopagitica*, which will be separately dealt with. For the moment we must continue the list of the Divorce tracts.

A third appeared on the 4th of March of the year following. It bore the, to us, singular and pedantic title of *Tetrachordon*— a title modelled upon the Gospel harmonisings of the Early Church.

The *Tetrachordon* was an accumulation of texts and arguments turning on the four Biblical divorce passages upon which he was chiefly engaged: in Genesis, Deuteronomy, St. Matthew, and Corinthians. He was as much concerned to emphasise the texts that seem to support as to explain away the texts that seem to refute his perpetual thesis for some vague very wide power of divorce—almost at the husband's will.

The *Tetrachordon* stands by his original thesis. He repeats in it of course his insistence that not the body but the mind is his concern, not the refusal of cohabitation but bad temper; yet there continues in all this his shirking of definition and clear thought.

But his vast reading comes into play with a vengeance! He marshals the reformers in procession. After the greater names of Luther and Melanchthon we have Fagius, of the Palatinate, and the wise men of Strasbourg; Farrerus, Sturmius, Musculus; Hermingius (of Geneva, an author highly esteemed), Hunnius of Württemberg—an amusing name for such a citizen of such a city. There is also the glorious vocable Bidenbachius—and there are many more. Nor does anyone remember this tract —same for one magnificent metaphor stuck in the midst:—"All the ecclesiastical glue that Liturgy or laymen can compound is not able to sodder up two incongruous natures into one flesh of true beseeming marriage." Indeed, indeed, "glue" is the operative word!

The *Tetrachordon* should also be remembered as the origin of Milton's very worst sonnet—and how bad it was the reader shall have later opportunity to know. But the *Tetrachordon* may well be forgotten in the blaze of that unique performance, the *Colasterion*, which appeared on the same day and was the fourth and last of the Divorce tracts.

The *Colasterion* is Milton's counterblast to an anonymous attack on the earlier Divorce pamphlets. It is an outburst of irrational foaming vituperation wherein you see the very inward of Milton, the man himself under the test of emotion at white-heat.

Here indeed you have the qualities of the poet out of harness, of the poet when he is thrown back upon his resources as a man, of the poet spurred on by that incomparable vanity which is the mark of poets, by that picture which they make of themselves to themselves as something sacrosanct.

Milton in defence of Milton is a raging torrent, and gives one the best of reading. Some mere mortal has dared to aim his base material jest at a divine seer. He must not be argued with, he must be blasted; and there is no doubt but that Milton believed from his inmost soul that the cataract of coarse invective which he poured out was a sort of Olympian thunderbolt. In the contrast between the two, the man who had criticised and the man who thus replied with a deafening amorphous roar, there is high comedy indeed.

Milton had outraged the moral sense of his time and people; he had dragged into the sacred certainties of the Saints something from the Anabaptists, something of anarchy. He had attacked marriage itself, its immutability. One might have thought that a man advancing thus into perilous isolation would have been conscious of such isolation—would be prepared to fence with and beat inevitable opposition. Not a bit of it! The situation left Milton as convinced as ever that he was the Heavenly Voice, that if he believed a thing and all others doubted it, it was because he was sane and all others were mad; because he was sincere and they mere advocates: or because he had the intelligence to see that they were too brutish to understand. Finding an opponent to his hand he flew at him as though that opponent did not represent what he did—the almost universal sense of society—but only some odious private attack upon himself.

To begin with, note the title. He calls his wild riposte *Colasterion;* a Greek word which has often been translated in this connection "punishment" but which is here more properly used in its special meaning of "torture-chamber." He presents his reply as a dragging of the culprit into his—John Milton's—private torture-chamber, there to be tortured as the blasphemers of God deserve.

It is a common trick, when controversy gets quite out of bounds and approaches the insane, for the violently angry man to make believe that he has caught his opponent in some humiliating posture. Thus he can do in imagination what in reality he cannot; he can pretend to himself that he has done what in the real world he would have desired to do. So Milton drags into this imaginary torture-chamber the man who has touched him on the nerve of his exalted self-worship, and there satisfies himself with torture which he is not indeed inflicting but which he comes to think he is inflicting.

Men who have fallen into this folly through lack of balance—and they are numberless—do as a fact achieve only one result: they provide great sport for the onlooker and even for the supposed victim of their onslaught, if that victim have a quiet head and enjoy the supreme blessing of an ironic mind.

Milton had discovered that the author (or chief author) of this anonymous very reasonable protest against his own sudden, most unexpected and revolutionary assault on Christian marriage had begun life as a footman. He had raised himself from such an origin and become a lawyer, a thing the more bitter when it is remembered what the profession of Milton's father had been. What on earth a man's having been a footman in youth could have to do with his arguments, turning on texts and doctrines, John Milton himself could not have told you—all he knew was that it would offend and wound to drag that footman origin in, and drag it in by the hair of the head he did whenever he could, all up and down the little piece of red-hot writing, until the abuse culminates in the phrase "rank serving man": and he will have it that one who has been a footman must be too interested in the misfortunes of housemaids.

"Observe," he shrieks, "the arrogance of a groom, how it will mount!" How dare a mere servant presume to question the heresies of a Milton! His business was to play valet to his master, and in criticising the tract on divorce the fellow "would untruss my arguments, imagining them his master's points." And since this arrogant groom had indeed mounted to be a half-scrivener, the horrid conjunction makes Milton shout "Mongrel!" loudly at the tire-man who had prospered. "His two faculties of solicitor and serving man compound into one mongrel."

The whole thing is "abuse at large." He prints upon his title-page "Answer to a fool according to his folly"; and that fool becomes "an illiterate and arrogant, presuming in what he understands not, to know Greek and not even able to spell it."

Again, Milton's opponent is "a gross sluggish overweening pretender." Then have at him again for his poor origins: he is "a mechanic." Milton further observes in him a singular note of stupidity; he begs us to hold our laughter if we can at this domestic, than whom "no antic hobnail at a Morris is more handsomely facetious," and who has "laid down his wallet to play the fool."

Milton goes further than this in the blindness of his rage—he goes as far as he can in sheer garbage. The opposing writer becomes "an odious fool who leaves the noysom stench of his rude slot behind him, maligning everything above his own baseness." Ah, "who would have believed so much insolence durst vent itself from the hide of a varlat," who becomes "an idiot by breeding," "a clod of an antagonist," and at last a "pork." The great man groans in spirit that he should have been put to the "underwork" of "scouring and unrubbishing the low and sordid ignorance of such a presumptious lowzel." "I endorse him on the backside of posterity, not a colt but a brazen Asse." "Thus much to this nuisance"; "this brain worm." Then he falls into that common error of an angry man, boasting that he is too proud to do what he immediately sets out to do most heartily. Milton will not dispute philosophy with the "pork"—"for he never read any." But dispute he does, and that with a raving and a foaming at the mouth which is really most excellent entertainment.

Moreover, in his banging about he spares no one; he is like a man who, having lost his temper to the pitch of madness, begins thrashing away at random, his unaimed blows falling on the spectators as well as on the fellow who first tickled him up. He bangs at the licenser for licensing such a thing, he bangs

at all the world. It reminds one of Bon Gaultier's parody of
Locksley Hall, a piece of humour now forgotten:—

> "Curséd be the damned Attorney,
>   Who his loathsome fees did earn;
> Curséd be the Clerk and Parson,
>   Curséd be the whole concern!"

It is a great feast. If all the other prose works of John
Milton perish—as cannot perish his immortal verse—may this
at least remain.

.   .   .   .

So end the Divorce pamphlets, a chapter by itself in Milton's works, worthily concluded by as exhilarating a spate of
vulgar invective as ever man penned.

But now the worst part of Milton's marriage ordeal was to be
eased. The Civil War was on the eve of its decision. The *Colasterion* was general reading in April and May 1645. In June, at
Naseby, the forces of the rebellion, twice their opponents in
number, destroyed the King's last army in the field.

Naseby it was that remade Milton's marriage—a replastering
concerning which we know not whether it gave him any
spiritual consolation nor even whether it suited the now peni-
tent bride.

The reconciliation did not come about on Milton's initiative;
it was the will of others that moved and controlled him in it.
The young wife who had fled in the summer of 1642, before
active military operations began, did not come back till the
summer of 1645, and but for Naseby she would not have come
back at all. So long as it seemed possible or even probable that
the King would win, that Royalist family of hers preferred to
keep their injured dove. But after Naseby it was another matter.
The King's cause was ruined, and the Powells, always out at
elbows, were thoroughly ruined with it. Of such moment was

that last left-wheel of Oliver's in the midst of the charge—of such distant effect upon the private lives of all England.

After Naseby Forest Hill was in the hands of the Revolution, it was only a question of time when Oxford would fall; and the Powells were now penniless. They must live on somebody, and their creditor, John Milton, was somebody to live on—to batten on would be a better phrase. The creditor John Milton let himself be managed.

Behind his back a plan was carried out. The Powells came up to London; it was arranged that Mary should be in the room next to one into which Milton was introduced. She entered, fell at his feet, and played the part assigned to her. "She had seen the error of her ways." "She had only acted as she had under the pressure from her mother," and so on.

He took her back, and not only her, but, soon after (to quote another poet) "her mother and her sisters and her cousins and her aunts"—that is, the whole Powell tribe. For the second time they got their meals free under Milton's roof, and, with these meals, swallowed their pride of Cavaliers.

Now to wind up the statement of this crash in Milton's life, after which the whole story of him is changed, let us remark how, in this also, Milton was a forerunner.

The destruction of indissoluble marriage as a fixed social principle, inherited from Catholic times, was bound to come sooner or later once the Reformation had got going. It came as a fact much sooner than any man would have predicted in those years when *The Doctrine and Discipline of Divorce* startled and shocked the Puritan world of the Civil Wars. That a Christian man should have but one wife and should cleave to her till death was still for the English mind in general, and even for much the most of those on the extreme left wing of the religious revolution, an awful sanctity—a thing not to be questioned for a moment. That was in 1643. Twenty-seven years later, when John Milton, the old man, was within four years of his death,

there happened a decisive thing. The indissolubility of marriage was destroyed in principle so far as England was concerned, and the right to divorce and remarry became part of
the national law.

It was a debate in the Lords, much contested, which ended
thus by a majority of two. The Protestant Bishops had been,
of course, divided. Two of their number agreed with this funda-
mental change in religion and so permitted it to pass the House.

The enormity of the moment escaped most men, and certainly nearly all the actors in that drama. The movement had
taken the shape not of a measure for divorce in general but of
a special act permitting a particular man, a peer and so a col-
league of those voting, to marry a second wife while his first
wife was still alive. In this form divorce remained in England
during nearly two hundred years; it was open to the very
wealthy alone, and even they could only obtain it by paying
the lawyers enough money to get a special Act of Parliament
through the legislature granting the privilege in each particular
case.

The horror which men felt at the new thing was sufficiently
proved by this—that for twenty-two years no second example
was attempted. Then, as the older England died, the thing became admitted among the small wealthy class which had taken
over power, ousting the King. After the first years of the
eighteenth century a divorce became pretty well an annual occurrence. Within a lifetime that rate had multiplied by three.
After 1857 divorce became of general right involving no personal bill in Parliament, but still only to be purchased at a high
price from the lawyers. But it became commoner and commoner thenceforward until, before the end of the nineteenth
century, it was taken as a matter of course in all classes of society above the labourers and became less expensive as it
spread.

To-day, as we know, the facilities for divorce are still hampered by a number of rules, false and true, and the universal spread of the new morality is only checked by the remaining expenses of procedure. Divorce has not yet become normal with the great mass of the English poor; it is not an accepted practice with the populace. But that will come, and the shade of Milton shall be satisfied.

Perhaps from over the edges of the Elysian fields he can look down and contemplate our modern happy carefree lives, our close spiritual unions, and discover how right he was in undermining that which our fathers once called the chief sacrament of human life.

Before I leave the unhappy Powell marriage let me add a note on how the bad confusion arose with regard to that all-important date in Milton's life.

It was taken for granted for more than two centuries after his death that his first marriage had been contracted, not in 1642 but 1643. The error was due to a date appended in the margin of the notes upon Milton's life written by his nephew Edward Phillips. Phillips mentions the move to Aldersgate (and here the date 1641 is put in the margin) and he goes on to speak of the work that was done there, notably the Anti-Prelatic pamphlets, and the *Areopagitica* (which came so much later): he says nothing of the pamphlets in between that point. He next goes on to mention the fact that to this house in Aldersgate Street came later John Milton's old father to live with him, and puts beside this the date 1643, which is accurate; but then his memory betrays him (he was writing between thirty and forty years after the event). He describes the marriage as having taken place shortly after Whitsuntide of that same year.

The real date was undoubtedly not 1643 but 1642. Scholars were indeed puzzled how to make a marriage in 1643 fit in with the date of the divorce tracts. The first divorce tract appeared as we have seen in August of that year; if Milton had married in the early June of that year and his wife had gone off upon her disastrous "holiday" in July it is morally impossible that the divorce tract should have appeared on the 1st of August 1643. He was expecting his wife to return at the end of September, and he did not fully appreciate what had happened to her until the end of October, following her visit to her home. When the date 1643 was still accepted scholars had to reconcile as best they could dates that were quite incompatible; they had to imagine moral miracles—a man nourishing the prospect of a public outbreak against his wife and against marriage in general while his wedding was in progress: a man carefully choosing a wife while planning a piece of writing full of allusions to his hatred of, and disgust with, her; and publishing it to the world in the very weeks when he was quietly awaiting her return from a visit to her parents.

But apart from this moral argument, which should be of sufficient strength, there is a material one which is conclusive. A quiet domestic undertaking of this sort, his ride to Oxford and then his return with members of his new wife's family to London, the whole gone through as though such peaceable journeys from the capital to the University were still matters of course, would have been impossible in 1643. That year was the first full year of the Civil War, and such a journey would have meant peril, the double crossing of hostile lines, or, at the best, special passes for all parties. These could not have been obtained, for Milton had already distinguished himself by appearing publicly upon the rebel side; Oxford was, after the King's retreat from London, the headquarters of the Royalist Army from the beginning of 1643.

The true sequence is as follows:—

Milton's ride from Oxford to London was undertaken at Whitsuntide (or a little after) in 1642. Whitsuntide fell that year on May 29th. The marriage was therefore presumably concluded in the early part of June. If Mary Powell stayed "about a month" with her husband in London (which was Phillips's vague recollection after all those years, and we must remember that he was only a child at the time) she would have gone off on that visit to her parents in the July of 1642. It is at the end of September 1642 that she fails to return as agreed "about Michaelmas"; his rising anger dates from October 1642, in the first months of active warfare before Edgehill. He is preparing his tract against divorce, a matter of very wide research and annotation, during the winter 1642-43 and spring of 1643, while his brother, living at Reading with his old father, goes through the siege of that town. Milton has the tract set up and proofs corrected in June and July 1643; it appears late in that July, perhaps on the very last day of the month, and is purchased by Thomason (as we know from his contemporary evidence in writing) on the 1st of August 1643.

All that fits in perfectly: it gives time for the repeated demands on the part of Milton for his wife's return, for the sending of the foot messenger, and the preparation of his violent public protest—somewhat delayed by the danger of assault upon the City (the occasion of his sonnet thereon).*

Historians have had the same trouble with regard to the real date of Milton's journey to Italy. This trouble is due to his own mention, later on, that he travelled to Italy immediately after his mother's death. She died in the spring of 1637, but he himself did not start for Italy till the spring of 1638: he says nothing about the intervening year and so it became telescoped up in the minds of some readers.

---

* This is not the only example of Phillips's inaccuracy. He puts down Milton's birth to the year 1606, whereas it took place in 1608. He makes him go to Cambridge at fifteen: as a fact he was sixteen and a half when he went up.

The *Areopagitica* was prepared in Milton's house in Aldersgate Street, and the moment in which it was prepared was significant. It was during the months of October and November 1644 that the pamphlet took shape, that is, after the heavy business of attack and defence in the matter of divorce had been fought out.

Politically the moment of its appearance had not the importance that has sometimes been attached to it. It was being written during the Rebel preparation for defence against the King's return from the West, during the march of the large Parliamentary force against Charles's small army, which ended in the second battle of Newbury and the bad bungling of that action by Manchester and Cromwell between them.

But the *Areopagitica* has no relation to the angry feelings of those days, when men on the Rebel side were divided into two hostile forces full of mutual recrimination. It was only by a coincidence that this little pamphlet of forty quarto pages appeared the day after Cromwell's attack on Manchester, the 24th of November—and it is characteristic of Milton that when he published this attack on the State's right of license he published it *without* a license.

It stands in a place apart. It is one of the divorce tracts in that it was an off-shoot from them, provoked by his irritation with the Censorship which *might have* interfered with his divorce propaganda. Also it belongs in time to this group, for it appeared midway between the second divorce tract and the third. It stands apart in another fashion (and not a very worthy one) in that it chimes in with the "Freedom of the Press" cry which filled the Liberal period of European politics, the latter eighteenth and nineteenth centuries: a cry hypocritical in the mouth of schemers, sincere in those of fools, and a mixture of

both in the mouths of you and me. From the French Encyclo-
pædists of the mid-eighteenth century to the last fossil remnants
of our own day, this cry, that the press should be "free," ran
a course of three generations. Now the *Areopagitica* with its
vague negative aspirations provoked nothing more than an
irritation against control, an irritation which never faced the
main issue: that of degree. *

There is another reason for specially noting this tract: Its
widespread reputation in the nineteenth century is a first-rate
example of confusion in criticism. Because the thesis was highly
sympathetic to the Liberal thought of the nineteenth century
and because Milton's defence of it was suitable to the false
idealised picture of the man which people then had in their
minds, *therefore* the pamphlet had to be a great example of
perfect English prose.

It is nothing of the sort. It is for the most part turgid and
when it is not turgid it is dull. But there are flashes of rhetoric
in it wherein the poet appears, and the moment the poet appears
in anything that Milton did you have a chance of coming
across something great.

The thesis of *Areopagitica* is that it ought to be possible to
print anything without restriction from the authorities. Now it
will be admitted by all sane men that a great many things cannot be freely printed, and that the attempt to print and publish
them at large should be prevented by the civil magistrate.
Granted any system of morals by which this or that act, *to
which many men will be strongly tempted*, is damnable, then
printed excuses for, or allurements towards, that act must be
forbidden: otherwise the code of morals, and the sanctities
which it enshrines, lie ruined.

Codes differ with differing times and places: that is a truism.
That they always *may* differ more largely than our experience
can conceive should also be recognised. Things of which we
cannot bear the thought may, in another society, have been

accepted; but there is always some code and some limit: therefore a censorship. Nor is that truth applicable only in morals; it applies also to the mere mechanism of the State. You cannot allow secrets which are vital to the armament of the Commonwealth against its foes to be bruited out to the world at large. There must be some restriction upon the publication of attacks upon individuals; there must be some restriction upon incitement to rebellion.

Clearly the whole value of any thesis upon freedom of publication lies in the establishment of these limits. Argument upon it, to be of any real value, must be argument for or against some principle which defines these limits, or at least for or against some set of limits clearly described.

Now Milton's *Areopagitica* has nothing of this. It talks confusedly and at large about the advantages of freedom in general, but leaves us without any guide as to the method or principle of its exercise. The note is struck by that translation from Euripides with which Milton prefaces the thing and which is quoted—or used to be quoted—in dozens of speeches and leading articles every year of the calendar in the height of the Liberal movement. But those verses, being but a poetic declamation, are empty of any precise meaning. Hackneyed as they are I will quote them, for they admirably illustrate the corresponding vagueness of Milton's own mind in the matter.

> "This is true Liberty, when freeborn men
> Having to advise the public, may speak free,
> Which he who can, and will, deserves high praise,
> Who neither can nor will may hold his peace;
> What can be juster in a State than this?"

"Who neither can nor will may hold his peace" is rather inflating the original Greek, which means simply "Let him who is not willing be silent." But it is better than Pope's use of inflation, as when he puts in a whole line of his own at the

opening of the Eighteenth Iliad. Milton was moved to just
poetry by the poetry of the Greeks, and that is not to be quarrelled with; what is to be quarrelled with is the unintelligence of
the argument. It is sometimes said that we must not expect intelligence in pleading, except the kind of intelligence that is shown
by the capacity for taking people in, but after all in this matter
of censorship a child can see that the whole thing turns upon
the principle you apply for the establishment of restraint. Some
things you must restrain, if you desire certain political results.
What are those things? What are the political results which
through restraint you desire to reach? Until you have answered
those questions you have answered nothing.

For instance, may a man print and disseminate broadcast
incitement to acts which are abhorrent to the existing morals
of the community—say, cannibalism? We get out of the problem to-day by pretending that we only prosecute such printing because it may lead to a breach of the peace. But that is
hypocrisy; such is not our real motive; and on the top of that we
do specifically define certain subjects on which a man may not
by law express himself. Society could not be carried on unless
limits of this kind were set. Nor let anyone pretend that there is
a real difference between openly proclaiming the institution of
a censorship and of licensing, and the exercise of judicial powers
to prevent publication. The result is the same in either case, the
motive is the same, and the machinery of prosecution is the
same. The whole thing is a question of two factors combined;
the factor of subject and the factor of degree.

Of course Milton was only acting as an advocate, and acting
as advocates always do from an immediate personal motive:
usually the motive of money, in Milton's case of conviction.
Being but an advocate he ought not to be too closely
analysed, but we must remember that he himself, for the honour it gave him and a substantial salary, was delighted to be an
official censor later on.

The *Areopagitica,* then, was only one more example of what we find continually in Milton's passionate pleadings—they are not the product of a reasoned creed, they are reactions against some private suffering of his own. He never said a word against marriage until his own marriage went wrong; he never said a word against licensing until they began to badger him for outrage of public morals in tracts which he had not submitted to the censor, nor until he was threatened with special proceedings against himself. There is less special straining of evidence than in most of his tracts and there is no extravagance of personal abuse; the occasion does not call for either of these. But there is no sufficient thought.

The *Areopagitica* suffers from two other defects which are common to nearly all Milton's prose work. The first is that it is very long-winded and is used as an occasion to show off the writer's wide reading, especially in things of the ancient world. The other defect in the *Areopagitica,* which also makes it popular—is its extravagant nationalism—which here reaches a pitch surpassing his other extravagances in that line. He had already said that "God always reveals the truth first to his Englishmen." Now vanities of that kind may make the writer feel comfortable, may even make him glow, but they are not of themselves a prose excellence.

It has been said by some more sober and accurate than the rest that at any rate the *Areopagitica* is the easiest to read of all Milton's pamphlets. That would not be saying much though it were true. To be readable is the first duty of a prose writer—or verse writer either for that matter. But who can call it readable?

Lest that assertion sound too abrupt and violent let me quote something which I think the reader will find sufficient proof. There is in the *Areopagitica* one famous passage of fine rhetoric —that is, a piece of writing from the pen of Milton the poet. It has been repeated a thousand times. I mean the passage beginning, "Methinks I see in my mind . . ." where he presents England, the mighty nation like an eagle, renewing its youth and the rest of it. It is almost the only quite lucid passage in the whole thing. But those who quote it forget the passage immediately preceding it. Now this I must beg the reader to allow me to quote verbatim, as a very good example of Milton's prose style—not at its worst (I have already cited a worse passage), but at its average.

"For as in a body, when the blood is fresh, the spirits pure and vigorous not only its vital but its rationall faculties, and those in the acutest, and the pertest operations of wit and suttlety, it argues in what good plight the body is, so when the cheerfulness of the people is so sprightly up, as that it has, not only wherewith to guide well its own freedom and safety, but to spare, and to bestow upon the solidest and sublimest points of controversie a new invention, it betok'ns us not degenerated nor drooping to a fatal decay, but casting off the old and wrincl'd skin of corruption to outlive these pangs and wax young again, entring the glorious waies of truth and prosperous virtue destin'd to become great and honourable in these latter days."

I don't say that this is incomprehensible. With diligence one can get sense out of it—but to call it good prose! With careful analysis one can distinguish the primary statement from the secondary ones; one might even go over the whole passage with a vigorous blue pencil and reduce it to order by a thorough remodelling—but that is hardly to present it as a masterpiece of expression.

Then look at the rubbish which comes after, when he addresses the revolutionary part of the House of Commons and the remaining handful of rebel Lords.

He tells these political outsiders that they above all other constitute a free and humane Government "which they by their valourous and happy councils have purchased for us."

[175]

Here the passage does not sin from confusion—it is its extravagance that renders it ridiculous. Whatever the ultimately successful but rapidly diminishing numbers of those wealthy men who had seized all power had achieved at the moment when the *Areopagitica* was written, it was absurd to call it *liberty*. They might plead the necessity of war for enormously multiplying the arbitrary taxation which they imposed; they might plead financial necessity for the arbitrary confiscation of land and goods of which they robbed their constitutional opponents for the support of the revolution upon which they were engaged; the Puritan faction into which they rapidly degenerated might claim to be the Servants of the Lord and therefore above criticism—but what the rebel leaders and their army certainly could *not* claim was the establishment of an urbane and rational freedom throughout English society since the King's power to maintain even justice had been weakened.

Milton's excuse is that he was pleading earnestly for the abolition of restraint in a particular field of discussion and debate—that he was addressing his plea to the only admitted authorities of his side, the rebel section of the Parliament—but then we must not say of his plea that it was filled with the same spirit of civic freedom, still less that it was a model of English. It has—like all Milton's prose—fine passages of poetic eloquence and it has, in an exceptional degree, a sort of gnarled swing which is effective indeed. But, though clearer than most of his tracts, it lacks that perfect clarity which is the test of civilised English.

Between his wife's return after the publication of the *Colasterion* and the sudden appearance of Milton as the defender of regicide, there is a gap of over three years; and this gap may properly be called in so stormy a life "The Lull."

They were the years—1645-48—during which the last struggles of the Royal cause were concluded, when the King was made a prisoner, sold by the Scotch, and at last his death plotted and achieved. Yet in the main politics of England during that decisive period the pen of Milton hardly appears.

The incidents of his life during this brief period may be briefly told. He moved in the autumn after his wife had come back to him from Aldersgate to a larger house close by in the Barbican, where he lodged his whole family, including his now aged father—driven out of his own house in Reading by the wars—his two Phillips nephews, and sundry pupils whom he continued to teach. He was not exactly (be it remembered) a schoolmaster, he had an ample livelihood and was under no necessity to teach; but he was a natural born pedagogue and the occupation which he had begun in the teaching of his nephews, and his reputation for learning, led friends to send him their sons in some small number.

While he was in this house in the Barbican the Royalist capital, Oxford, fell—and that was the month, July 1646, when the Powells in their destitution were taken in by the son-in-law whom they had treated so badly; and at the end of the same month his first child was born, and christened Anne.

With the opening of the next year (1647) his wife's father died, and two months later his own. His father-in-law's death brought him nothing; for the man was bankrupt and in a worse posture even than he need have been through the harshness of the victorious rebellion towards the defeated Royalist party;

but Milton was in better circumstances through the death of his own father. He moved again, going out of town westwards to the limits of the built-up area, taking a house in Holborn with a pleasant south view at the back over the open green space of Lincoln's Inn Fields, a square of eleven acres round which as yet there were no continuous houses save to the north—though the opposite side was in process of being filled. The west side was open land, and from the windows of Milton's home one could see the sun setting behind hedges and trees.

It was in the early autumn of 1647 that he came under this new roof; and for a year more he was not stirred to anything remarkable. All quarrels had been patched up; the Royalist brother Christopher, with his Catholic leanings and general opposition to his elder brother's attitude, was making his peace with the victorious Puritans and compounding for his own property in Ludgate Hill—a house worth from £240 to £250 a year.

John Milton wrote, I say, during this comparatively peaceful "smooth" which marks the centre of his life's tempest, little or nothing remarkable. He found an outlet for his unquenchable energy in beginning a history of England, chiefly interesting for one veiled allusion to the lawfulness of a plurality of wives. He also wrote very tawdry metrical translations into English of the Psalms. By way of original English verse these are the years in which he produced nothing else but the sonnet to Lawes, the sonnet against the Presbyterians, the sonnet in memory of the worthy Mrs. Thomson, and quite at the end of the business the sonnet to Fairfax: none of these are of a high level and one is of the lowest. The really notable thing in these three and a half years is his first open publication of and his collected verse at the beginning of them.

It was in the early autumn after his wife's return, on the 6th of October 1645, that the "Poems in English and Latyn by Mr. John Milton" were registered at Stationers' Hall; a very small volume of 120 octavo pages. It was not in the hands of the public until the first days of the following year, the 2nd of January 1646. Here we have all Milton's early lyric work and ten of the sonnets.

It seems strange, to us, that he should have waited so long before making the collection; but the delay was consonant with his character. He had, as we know, always thus postponed presenting his *verse* publicly, both for the sake of perfecting at leisure and from his certitude of future fame. He already had his small appreciative audience of verse-readers and already a vague reputation as a poet over a circle larger than that audience, but he was still in the eyes of the world (and perhaps in his own) the pamphleteer, the man who had engaged in printed public controversy on the scandalous point of divorce; a moral rebel. Now, in 1648, at the end of this quiet interval he was to attack again with all the old violence and much more than the old success, but a front wholly new.

For there are two quite separate chapters in the polemic of Milton; the first is all connected with his most unpopular campaign for divorce; then after this interval of three and a half years comes the second group, devoted to the killing of the King, the defence of that deed and the taking up of the quarrel between the triumphant republicans and the outraged conscience of Europe. Even while the King was wrestling and straining for his life against the net closing round him, even in the last weeks before the tragedy of Whitehall, Milton was working at something that should resound throughout Europe —he was preparing (while the King still lived) a defence and plea for the putting of him to death.

It is not known when Milton first sat down to write—still less when he first conceived—the idea of the *Tenure of Kings and Magistrates*. Indeed in this case as in so many in Milton's life, we are badly served by contemporaries. There were few, perhaps none, of the same standing in European letters during the mid-seventeenth century of whose methods and dates of work we know so little. But we have certain presumptions to guide us.

Here is a piece of composition which is drawn up with deliberation and constructive skill. It is not a passionate outbreak like so many of the earlier and later pamphlets; it is the work of a man who has made up his mind to do a particular thing, to think it out, and to do it thoroughly.

So far, so good—now we further know from an inspection of all Milton's career that he never pointed the way publicly to others in politics or in religion. He was a pioneer, a forerunner, of what the modern decline in religion has led to in three capital points of the Christian culture—indissoluble marriage, the doctrine of the Incarnation and the Omnipotence of God's creative power. But his attack on the first he had hoped to be anonymous; the two last he deliberately kept hidden, and his attitude on them remained secret for the better part of two centuries.

He had appeared as a pamphleteer against Prelacy, but had waited until others had already virtually won the victory—at any rate until long after the battle had been joined. So it was to be in all his later work, for to the very last abortive tract in which he attempted a settlement of the republican quarrel after Cromwell's death and on the eve of the Restoration, he always followed, he never led in his public utterances.

Therefore we may presume that he did not consider a plea

for the trial and execution of Charles Stuart until it was known that such a policy would be adopted. And, by "would be adopted" I mean that Milton did not write in favour of Charles being killed until that policy was beginning to appear as official: as the policy of those who would have the power to execute it.

Now it is exceedingly difficult to fix the date upon which even a well-informed man, who could hear of political matters from within and who was on the victorious side, would first have appreciated that there was a probability—later a certitude—that the King would be put to death. The fullest writers hesitate to this day upon the moment when Cromwell himself came to that decision. What we can say with certitude and on full testimony is that the group of men who were already the most powerful in England began to call for the King's blood in the spring of 1648, before the Second Civil War was in full swing; well before the Preston campaign decided it. But until the battle of Preston (August 1648) no one could be sure that these men would be masters in the end.

After the battle of Preston the thing was beyond doubt. These men had *then* achieved the power of ordering what they chose, it was *they* who would be the rulers of England. If there was to be one ruler substituted for the legitimate King he would come from amongst them; and it was already pretty clear who that man would be—Oliver Cromwell. We have therefore (not with any certitude but as a strong presumption) for a limiting date the early summer of 1648—six or seven months before the deed was done on the scaffold in front of the Banqueting Hall.

Now the *Tenure of Kings and Magistrates* would not take all that time to write. It has few references. It contains only sixty-nine numbered paragraphs. It is more likely, then, that it was not begun until much later in the year, when the trend of things had become obvious, well after the unfortunate Charles Stuart had been shepherded by his enemies into the

Isle of Wight. There is even a certain amount of internal evidence in the booklet to show that the bulk of it, at least, was composed later still, when the imminence of the King's fate was clear—that is, in the winter, say, during November at earliest, more likely December, or even, perhaps, January 1649.

On the other hand we know that the thing was finished before the axe fell on the 30th of January 1649; and the MSS. appears to have been touched up in the last days before the tragedy, perhaps during the trial itself. The King once dead, Milton published, a few days later, this demand for his death and this considered argument in its favour.

It would, of course, be a complete misjudgment of Milton to say that he wrote this defence of those who killed the King because they were going to be the depositaries of power. He wrote because he agreed with them, because he was himself a convinced regicide, because he was strongly of their party, an enthusiastic adherent not only of the comparatively small republican party which was to control England for eleven years, but of the far smaller faction which thoroughly approved the killing of Charles Stuart. Nevertheless thus to proclaim himself publicly the advocate of the most extreme policy, to make himself a sort of accredited apologist for what the mass of Englishmen regarded as a monstrous crime and what shocked all European opinion, was on the part of Milton the considered adoption of a standpoint and a label. He had not only publicly taken up a very definite position on the side of the small but victorious minority, now pointed at by all Europe and the mass of Englishmen as murderers of their King, but he had affixed a title to himself—he was already as it were official. He was already informally, but actually, part of the small governing group which had usurped power.

It might be suggested that the whole thing had been planned. It might be suggested that Milton had been approached secretly by those who had the thing in mind, that is, by Cromwell's faction—or even by Cromwell himself. It might be suggested that this, the first of his regicide pamphlets, was (after a fashion) written to order as the rest certainly were. That suggestion would fit in with the circumstances.

But such a suggestion would probably be erroneous. We have no evidence to support it, and it is upon the whole not probable. It is more consonant with Milton's temperament that, first, he should have approved of the death of the King; next that he should have sat down to codify his approval in a set piece on paper—to demonstrate and affirm it in lasting fashion when once he was sure (or thought himself sure) that those who intended the killing of the King would keep their power indefinitely.

The *Tenure of Kings and Magistrates* was that one of Milton's writings which later most nearly endangered his life. It was of more effect in this than was the *Eikonoklastes* which followed it, for in it he set forth definitely, and as a principal advocate, the claims of the regicides; pleading repeatedly their moral right to put Charles to death. That demand for death appears on the very title, and, out of the many decisive passages to such an effect in the body of the work, these critical words may be quoted:

"It is lawful to depose him" (the King) "and *put him to death.*"

There it stood in black and white; there was no escaping it. Milton had struck the nail fair on the head and clinched it down.

The man who wrote that was already prominent in English life, already known in Europe for one of the principal English writers, capable of influencing English opinion, sought after by the English factions for his talent as a pamphleteer (which we now know to be exaggerated, but which his contemporaries extolled) and famous for his scholarship. And such a man, a bare fortnight after the head of the King had fallen, came out

[183]

with such a sentence—the centre and kernel of all he had to say of the thing that had shaken all Christendom!

From what Milton did on that day there was no going back; he could only have done it under the supposition—a piece of very bad judgment—that in killing Charles they had killed the Dynasty.

They had indeed killed Monarchy as far as England was concerned—from that moment all the power of Kingship so rapidly disappears that within a lifetime it was gone. But he must also have been certain that there would not be even a technical Restoration, for he was as yet under no obligation to defend any official thing; he was still free to hold his peace. And yet he chose that very moment in which to appear as the chief apologist of what had been done.

Moreover it was evident that the tract had been carefully arranged while the King was yet alive. Even if the few days between the execution of the warrant and the publication of the booklet had been sufficient for the writing and printing of it—which it certainly was not—the thing shows by internal evidence that it was written, all but a few retouches, before Charles's death. Milton had deliberately prepared his argument in favour of that death, he had deliberately ranged himself with the regicides before as yet they were regicides. He had deliberately and openly chosen the company of those who had accepted the burden of shedding the Royal blood.

As might be expected there is nothing novel in the argument. The plea for tyrannicide is as old as the world; the conception of the nation or the tribe or the city as the ultimate authority and of the Prince as no more than the officer of that authority is, if not as old as the world, at any rate as old as clear thought. It is the principle of the Social Contract, the principle which you find in one form or another running throughout European political philosophy—and nowhere more clearly affirmed than by the scholastics of the Middle Ages. "All authority is from

God." Yes—but the community is sovereign; and that which is responsible to God is the community, for civil action.

"No man who knows ought" (writes John Milton) "can be so stupid as to deny" that age-long doctrine. True, though many fools have denied it, in their confused horror of the violence which accompanies revolution and their inability to distinguish between the real and the ideal order. A real contract of men coming together to form a community there has been many times in human history; but in the great mass of events such things are rare, communities rather grow than are made. But the idea that there lies a contract behind government and governed is necessary and axiomatic, if the conception of justice in government is to be admitted at all. Milton then had nothing new to say; what gave the appearance of this piece of writing immediately after Charles's death so considerable a place in the poet's own story and in that of his country, is the strictness of its affirmation, and the moment in which it appeared.

For the rest it was an *ad hoc* piece of work, in which side by side with the very general principle which it sets out to defend, he puts in a mass of very local and temporary considerations and a good deal that is trivial.

There is the usual weary list of citations from the Old Testament, and an odd quotation from Seneca—of all people!—where that sententious millionaire puts into the mouth of Hercules the phrase, "that there is no sacrifice more acceptable to Jove than that of an unjust King." He appeals to St. Paul—to whom, by the way, he gives his full title; not here calling him "Paul" after the Puritan habit. Perhaps he thought that as he had summoned the Apostle of the Gentiles as a witness on his own side special politeness was, for the moment, due to him. It recalls the Bishop who said: "You might at least call him 'Mr.'"

Milton also had a dig at the Dutch, among whom Charles's son had found asylum and who had tried to save the King. The feeling of the Dutch on what their fellow republicans were doing across the water was one of sharp annoyance to Oliver Cromwell's group, and Milton reminds them of the anomaly appositely enough:

"In the year 1581 the States of *Holland* in a general assembly at the Hague, abjured all obedience to Philip, King of Spain; and in a declaration justified their so doing; for that by his tyrannous government against faith so many times giv'n and brok'n he had lost his right to all the Belgian provinces; that therefore they depos'd him and declar'd it logical to choose another in his stead. From that time to this no state or kingdom in the world had equally prosper'd: but let them remember not to look with an evil and prejudicial eye upon their neighbours walking by the same rule."

There is one last thing to be noted about the *Tenure of Kings and Magistrates*. He delayed to publish it until after the King's death.

Now that is not to say that he did not definitely affirm the justice of the act, still less that he feared to associate himself with it. It having been done he adhered openly to the men who did it; but it is significant that he did not want anyone to be able to say that any writing of his had been in any degree the *cause* of the King's death. He is at great pains to point this out. The mass of the book was presumably written before the King's trial, and Milton insists upon the fact that as it did not appear until after the axe had fallen it could not have hastened that fall. There is here what we shall find later in the *Eikonoklastes*—a hesitation within the man, not to take side definitely with the victors, still less to hide his political sympathy with them, but to be in physical contact, as it were, with the act of blood. Something about it repelled him: not in idea, not in theory, but in his nerves.

Whether he had written it in secret connivance with Cromwell's faction or spontaneously (though by calculation), the

Tenure led at once to the offer of a great public position for Milton under the new republican government. It was proposed by those who had seized on power that he should be taken on as Secretary of State. He was appointed to write letters to foreign courts, to receive them, and to deal with diplomatic correspondence in the accepted international language of the day, which was Latin.

Hence his nephew Phillips calls him "Latin Secretary," but in truth he was what we should call to-day Secretary for Foreign Affairs, with this difference, that to-day the Secretary for Foreign Affairs is responsible for foreign policy, whereas Milton was only the employé, and secretary in the literal sense, of the Council, which directed affairs and paid him his salary.

It was a fairly good salary, close on £2,000 a year; it involved work that was congenial to him, and though he was now in even better circumstances than he had been in his old house in the City the additional income must have been welcome. He left the house in Holborn in the course of the year and took lodgings in Old Scotland Yard (which stood exactly opposite where the Admiralty stands to-day) pending his removal to rooms in Whitehall itself. The giving of such a post to the man who had publicly affirmed before all Europe his approval of the King's execution, the making him the vehicle through which other Kings had now to approach the English Government, was characteristic of the revolution which had taken place.

For it is the mark of all revolutions that if they are to have even a temporary success, they must vigorously take the offensive and maintain it. We have seen it done at Moscow in the last two years, and we have seen the success of that policy. It is always so; a revolution which comes off and maintains itself is accepted by those against whom it is directed. The foreign governments were, one after the other, bound to recognise the new usurping system imposed upon England by force; and before many years were over those foreign governments were taking it for granted that Cromwell's family would be the beginning of a new English dynasty, and France and Spain were seeking its alliance.

For it is another mark of successful revolutions that foreigners always think their effects more firmly rooted than they are, and always take the *de facto* revolutionary government for something generally popular. But the English revolutionary government was in truth nothing of the kind; it was detested; and the feeling against it was so strong that the authorities were alarmed. The proof of that feeling was the sudden and enormous success of a book purporting to be written by the late King, describing his sufferings and registering his piety. It was given the Greek title of "Eikon Basilike"—that is, "The Royal Image," or the "Portrait of the King"—and people could not buy it up fast enough.

This time there is no doubt as to what happened. Milton received an order to reply. It took him some time; the "Eikon Basilike" had come out in early February 1649; Milton's reply, which was not successful, was not completed until October.

The *Eikonoklastes* is of higher interest than most of Milton's prose writings for the reason that it gives really valuable evidence as to the state of mind of England as a whole in the supreme crisis of the Revolution—the killing of the King.

Its being ordered by the republican government is a permanent testimony to the Royalism of the English people, to their hatred of the Puritan revolution and to the isolation of the regicides. These last were not what nineteenth century official history represented them to be, some great part of the nation, even half or more than half; they were a small body of men who had come into power by a series of accidents, not of their own design, and who found themselves under the constraint of destroying Charles or of seeing their own future imperilled, and, in the case of many of them, their lives.

Even so, the most of them were reluctant to kill the King, and driven to do what they did by the more determined, the more clear-headed and the more far-seeing among them—of whom by far the strongest and most perspicacious was Cromwell.

The *Eikonoklastes* appears thus as an essential piece of historical evidence in two ways; first, it testifies to the weight, extent and violence of English feeling against the crime which had been committed; and secondly it testifies to the way in which the shock of that crime had been so great as even to affect Milton himself. For it is almost the only one of his pamphlets in which there is a half-hesitant tone. There is even something about it paralysed, appearing from time to time in the halting sentences; there is a fear of assuming blood-guiltiness.

It was not indeed that piece of his which was most to imperil him, after the Restoration: that, as we have seen, was the pamphlet appearing some months earlier, coincidently with the King's death but written before it—the pamphlet on the right by which Kings and civil magistrates hold their power. That first pamphlet, the *Tenure of Kings and Magistrates*, had been produced by a man who was still a private citizen, but the *Eikonoklastes* is a piece of official writing put together by its author as an official apology for what a government already established had done, and put together by that author because he had become the salaried servant of that government.

It was even (as Milton himself says, and he may well have been telling the truth in this) written to order. At any rate he used this as an excuse for its appearing at all. He says in so many words that he would not have written it had he not done so under command, being bound in duty by his new position in the service of the new revolutionary government.

The title means of course "the image-breaker," because it was written in reply to that book which had swept all England with such enthusiasm—the "Eikon Basilike." He gives the title in Greek because that book against which it was a reply appeared with a Greek title also—it was not a Miltonian affectation of learning. And we should remember that in the use of these words, *Eikonoklastes*, there is a connotation of idol-breaking. That should be evident in itself, but he emphasises it by allusion to those Byzantine Emperors who under the impulse of the Mohammedan example tried to destroy the use of images in the Christian Church.

The "Eikon Basilike" was published under the guise of Charles's authorship. It was as a fact written by Gauden, and the fact that it was not the King's was suspected from the moment it appeared (immediately after Charles's death). Milton alludes to that doubt. But on this point, as on almost every other throughout the pamphlet, he is singularly reticent and moderate, his extravagant temper only breaking out now and then in single phrases, such as that in which he sneers at the dead King's

Courtly life prior to the Civil War ("as though a King had nothing else to do but eat and drink"). That was on the old note of absurdity into which Milton was for ever falling: Charles in those years of excellent Government (as prosperous years as England had ever known) was working hard at his trade of Kingship, supported by others whom he inspired, nominated and controlled and who worked as hard as he did himself. But take it all round, it is the most chastened of Milton's controversial writings.

The immense success of the "Eikon Basilike," running through fifty editions in a torrent of print, could not be hidden. It had somehow to be met. And Milton himself calls those who in their myriads worshipped the dead King, "the people of England." He calls them, on account of that worship, "an inconstant and irrational and image-doting rabble"; but even in so calling them he admits the power and universality of their loyalty and its evidence in the book which had so moved them.

It moves us no longer, nor indeed is it moving. Gauden's compilation had the dulness of most contemporary work on either side; moreover it suffered from plagiarism—in some places gross and obvious. That a book so bad should have had the immense success it did is a further proof of the popular emotion in the matter of the King.

It will be remembered that Milton had been given his new official position of Latin Secretary, which involved the reading of much matter hostile to the Government as well as the overlooking and occasionally writing of foreign dispatches towards the end of March 1649; that is, rather less than two months after Charles's death. It was during those two months that the "Eikon Basilike" was running through its first huge circulation. It will also be remembered that it was shortly after his appointment that Milton moved from Holborn to Spring Gardens, so as to be near the Council which he served; and it was here that he prepared his official reply, which was ready by at least the end of September, before he moved on to his new lodgings in Whitehall. The pamphlet came out much in the same shape and size as the other on the 6th of October, printed by the man who had become the official Government printer, Matthew Simmonds, who had already printed for Milton before, and who was still established at his sign of the Gilded Lion in Aldersgate Street, near Milton's old home.

Milton followed the "Eikon Basilike" exactly, point by point, a mechanical method which in itself argues lack of enthusiasm in the writer.

Under the sobering effect of those strong emotions provoked by the killing of the King his style came near to being purified. Indeed the preface to the little book is shorter than most of his stuff and almost crisp, at least in the first paragraph of that preface. But immediately after he relapses into his confused otiose manner, with sentences as long as boa-constrictors and at his worst he is just as bad here as in the most involved of his writings. It is worth while giving a specimen of it, for the length of which I apologise—but seeing that the whole page consists of one gigantic sprawling sentence I do not see how the citation can be shorter.

"And furder, since it appeares manifestly the cunning drift of a factious and defeated Party, to make the same advantage of his" (Charles's) "book, as they did before of his Regall name and Authority, and intend it not so much the defence of his former actions, as the promotion of their owne future designes; making the Book their owne rather than the King's, as the benefit must now be their owne rather than his, now the third time to corrupt and discover the minds of weaker men, by new suggestions and narrations, either falsely and fallaciously representing the state of things to the dishonour of the present Government and the retarding of a generall peace, so needful to this afflicted nation, and so new obtained, is, I suppose no injurie to the dead, but a deed rather to the living, if by better information given them, or, which is enough, by onely remembring them the truth of what they themselves know to be heer misaffirm'd they may be kept from entring the third time unadvisedly into warr and blood-shed."

You see, it is as intolerable a rigmarole as that other which I have quoted from the *Areopagitica*. No man reading it through at a reasonable pace for the first time could understand clearly what it was driving at. If you read it slowly two or three times over you will find that he is proposing by his *Eikonoklastes* to undo that work which the "Eikon Basilike" had done, namely, filling men with a false enthusiasm for Charles and preventing their settling down under the usurpation of the Army and its politicians.

Milton was writing under that universal fear which all the regicides were feeling, lest the enormity of their outrageous act should provoke a third Civil War. But the nation was weary of bloodshed and of the effort of arms, while the Army was now so well organised and so large that further active effort for the restoration of the old Constitutional Government of England—the Monarchy—stood for the moment no chance.

Apart from its testimony of which I have spoken and its dreadful style, the *Eikonoklastes* is also remarkable for something new in political doctrine, and one has a suspicion as one reads that this novelty was not wholly congenial to Milton. He seems to be writing to order in this particular matter, as he affirms he is writing to order in the general thesis.

The novelty consists in the affirmation that Kings are not only subject to Law, but especially to *Parliament*—English Kings to the English *Parliament*—which he calls the second of the King's two "superiours." The King had two "superiours"— the Laws and his Court of Parliament.

Such a doctrine had been heard in the mouths of enthusiasts during the heat of the struggle, but it was wholly new, and in English ears quite unnatural. This "Parliament" was a wretched

[193]

remnant of that Rebel fraction (itself never much more than half) of the original House of Commons; and that original House of Commons had been in no sense the People of England. The suffrage was restricted and capricious. In the counties the vast majority of the nation, only a minority could poll. The boroughs were controlled. The House of Commons was no more than a body of country gentlemen with a sprinkling of lawyers and merchants among them.

Milton of course was familiar, as was all the educated England of his generation, with the doctrine which the Jesuits of a previous generation (especially the Spanish theologians with the great Suárez at their head) had restated, and which runs through the more vigorous preceding pamphlet on the tenure of Kings—the doctrine that the community is sovereign and the Prince or Civil Magistrate no more than the servant of that Sovereign. But for a man of his intellectual power to identify the little knot of regicides with the community has about it something ridiculous; and it looks as though Milton were sensitive to the anomalous position in which he found himself. He says rather touchingly that it is an odious thing to have to attack the dead, and he curiously insists that he is not doing it from any love of fame. No one I think would have suspected that motive in such a work. Yet he does go too far in vilifying the dead when his pen runs away with him, even here, or when he feels that there is a bit of special pleading to be done even at the obvious expense of truth.

Thus he actually accuses Charles of abetting the rebellion in Ireland, the anti-English nationalist movement in 1641, eight years before. It is one of those irrational charges which are brought out against opponents in the white heat of civil war. It may have been believed by the *merely* fanatical, but can it have been believed by Milton? He was a fanatic by temper and by family history, as we have seen—or at least he was a fanatic in one particular—but he did not undertake this particular pamphlet in the mood of a fanatic.

It may also be questioned whether he believed the figures he put down for the massacres which took place during the Irish Rebellion: "the horrid massacher of English Protestants in Ireland to the number of 154,000 by their own computation." It seems a proof of his weakness in the task and even his distaste for it that he thinks to strengthen the argument by saying that Charles had brought "no solid evidence" to exculpate himself of a charge which no sane man would have expected.

Let us note before leaving the *Eikonoklastes* that Milton shrinks from the picture of what was done on the scaffold. That he should so shrink is powerful evidence of the reluctant mood in which the thing was done—for one would naturally have expected a man of Milton's temper to have exulted in the violence of the act. On the contrary, he is embarrassed by it. In only one phrase, a hurried couple of words, does he support it— calling it "condign punishment." For the rest, he brings up old legends from Greece and Britain, Hebrew curses also of course; but he was clearly getting over the worst as hurriedly as he could.

How many Englishmen were there, even among the small body of the new rulers, whose opinion counted and whose reputation was of value to them, who approved in their hearts and thoroughly of that "cruel necessity"?

The next task upon which he was officially engaged as a prominent and highly salaried official was one in which he undoubtedly failed. He was called upon to reply to Salmasius— a man in the very forefront of European Latinity and controversy. Salmasius had been put up to express the indignation of Europe against the killing of Charles Stuart. His attack had been of the greater weight because he was a Huguenot, and wrote under the protection of the Protestant powers, notably

Holland and Sweden. It was a great opportunity—and Milton missed it.

His answer, the *Defensio Pro Populo Anglicano* was his task during the greater part of the year 1650, the second year of his Secretaryship; and the performance is bad in substance as in effect. It does not tell, because it is thoroughly out of proportion. What sense was there in representing Charles Stuart almost as a debauchee, or of reviving the idiotic calumny that in company with Buckingham he had killed his own father by the use of drugs? Yet Milton commits that folly. Yes, it was a bad performance; but it had at least this effect (of a sort which would please Milton above every other result) that it got under his enemy's skin. Salmasius and those who stood with him more than equalled Milton in the vileness of their personal abuse when they in their turn produced a counter-reply.

It was the moment when this great poet, very learned, and very unbalanced man, was about to suffer the awful catastrophe which he met with such courage—and which he overcame by that courage—his blindness. It was the *Defensio* which began the destruction of his sight. He actually glories in the trial, which came to its fulness within eighteen months. Before the spring of 1652 he could read no more: those who hated him told him that it was the judgment of God on one who had deliberately helped to procure the death of the Innocent and the Anointed; he himself called it a worthy sacrifice offered in defence of the cause he served.

Here let me digress to note what appears almost suddenly and most prominently in this second turning point of his life: it may be called "The Fortitude of Isolation."

If it was a defect in Milton (and it was not only a grave defect but an inhibiting and corroding fault of pride) that he was bound up in himself, almost to the exclusion of other interests, yet this fault carried with it a quality which Pagans would call a virtue. The segregation of his soul, its imprisonment within the walls of self, now not even provided with windows but all dark, did breed in him a rigid moral texture. It gave him an armour against the worst that fate could do, a plating of steel invincible.

Consider in what succession fell upon him those shocks, any one of which might have unhorsed a rider less muscled. First comes the death of Mary Powell, the first wife, a few weeks after his blindness had become total. He is left with three young children, girls, the eldest barely six years old, the youngest a baby. As the years of his loneliness pass he is the centre of violent attack, it rouses him but it wounds. After four years more of such loneliness under his own roof he ventures to marry again, and that marriage by a singular chance might have given him back his happiness. Catherine Woodcock must have had some uncommon gift, for she could elicit in Milton, as it would seem, a brief but profound affection. He had felt none such since Deodati died, and one might have thought him incapable of a renewal. So rare a gift was immediately taken away; he had that companionship, that one real companionship, for barely fifteen months. He had married her a little before his forty-eighth birthday, in the November of 1656: by the February of 1658 he lost her—dead in childbed with the child.

The uncompanioned darkness had returned, re-enhanced, made absolute. He met the challenge by sitting down to begin his great epic. Next, in two years his whole world collapses about his head. The Republic is ruined. His party is proscribed. He goes in danger of sudden death. He is in hiding. He passes weeks in expectation of the scaffold. His sleep has gone. He is under arrest for half a year, and still the unchecked power remains in him; with all his regular income disappeared, with half his capital destroyed, largely abandoned, he still writes on. And those very years were the years in which he was in the thick of *Paradise Lost*.

[197]

His children, or the eldest at least, are an increasing burden. They steal his books, they conspire to rob him for petty cash and his servant abets them. The household could not continue thus, and he marries again. It is a tolerable companionship for a man now old, and supports him well enough through the eleven years he still has to live; but he is wholly dependent, he must trust to the hand of others for the perpetuation of the verse which was his past, his intimate, his permanent and almost his sole concern—and in all that he stands firm. Not without complaint, for the conception that a man must hypocritically pretend indifference to misfortune is modern. Not without high protest, which has given us *Samson Agonistes:* not without anger. But without yielding—without so much as bending the blinded head.

It is a fine passage of arms indeed between a man and his fate—and a strengthening to all who read it. This "fortitude through isolation" appeared in another matter which required indeed no great effort in him, but was characteristic all the same; I mean the fashion in which he faced impoverishment.

It is always necessary to know a man's attitude towards money in judging him, because a man's attitude towards money is one of the most illuminating points one can choose for the examining of his character.

Not a few of the great poets have been mean; some avaricious, and most of them a good deal too much preoccupied, when they once began earning unexpectedly, with how large the lump would be likely to grow. Corneille is an example in point. Harcourt, the Duke who was governing Normandy when the Cid came out, asked Corneille as a fellow Norman (but also as a lion) to dine with him; and he wrote an amusing letter about it (as is the habit of the great behind the backs of the middle-classes) describing Corneille's conversation. It seems to have consisted mainly in anxious inquiry as to what the Duke thought about the chances of the play and the future box-office receipts. It was all very well for Harcourt, who was indefinitely rich, to be amused—but box-office receipts do matter to people of a lesser fortune.

At the other end of the scale there is your legendary poetic spendthrift. Ask the man in the street what poets do about money, and he will tell you that they are always out at elbows and in debt, and, when they have anything, spend it all on drink. That has not been true as a whole of the great poets; Shakespeare was careful to accumulate, so was Tennyson (whom I hope I may call a great poet even to-day); still, the spendthrift poet is a recognised type all through history.

Now Milton in all the record we have of his money-dealings preserved an honest mean; he had not inherited his father's character in the affair, we cannot trace him as a money-lender though he did take advantage (as we know) of a debt. He tried to improve his fortune by reasonable investment, and on the whole was unfortunate, but not desperately so. He was cautious in this (as in nearly everything else) for there was nothing loose or at random in his composition; and only when his vanity was offended, so that he fell into one of his fits of rage, was there any sign of extravagance about him. We know that when assessment was made for paying the Scottish blackmail in 1641 he defaulted; the Treasury wanted to get what would be to-day £60 or £50 out of him, and he did not pay. He had the excuse that he had never been sympathetic with the King's policy.

On the other hand, when it came to subscribing for the victims of the Irish rebellion, he paid up strictly enough; nor was his punctuality due to the fact that (as some have surmised) it was not a subscription to a public cause but an investment. It is true that many of the subscriptions to advance the English cause in Ireland were investments and nothing else—this was notably the case with Cromwell. They were speculations perhaps rather than investments, you paid so much for the expenses of the Conquest and if it came off you would make a good thing out of it. But there was a risk, it might fail—in which case your money would be thrown away.

But Milton's case was not of this kind; he paid what was genuinely a sum for relief, and so far as we can judge those payments gave him no return and were not even supposed to be recouped. They were like the sums given now in relief after some great public catastrophe.

Take the known evidence on the life of Milton all round, and we find him not indifferent to money but honourably moderate in his attitude towards it. And it is the more to his credit because in the world to which he belonged, the rebel Puritan world, money held far too great a place. He was not a man to be silent when he thought himself aggrieved; he complained bitterly of this and that; yet I believe there is no case of his complaining of mean treatment in the matter of money though he suffered pretty badly in that regard. In the matter of his wife's desertion, for instance, that bad blow was accompanied by two financial losses; first his father-in-law never paid the debt of £3,000 which had been outstanding for more than a dozen years; secondly, he never recovered the dowry of £6,000 he had been promised—he seems never to have had a penny of it. In the midst of his angry speculation upon all this misfortune he keeps silent upon the money side of it.

Then again, when the ruin of his cause at the Restoration had rendered him a comparatively poor man, his emotion is aroused by everything except his loss of fortune—by the crash of the "good old cause," by the merriment of the new Court, by the ungodly happiness in place of the old gloom and savagery of the hated Puritan rule, by everything except the loss of fortune.

The absorption in his task which permitted his indifference to money had another effect; it limited his sense of humour.

There is sufficient record of his tendency to sarcasm; but of direct humour very little evidence.

There is indeed in the whole of his career only one incident which seems to show, harsh though it is, some gleam of real humour. It was the trick he played upon the engraver of his portrait.

When the first edition of his collected poems was published in 1645 a portrait was appended purporting to show him as he was in his twenty-first year. But he was represented as a man in middle life, gloomy and one might say repulsive. Milton did not demand the suppression of the print, nor its replacement by something more congruous. He only asked the engraver to put under it by way of motto certain lines in Greek carefully written out. The engraver knew no Greek, but faithfully copied them. And those lines were to this effect:

That no one, seeing the portrait, could possibly have guessed it to be Milton.

However, his inability to correct lines where he fell into the grotesque, an inability which he shares with so many other poets, does not mark a general lack of sense of humour, but rather a particular one. He did not detect the comic side of his own failures. Perhaps he would have cut out those bad lines more readily if they had been written by somebody else.

From this digression on the "fortitude of his isolation" let me return to the main sequence of the man's activity.

We are at the moment when, after 1652, after there had fallen upon Milton the awful doom of blindness, he had lost his first wife and was left alone with three young girls to bring up as best he might and all his movements dependent upon others.

Even in that moment came the second great broadside from the Continent against the regicides who had mastered England. There appeared in the summer of that year, published in Holland, another Latin attack whose title, translated into English is: "The Cry of the Royal Blood to Heaven against the English Parricides." They were the days in which his first wife Mary Powell died, and in which his little son died also; yet he was more concerned with answering the attack than with any mourning of his own. He took his time; and in the second year following, 1654, he published the second apology, the *Defensio Secunda*, violently attacking those who had given him so much provocation—but whom he had himself been the first to insult.

There is far more driving power in this second than there had been in the first *Defensio*, because it was now John Milton's business to talk of John Milton—and that was a subject on which John Milton's energies were roused to their highest. As against the jeers and falsehoods directed against him he trumpeted his own praise—and got the best of it. That he had been refused his Fellowship at Cambridge had been represented as a public disgrace; he was told that he had "suffered expulsion," he had been told that Cambridge had "vomited him forth," his leisurely and pleasing travels in Italy had been represented as a flight from disgrace at home. Calumnies of that sort were not difficult to refute, and the refutation was well done.

Perhaps the most interesting point in the *Defensio Secunda*, quite separate from the amusement one gets out of Milton's violence, is his treatment of the crucial point in the relations between Cromwell and the King.

It has been debated from that day to this whether Cromwell did or did not lure Charles Stuart into the Isle of Wight—lure him thither as into a trap. I have never myself believed that there could be any doubt but that Cromwell acted thus: and I doubt whether the opposite thesis would ever have been presented but for the hero-worship which mars and warps all attempts at writing true history on the Protector. I have given the evidence elsewhere, I will briefly recapitulate it here.

First, Whalley, Charles Stuart's jailer at Hampton Court,

was Cromwell's first-cousin and close confidant; and he was undoubtedly chosen on that account for the post.

Next, on the evening when Charles escaped, Whalley, while pretending to put on a specially strong guard, deliberately left the obvious avenue of escape—the door on to the garden by the river—without sentinels. The anonymous letter which was designed to frighten Charles into escaping (though he himself disdained the imputation of fear in the matter) was believed by the man who knew most about it, the Chaplain and intimate of Whalley, to proceed from Cromwell himself.

Thirdly, Charles Stuart's great friend, who was watching to help him, Ashburnham, had lodgings just over the river from Hampton Court—and Whalley was cognisant of every movement there. He therefore knew very well that Whalley had made preparations for Charles's escape, and had just before that escape given up his lodgings. Yet he let all this go through without interruption.

Fourthly, Ashburnham took the King to Southampton Water because he had heard that a ship would be ready to take him to the Channel Islands. Someone must have given Ashburnham to understand that a boat was waiting in Southampton Water to take the King away if he could get thither. But when Charles and Ashburnham got there they found there was no boat—hence the necessity of throwing themselves upon the mercy of the Governor of the Isle of Wight. In this matter either Ashburnham was a traitor or a dupe, and no one with any acquaintance of Ashburnham's character could believe him a traitor. Indeed up to the last he was prepared to risk his life, and it was only Charles Stuart himself who prevented him from killing the Governor of the Island while there was yet time. And that Governor, be it remembered, was not only Cromwell's relative but his dear and close confidant as well as Whalley.

We have of course in support of all this the famous words

of the poet Andrew Marvell; and I think the positive evidence sufficiently supplements Marvell's general statement to make it certain history.

However, as I say, those moderns who are obsessed by hero-worship in the matter of Cromwell try to argue even against this convergence of evidence.

Now the interesting point about Milton's attitude in the *Defensio Secunda* is this: The whole of Europe took it for granted that Cromwell had acted after the fashion I have described—intending to entrap the King as the first step to his destruction. Salmasius in his book against the regicides affirms it strongly. Milton was put up officially to answer that affirmation, among others, and we note with particular interest that he could not make out a sufficient case for his master.

Cromwell saw Milton; Milton was the employé of Cromwell at the time, he had before him all the documents and any facts which Cromwell could have given him in his own defence —and yet that defence is at once hurried and weak.

Milton begins by saying, in effect, this: "If it were true that Cromwell had successfully lured the King into a trap it is very inconsistent in Salmasius to call the King wise and prudent," and so forth. But he does not directly deny Cromwell's guilt. Next he advances the argument that Cromwell should not be accused because he was not in Hampton Court at the actual moment of the flight—and that argument is worth nothing. He could have left orders, and Whalley, who was in command at Hampton Court, was Cromwell's *alter ego*—the close relative who did all that he was told.

Having said so much, and it is very little, brief, hurried and confused, Milton turns away from this capital point of all and refuses to discuss it further. I do not see how anyone can read this passage in the *Defensio Secunda* without seeing that it strongly supports the universal opinion that Cromwell was the author of the King's flight—its direction and its tragic end.

For the rest the *Defensio Secunda* is scurrilous (as indeed had been those against whom he was writing). It was followed by yet another piece of Latin, further attacking the half-Scottish, half-French More—first suspected of being, then known to be, the author opposed to him.

The thing is another torrent of abuse, as gross as can be, personal, and indecent, and unreasoned. It is a pity that it should have been written in Latin; had it appeared in English it would rival or surpass the *Colasterion* as a subject of amusement. More had got into a scandal, and Milton took full advantage of that. He, More, the Calvinist clergyman, had seduced the serving-maid of Salmasius, a certain Pontia—and you may imagine how Milton lets himself go on that! The target becomes "a compost of iniquity," "a devotee of Priapus"; "his damnable bosom" is the seat of "a never-dying worm," he is "a foul miscreant and a base one." "Shall I call him" (asks Milton rhetorically) "a man or an excrement?" And there is no doubt which alternative he decides on. "You pass," he says, "from adultery with serving wenches to adulteration of the truth." And he presently adds a Latin phrase which may be translated "this man's lust is always falling upon kitchen wenches."

He also says that his opponent picks his nose.

Now all this is excellent fun, and we must be grateful to Milton for giving us such capital display of thwacks and bangs. But as a reasoned defence of what he calls "the British people" (by which he means the small minority of extreme Revolutionaries, and the wildest part of the Army, used by the calculation of Cromwell for the killing of Charles I) it is not pleading, it is hardly argument. The only historical value of this piece of Billingsgate, apart from the passage on Oliver Cromwell's responsibility for the King's death, lies in the picture he gives of himself, as also in the example it affords of his methods of controversy.

With this virulent, white-hot yelling against More the

regicide pamphlets may be said to end. In the four years that
remained before Cromwell's death, the nearly six which were
to pass before the whole republican cause which Milton had
served fell to the ground, he still wrote fitfully (or rather dictated, since after the loss of his sight he had to depend upon
dictation) and even to the very last he was still unable to suppress the itch for pamphleteering. He wrote public advice to
Oliver's son in the first months after the Protector had passed;
in the following summer (less than a year before the return of
the King) he was still worrying in print against an official
clergy and an official Church. He cried out against the last
suppression of the Parliamentary remnant by the Army, he
cried out against the restoration of Government by one man.
Even as Monk was in the very act of ending the dragging farce
—even as the approach of the young King could be felt and
heard—Milton was still pouring out a final tract of advice and
warning. It was futile, and much too late.

It is the privilege and pleasure of poets to suffer illusion
in things mundane. Of all the men gathered together in the
small group which had mastered the now suddenly angry mass
of Englishmen Milton least understood what was toward.
Among the rest there were some who had their suspicions in
varying degrees, the industrious Thurloe perhaps saw the danger most clearly—but nearly all of them saw it, except Milton.
When Cromwell should no longer be physically present among
them, his ghost would not suffice to keep upright the unnatural
balance. Hence the hurried nomination of Richard Cromwell
when the end came, and the affirmation that Oliver in the last
hours of delirium had named him successor. Hence the pomp
of the obsequies.

The memory of Oliver's victories, the respect in which his
soldier comrades held him, had been the cement which kept
the thing together; the disruptive force which was to break it
up and did in fact break it up sooner than had been expected

even by the most anxious, was a mixture of ill-ease against restraint and protest against taxation. This last all that mass of Englishmen who were still small owners, and their superiors, the squires and the merchants, could understand after a most direct fashion. Every man who had to pay Oliver's novel and crushing taxation was now in protest.

The Protector himself had said that nine men out of every ten were against him, but that he was safe because he had put a sword in the hand of the tenth man. He miscalculated. There is no permanent government of men save by persuasion. His fame, and the regard which England under him had excited in foreign nations, was part of that persuasion. He no longer there, men would be increasingly difficult to persuade.

Yet did John Milton to the end imagine that his republic would endure. Up to the very last he was ready to pamphleteer away and help to settle matters in spite of the brutish multitudes who were howling for their King.

That King returned. Upon his birthday, the 23rd of May 1660, Charles Stuart, the second of that name, landed on Dover beach, to the thunder of the guns. The Monarch, though not Monarchy, was restored. The nineteen years of Polemic were over, and so—it might be thought—was the opportunity for Milton's pen, whether in verse or prose. But things stood not so; Milton was to re-arise; nor was this to be the fruit of any chance —he was to rise as from the dead by the power of his own will, by the exercise of his own superb tenacity.

Part Five

The Sonnets

The Sonnets

THE sonnets of Milton must be considered *as verse* by themselves, disconnected from the rest of his writing.

A sonnet demands high verse more essentially than does any other looser form. If it fall to a standard tolerable in things less packed, it is damned. If it contains one really bad line it is as intolerable as wine with a dash of vinegar in it. In all this the sonnet resembles the epigram: which is either perfect or to be rejected. Now this character in the sonnet Milton never felt, though in all other verse he laboured to achieve.

Although his whole soul was classic, and the sonnet, even when it is not strict, requires the classic temper, yet are Milton's sonnets so uneven as to stand apart from all else he did in rhyme, because in them his classic spirit wavered.

Although each of his English sonnets (save the early one *To the Nightingale*) is concerned with some event or friendship in his own life, although a good half of them are actually political, yet must they be set aside from the accidents of that life and treated in a department of their own.

The reason is this: that the sonnet is the prime test of a poet. The writing of verse, like all activity, is strengthened by limitation, and the poetry of a mind classical is braced up (and thus strengthened) by fixed form and rule. Thus those who shall come to question the greatness of Shakespeare—and a reaction sooner or later will certainly do that—can be answered abruptly by the example of the sonnets. In that mould he excelled himself—and all others.

Therefore when we are judging Milton as a poet we must make a particular test of what he wrote in this shape. Omitting the imperfect Italian experiments (which count no more than Swinburne's experiments in French) we have of his sonnets eighteen remaining. They must be carefully considered and judged aright, and as it were with a fresh eye—like one who should come upon them for the first time. For Milton's place as a poet has been so confounded with his religious and political significance that his verse is most uncritically placed, especially those parts of it which cannot be placed too highly.

Let us note in the first place that the example of William Shakespeare has here (as elsewhere) little moved him. With the exception of the sonnet on his blindness, "When I consider how my days are spent, E'er half my days in this dark world and wide," etc., none of them are influenced by the Poet who not only provided the highest of all models, but lay most immediately to his hand. One would have thought that such an example would have filled the whole mind of the young man, being an example contemporary with that mind in its first enthusiasms. Repeated by friends, circulated among them in manuscript, Shakespeare's sonnets first appeared in print immediately after Milton's birth, and must have been before him as new and famous stuff during those first creative years at Cambridge. Yet they touch him not. The twin spiritual parents of Milton's sonnet are Spenser and Petrarch: Petrarch through that passion for learning foreign languages which possessed him as a boy, so that Petrarchian verse was early familiar to him; and Spenser because Milton, like all his generation, was moved by Spenser as by no other. They got from him that spendthrift spirit in words, that lack of economy, which was also Milton's chief defect—just as the most intimate sense of rhythm is his

chief quality. Indeed the defect and the quality are comple-
mentary.

It is not to be denied that in Milton's treatment of the sonnet
he ignores what is most essential to its effect—especially in the
English tongue. He ignores the contrast of the octave with the
sextet. A sonnet has been called the expression in verse of a
single thought. That definition is insufficient: a sonnet is rather
the expression in verse of a thought and the consequence of
that thought. "If this . . . then that." "How is this . . . it is
thus." "Is this so? . . . No, it is otherwise." "Though . . .
yet," etc.: and this duality appears in the division of the sonnet
into two parts.

This double formation is of the essence of the sonnet, as
Shakespeare intimately understood. If the sonnet is divided into
its octave and its sextet—which division makes it what it is—
there is a reason for the separation of the two and for contrast
between them. The first eight lines make a unity which asks a
question to which the last six lines give the reply; or the first
eight state an unfinished mood which the last six follow up
and determine; or the first eight express some complaint which
the last six relieve by denunciation; or the first eight announce
the subject of strong love, which the last six proceed to adorn
and confirm. The sonnet to work with full force must have
this central hinge. For the sonnet is feminine and needs a waist:
the limber must be followed by its gun.

Now with Milton that dualism in the sonnet is missing. Nor
can I believe it to be missing through deliberate intention; it is
missing because it is not understood. The only exceptions (and
these are hardly exceptions) are the sonnet on his twenty-third
birthday, and that imploring protection for his house against
the King's army in the Civil Wars. On both of these one can
pause fully at the end of the octave, and take up the sextet in a
new tone. Indeed in the first example (that on his twenty-third
birthday) you have actual contrast. "Though this . . . yet

that." In the other, the sonnet to protect his house, there is no contrast, but there is a second springing forward of the verse. (For the truth of this, read either text aloud, as I shall present them in a moment.)

In the greater part of them, however, he was so contemptuous, careless or ignorant of the sonnet's dualism that his eighth and ninth lines actually belong to one and the same sentence. Even the splendid sonnet on the Vaudois, standing among the very summits of English verse, suffers that lack of pause; and of course—since it suffers the lack of pause at the centre—a lack of contrast between what should be the first and the separate second part.

> (8th line) ". . . their moans
> (9th line) The Vales redoubled to the hills and they
>   To Heaven. . . ."

As a fragment those lines might be a piece of blank verse from *Paradise Lost*—they are in no way the cessation and rebirth which should mark the sonnet.

Let not this point be judged insignificant: the sonnet (the English sonnet at least) lacking this division, is not itself. It may be of the purest, the noblest, the most inspired quality; it may be poetry at its climax; but it will have something about it not that which the sonnet, as a sonnet, should present.

Here is the sonnet on his twenty-third birthday, which may have been the first he ever wrote, though when he produced his collected edition he put it second.

> "How soon hath time, the subtle thief of youth,
>   Stolen on his wing my three and twentieth year!
>   My hasting days fly on with full career,
>   But my late spring no bud nor blossom shew'th.
> Perhaps my semblance might deceive the truth
>   That I to manhood am arrived so near:
>   And inward ripeness doth much less appear,

That some more timely-happy spirits endu'th.
Yet, be it less or more, or soon or slow,
   It shall be still in strictest measure even
   To that same lot, however mean or high,
Toward which Time leads me, and the will of Heaven.
   All is, if I have grace to use it so,
   As ever in my great Task-Master's eye."

The fourth line is Shakespeare to a fault, the eighth line (rhyming with the fifth)—"That some more timely-happy spirits endu'th" has a forced rhyme for the very purpose of keeping to the regularity of the sonnet form. Then comes the rightful break between the octave and the sextet: the thought, and the consequence of that thought. The octave has said, "I am behind-hand with my young life"; the sextet says, "But keep an eye on me, I shall achieve my business."

In the sonnet which he affixed (or meant to affix), to his door, all those years later, when the King was marching on London, you still have the strong sense of form compelling him to give the sextet its due separation. Here is that fine thing, the finer because it rolls up so grandly towards its end.

"Captain or Colonel, or Knight in Arms,
   Whose chance on these defenceless doors may seize,
   If deed of honour ever did thee please,
   Guard them, and him within protect from harms.
He can requite thee; for he knows the charms
   That call fame on such gentle acts as these,
   And he can spread thy name o'er lands and seas,
   Whatever clime the sun's bright circle warms.
Lift not thy spear against the Muse's bower:
   The great Emathian conqueror bid spare
   The house of Pindarus, when temple and tower
Went to the ground; and the repeated air
   Of sad Electra's poet had the power
   To save the Athenian walls from ruin bare."

It is not a clear antithesis of "When I . . . Then I," which is the best, purest and strongest form of the sonnet; but at any rate it has its distinct second stanza. If it is not what a sonnet should be—a thought, and the consequence of that thought— it is at any rate a thought, and the repetition of that thought. And Lord! what a triumphant repetition!

Well, then, here is Milton's chief defect in the matter, he thinks it indifferent whether the sonnet have a waist or no. All the genius of English verse clamours for dualism in this form, but Milton does not feel the necessity for it, though he is a high-priest of the English tongue. Is this the effect of Spenser on him, or Petrarch, or is it an original blemish?

Hardly Spenser: though he often does not break the run, yet his eighth line nearly always completes a phrase. Though the ninth often rhymes with the eighth in Spenser, yet the octave rarely runs confusedly into the sextet. Sonnet XXIV of the *Amoretti* is an exception, and LXXVII, somewhat; but none of the others, I think.

Petrarch's model I am not competent to analyse, but so far as my fragmentary knowledge permits me to judge the 281 sonnets of the edition before me (Soave's of 1805) that Master (like Spenser) commonly, though not always, achieves the octave and there draws breath. Thus, at random, number 65 ends the octave thus:—

"Poi che l'alma dal cor non si scapestra;"

or 71:

"Quanto bisogna a disfogare il core;"

or 103:

"Il Sole, e'l foco, e'l vento, ond'io son tale;"

or 225:

"Ne d'Amor visco temi o lacci o reti,
Ne' nganno altrui contra'l tuo senno vale."

But John Milton spills over from octave to sextet like a man pouring out wine with his head turned and overflowing the cup.

Look at these three examples of eighth and ninth lines all continuous. The first from the sonnet to Cromwell:

> ". . . and Dunbar field resounds thy praises loud
> And Worcesters laureate wreath."

Then this from the sonnet to Fairfax:

> "Moved by her two main nerves, iron and gold,
> In all her equipage."

This last from the sonnet *On his Blindness*:

> ". . . But Patience, to prevent
> That murmur soon replies."

In each there is a complete indifference to the required break.

Next we must note how strangely uneven are these eighteen sonnets. Not only is there a gulf between the worst and the best, but there is unevenness in the texture of each individual sonnet. Time and again there is a line, a phrase, even at the best a word, which lets the reader down with a shock.

Now it must be admitted that to avoid such exceptions has been, for most poets who have attempted the sonnet, impossible. Even for some poets who have excelled in the sonnet the absence of such shocks has clearly proved impossible. Indeed that is the whole point of the sonnet—its incessant demand for perfection: and perfection is not for man. It is because the sonnet demands perfection that all true poets feel themselves challenged to attempt it; and there is perhaps not one of those who have attempted it, since it was first happily imported into this island not 400 years ago, who does not die bitterly regretting this expression, that line, in some sonnet of his which he has hammered at in vain and failed to repair.

[217]

If Wordsworth, for instance, has, through religious prejudice, been over-praised (though certainly he proved himself
upon occasion a master of the sonnet) yet in one of his best
("The world is too much with us," etc.) he thrusts right into
the living organism of the thing the horrid, wounding deadness
of "standing on this pleasant Lea." Nor is the phrase "getting
and spending" up to the mark.

To appreciate the contrast between the good and bad sonnet
in Milton, consider the worst. It was provoked by precisely
that emotion which in prose produced the opposite effect—I
mean epileptic anger against those who had offended his vanity.
The *Colasterion*, for reasons Milton never intended, is the most
readable of all his prose; anger expressed in violent vituperation
has, for once, rendered him quite clear—and most entertaining
as well. But what rubbish is this, upon precisely the same theme
—excited anger against those who criticise his novel views on
marriage and his patronage of divorce.

"A book was writ of late called *Tetrachordon*,
    And woven close, both matter, form, and style;
    The subject new: it walked the town awhile,
    Numbering good intellects; now seldom pored on.
Cries the stall-reader, 'Bless us! what a word on
    A title-page is this!'; and some in file
    Stand spelling false, while one might walk to Mile
    End Green. Why is it harder, sirs, than *Gordon*,
Colkitto, or *Macdonnel*, or *Galasp*?
    Those rugged names to our like mouths grow sleek,
    That would have made Quintilian stare and gasp.
Thy age, like ours, O soul of Sir John Cheek,
    Hated not learning worse than toad or asp,
    When thou taught'st Cambridge and King Edward Greek."

For badness on this level it is no excuse to say that it was
"intended comic"; there is no reason why the grotesque or the
comic in verse should not be good. On the contrary, it is pre-

cisely comic verse which has nothing to sustain it save its own excellence of construction and which therefore the writer of it is bound to perfect *ad unguem*, and it is the common experience of those who have attempted it that no kind of verse needs more the careful and repeated attention of the artificer. But the construction and texture of these fourteen lines—one can hardly call them a sonnet—are merely contemptible. He uses the clumsy effect of rhyming with a half word in a deliberately clownish way, and seeks with awkward humour for difficult rhymes—"Tetrachordon," "pored on," "Gordon."

What can excuse "O soul of Sir John Cheek" (and by the way, the spelling he gives that famous name, the great Cecil's brother-in-law, should be a warning to all those tiresome modern critics whose idea of their trade is to discover misprints and slips in spelling). But worst of all is the final line, which, in a sonnet, should be (if anything) the best: "When thou taught'st Cambridge and King Edward Greek." It is to be hoped that Milton blushes when people bring up that line to quizz him on those edges of the Elysian Fields.

But it is to be doubted whether he will take the quizzing kindly, for Milton never seems to have regretted anything he did—not even the dreadful time he gave the first Mrs. Milton!

As for unevenness within what are otherwise tolerable sonnets, take such a line as "Madam, methinks I see him living yet" coming immediately after the famous "Killed with report that old man eloquent." Or take the previous, "But this is got by casting pearl to hogs," coming straight upon the strong line, "Which after held the sun and moon in fee." Or again, in the sonnet to Sir Harry Vane, "Both spiritual power and Civil, what each means." We need not quarrel with the presence of the extra two syllables; indeed, redundant syllables, properly and occasionally employed, are excellent, even in the strictest rhythms, as no one knew better than Milton himself, with his

[219]

introduction of triple feet into the solemn decasyllabics of his blank verse. But what one may quarrel with and condemn unreservedly are redundant syllables that do nothing but trip up the tongue as one reads, which are not intended to be redundant but are only an effort to get a long word in by slurring it over. And as for the line as a whole, it is prose, and dull prose at that.

There are but three of Milton's sonnets which are wholly free from such shocks of the prosaic or the unworthy or the ill-fitting. These are the "Captain, or Colonel, or Knight at Arms" (for "Colonel" had three syllables, so the first line is good enough); the sonnet on the vision of his dead wife; and of course the supreme sonnet on the Massacre in Piedmont.

However, to say that any man attempting to write eighteen sonnets has written three good ones and one very good is high praise. A perfect sonnet is, for the poet, full marks, as is not a perfect anything else. And to get one set of full marks and two ninety-five's out of eighteen papers is good going.

Praise a man for his best, and praise Milton for that glorious gift to immortality, "Avenge, O Lord, thy slaughtered saints whose bones Lie scattered on the Alpine mountains cold."

"Avenge, O Lord, thy slaughtered saints, whose bones
  Lie scattered on the Alpine mountains cold;
  Even them who kept thy truth so pure of old,
  When all our fathers worshipped stocks and stones,
Forget not: in thy book record their groans
  Who were thy sheep, and in their ancient fold
  Slain by the bloody Piedmontese, that rolled
  Mother with infant down the rocks. Their moans
The vales redoubled to the hills, and they
  To Heaven. Their martyred blood and ashes sow
  O'er all the Italian fields, where still doth sway
The triple Tyrant; that from these may grow
  A hundred fold, who, having learnt thy way,
  Early may fly the Babylonian woe."

The thing is so good that it swallows up its own defects. It covers them with the cloak of its achievement; just as the push and width of Shakespeare when he is galloping at large quite swallows up his defects by the way. For very good verse may be compared to a young horse, off and away upon the hills at morning, who now and then seems to stumble but is right again in a split second, having such strength in him that he at once recovers and makes of the whole effect of his charge one thing.

That sonnet has no proper break in the middle, as I have already pointed out; its appeal does not run in a crescendo as that of the sonnet should; and it "dates"—for who is now concerned to *fly* the Babylonian woe—however much they may dislike same? We have other fish to fry, and when we must be with the Babylonian woe (or giant Pope, to give it its other name) we are ready to be spit-fires, or silent contemners, or secret intriguers—but at any rate no longer refugees.

The splendour of this piece of verse lies (if you will forgive my saying it) in its sound. And it is folly indeed to belittle sound in verse, as though it were a secondary thing. It is primary. It is by the sound of verse that you know it. Good verse is a music, shrill or deep, calm or ecstatic—but it is a music always if it is to be poetry, and when the music fails the poetry fails with it.

See how John Milton has, not without art, but more by some sudden inspiration of anger, produced music here.

It is the rolling of an organ, sustained, modulated, appealing, overawing from the first line to the last. It has such inspiration that what should be in any other a defect (the assonance of all the last syllables in the first eight lines) here passes unperceived—or rather enhances their value. For those long syllables, and the images they call up, "moans," "roll," "old," "bones" and "soul" make a recurrent noise like the waters of the Alpine hills, and give the full note required.

As for any man who quarrels with the bad history of it, and

thinks by that to diminish Milton's triumph—he knows nothing of the Poet's trade. Bad history makes good verse—witness the *Song of Roland*—and verse more powerful than this has never been written in the English tongue. It not only sounds, it burns; it not only burns, it engraves. It is one thing; complete in its noise and in its meaning, from its surface to its depths, in its under and its over tones and in the immediate full sweep of its being. It is a living thing.

Bad history it certainly was; the story of the Vaudois (as the French called them and as most of them called themselves) or the Waldenses (to give them their official and Latin name) is that of most angry quarrels of this kind, having what are called "faults on both sides." But the impartial Pagan would I think give more blame to the Waldenses than to the angry government which at last lost its temper.

They were the last fossil of that great Manichæan assault upon our civilisation, which had filled the Middle Ages. They had suffered centuries of suppression by war and inquisition and the hatred of their neighbours.

They were now dwindled to a few Alpine rustics of the upper valleys between Pignerolo and Susa who had been so cut off from civilisation that even their strange religion had grown atrophied. They coveted (as the upland people always do) the better pastures and corn lands of their neighbours downstream; and as these wealthier neighbours downstream had not suffered isolation but had the fulness of religion about them the friction between the two, when the Reformation broke out, got an added excuse of religion. Then their legitimate Government of Turin, the Counts of Savoy, rather tardily woke up to the disorder, and mixing the religious with the political motive (as was inevitable at that time) sent troops who massacred and spread a terror.

The thing was turned into a point of honour between the Catholic and Protestant camps, who had just been liquidating their quarrel in the spluttering out of the Thirty Years' War. Opinion was the more inflamed because this persecution had come so late in the day, after the main religious wars had died down.

Cromwellian England, immune through sea-power, was the stronghold (and through the recent victories of the rebellion the victorious stronghold) on the Protestant side of Europe. Cromwell interfered. He was specially exasperated to note among the soldiers guilty of these atrocities, refugees from that Ireland where he had himself behaved so horribly. He demanded that the chastisement of the mountaineers should cease —as Spain might have demanded that the destruction of the Irish should cease. Though the English nation was still small compared with the great Continental powers, the French were eager to get the aid of the well-trained permanent professional soldiery which Cromwell had at his disposal—therefore Cromwell was listened to and the persecution ceased. The Regent of Savoy was a French Princess. Mazarin brought pressure to bear on her, and the thing was over.

The sonnet was written before this policy had matured; it was a sort of announcement by fanfare of heralds, and thoroughly does it carry out its rôle—"Sound trumpet, sound." And sound it did indeed!

I cannot leave it.

My mind returns unceasingly to those recurrent deep omegas at the end of line after line, rolling like a deep surge on a beach; recurrent, yet not monotonous, unique in our language. How could he bring in that long "o" of "bones," "cold," "old," "rolled," "sow," "grow," "woe," line after line, loud at the end of each, and yet conceal his effect? No one knows how those things are done—least of all the man who does them. But when they are done they take root for ever.

It remains astonishing that a man who could do so well in a particular form should also do so ill—or rather that, doing so well, he published what he did ill. He had tendencies that way all his life, even during his best lyric period in youth; though then it will be remembered he at least had the grace to set aside his breakdown on the theme of the Passion.

Perhaps his inclusion of so many thoroughly mediocre and more than three right-down-bad sonnets, like his also very bad translations of the Psalms, was due to something which hamstrings a good many poets of the first class in the middle of their lives: a new uncritical pride.

The thing happened to Tennyson. It was in middle life that he did his worst, and pretty bad it was. And the reason seems to me explicable. Your good poet in youth is diffident, because he is, by the nature of his calling, sensitive. He is athirst for fame, he has heard the unmistakable note of his great predecessors, he despairs of rivalling them, he keeps back what he writes, he is abashed by the least discouragement, even from the most incompetent. Then in time, perhaps in the late thirties or after, he finds that men begin to praise him; he begins to worship his own work. As he approaches middle age he is flattered by the parrot repetition of these praises among the rich, who have heard from their betters below them that he has a reputation. He is too much pleased also by the adulation which now also begins to be paid to him by certain juniors. His old diffidence is altered into a new confidence and, since poets are as vain as they are sensitive, an over-confidence. He comes to think that such as he are permanently inspired.

The error increases through the falsity of fashionable praise. His worst lines, his mannerisms, are dwelt upon enthusiastically by fools; he snuffs the incense, and though he may have known on writing it that this or that passage was weak, this or that line pedestrian, yet he reads into them, after a while, a subtle beauty which they do not contain, and prints what he ought to have suppressed.

This was particularly the case with Milton—a man always

too sensitive and always unfortunately vain. When we remember that the sonnets were written, especially the worst of them, just at the moment of his life when he was becoming famous as the champion of a victorious cause, I think the publication of what is bad among them is sufficiently explained, though what is bad outweighs what is good. Nor did Wordsworth (the worst of critics, whether of himself or others) ever express an unsounder judgment than when he wrote his own bad sonnet on Milton, proclaiming Milton's sonnets to be so many trumpets. Some of them were. "Parts of it are excellent."

Note this further defect in Milton as a sonneteer; that whereas in almost every other form of verse he attempts his ear is invariable, his accuracy of rhythm, his multiplicity of rhythm inevitable, yet when he is bound under this strictest of all forms he boggles, making that worst of all faults in English rhythm, the introduction of the unwanted spondee.

I call it spondee for lack of a better term. "Spondee" means strictly two long syllables, but two English syllables may succeed each other one of which is not long in the sound but halted by the nature of the consonant—for instance, the phrase "bad lot" although "a" and "o" are both short. "Bad" might be long anyhow, because there is the "d" and the "l" after it, but "lot" does not become short, as it would be by itself; it becomes long by finding itself in this association.

Consider in the fine sonnet "When the assault was intended to the city," the fifth and sixth lines:

> "He can requite thee, for he knows the charms
> That call fame on such gentle acts as these."

The rhythm of the first line sinks and rises admirably, and then at the beginning of the second you get the nasty stumbling check of the spondee "call fame." It is impossible to pronounce that line so that it fits in: it stops the whole movement. And this is remarkable because the rest of the piece is a trophy of superlative rhythm. Read it again. The very punctuation suits the singing of this great song; and the three last lines have all the appeal of a sighing wind coming at evening over fields and trees. In those lines the word "repeated" is the pivot of the measure; and no one but Milton would have hit instinctively upon that word.

It is further to the high praise of Milton that he never took refuge in a trick—which refuge in the case of the sonnet is more abominable than any other. That he disdained tricks always I have already emphasised, and I wish to re-emphasise it in the case of the sonnets. He had indeed one individual manner, the beginning of a sonnet with a proper name; but that is not properly speaking a trick, it is indeed a short cut to lyrical effect. It is an emphatic signature, as who should say, "I, John Milton, now address this person." Of that worst trick in English, exaggerated alliteration, there is no trace in these exercises; nor is there of repetition (an excusable trick), nor of that very base trick—odd words. Indeed Milton had a fine contempt for odd words, well knowing that a man who cannot cook without too much spice is no cook.

And, talking of odd words, Keats exaggerated adjectives ending in "y." He did it no doubt to escape the intolerable repetition of our adjectives ending in "ing"; but it was an affectation. Now we may note in Milton's sonnets one such example—the word "bloomy" in the ode *To the Nightingale*, "that on yon bloomy spray," whereas the common word is "blooming." But Milton can plead that the word he used was nearer to his own time. Keats used such as deliberate archaisms. It is witness to the inhabiting Muse of Milton that even during those sonnets where he was guilty of such bathos, of such descents, the poet in him springs out everywhere. Let us note this even in his worst efforts; that power in him still lifts him, at moments, to the skies. The sonnet to a virtuous young lady, for instance, is not eminent, but what a memorable line is the penultimate one thereof,

>"Passes to bliss at the mid-hour of night."

Or in the mediocre sonnet to Vane, do we not find the good drum-beat of place-names as in his great epic?

>". . . When gowns not arms repelled
>The fierce Epirot, and the African bold—"

Yes: the triple drum-beat of "African."

And in that yet another mediocre piece to Lawrence, "The lily and rose that neither sewed nor spun." That line is perfect, in its smoothness, in its lilt, its escape from the repetition of a well-worn text; its balance of the long vowel with the short; its exact conclusion.

In the sonnet, also mediocre as verse (though not as doctrine or as morals), the second sonnet to Cyriack Skinner, which he so cautiously kept back from the public, and in that on the recurrent theme of his blindness, what could be better than the substantives with just one adjective among them, graving a picture of his isolation. He is speaking of his eyes now three years blind,

>"Nor to their idle orbs does sight appear,
>Of sun or moon or star throughout the year,
>Or man or woman."

That is a final way of writing.

That his sense of rhythm is exalted, triumphant, in the three great sonnets, we might expect. I am ashamed to repeat such a truth. They are monuments of English because he has so used that sense therein. They have never of their own kind been surpassed; nor, it may be presumed, will they ever be. And the highest among the trinity is that which sounds the military trumpet for the charge—for the host of Heaven to avenge the highland raiders of the Alps.

We must not leave the sonnets without putting them into their proper place amid the incidents of Milton's life as a man. As the works of a poet, showing his deficiencies, even his absurdities, and also his unequalled magnificences, they have their chief places of interest: but we are also dealing in this book with John Milton the human being, and it is much to our purpose to see how they fit in with the eruptive, combative, crammed business of his life.

From this aspect we note to begin with that they accompany him throughout that life. Alone of all the moulds into which he poured his molten gold and dross he kept the sonnet with him from the spring of youth to the breaking down of age. It is a tribute to him to remember this; and there is a reason for it. A man who has begun to write sonnets in his youth discovers that they take long to complete. There never was a sonnet worth keeping that was written off-hand—as a song, a chorus, an epigram or the spouted lengthy passage of an epic may be. For the sonnet is not a cry, nor the voice of an emotion; it is a thing made, and made slowly; an exercise in verse by man, the creator of his own world. Therefore it is that when a poet achieves even one success in this form he can lie down contented; he has done a thing necessarily enduring.

What is called the second of the sonnets (but Milton put it after his Italian exercises) was, as we know by its matter, written, and presumably *first* worked on, not much later than his twenty-third birthday in November 1631. How much further it was worked on we cannot tell. That to the Nightingale came earlier in Milton's own order of arrangement, and may possibly have been written earlier (the title is not his own). But the sonnet touching his twenty-third birthday is the fixed date for which we have a beginning. The last one (upon his dead wife) cannot at the earliest belong to a date before his fiftieth year (1658), when she died. It was transcribed (for he had been blind six years) in the hand of that same secretary who took down later his secret speculations against the Trinity.

What is as characteristic and as remarkable is that the list of these few exercises not only runs through his life from one end to the other, but is well spaced along the way. The sonnet imploring the King's soldiery to spare his London house belongs on the face of it to the late autumn of 1642, and must be round about the days just before the middle of November when the King's Army was standing within a march of the City. He had, in his alarm, stuck it up on his door, as we know from the original manuscript—though he himself, perhaps in shame, struck out the inscriptive words.

The sonnet reckoned the ninth comes two years later, the sonnet reckoned the tenth (to Lady Margaret Ley) a few months after, or in 1645 at the latest. The two bad sonnets complaining of the attack on his defence of divorce similarly date themselves—the last, we know, must come after the attacks and therefore be of, or later than, 1645, when Milton was a man of thirty-seven; though he did not print them until later still.

The next sonnet could hardly be, at the latest, beyond 1646. Then come that to Lawes and to Mrs. Thomson; that to Fairfax cannot be earlier than the fall of Colchester in 1648, nor much later—for a very few months after that Fairfax was on the other side of the hedge.

Milton's sonnet to his employer and master Oliver Cromwell belongs to 1652, definitely fixed to May of that year by its title and matter, though it did not appear published for more than forty years; and the one to Sir Harry Vane must have come immediately after, for within a few months poor Harry Vane was no subject for the pen that would belaud Oliver—he had been turned out ignominiously along with the other poor remnants of the Long Parliament, for the epitaph of his meddling and vanity (not unmixed with diplomatic skill), of his despicable action in the matter of Strafford and all the rest of it was contained in Cromwell's own loudly bellowed phrase now familiar to all, as he drove the Parliamentarians forth: "Sir Harry Vane! Sir Harry Vane! The Lord deliver me from Sir Harry Vane!"

The incomparable Vaudois sonnet can also be fixed with a superior date at least, for it cannot be earlier than the attack on the rebels in 1655. It is worth remembering that this masterpiece was dictated (by a man already blind) as also the one to Cromwell. Milton himself puts the latter down after the "Avenge, O Lord. . . ." And so to the last.

He was twenty-three when he began (as poets do) to see what he could do within the discipline of that form which has so stamped European letters with its strict command: he was a man blind, widowed, and approaching old age before he ceased. And let it be remarked that the sonnets continue to appear during all those years of controversy, barren of other verse. Those years begin with the uprising of violent political conflict, continue through the Civil Wars and deny him the presence of his Muse in any other manner, until the great resurrection of *Paradise Lost* five years after the breakdown of that military despotism which had seemed to him the victory of God.

All those years are filled with the political pamphlets, and thick and tortuous railing, and pedantry, and long and laboured undecipherable sentences.

Those years had seen his outburst against the Christian doctrine of marriage, his consequent demand for freedom in such expressions, his plea for the killing of the King; his more sober and half-shocked attack upon the memory of Charles, even after death, in the *Eikonoklastes*. They had seen the procession of minor writings through the end of the Commonwealth, all his official labours in the Secretaryship, all the burden of work which, before and after his blindness, had for the moment exhausted even *his* exceptional energies. It would seem as though the tempest of the Civil Wars and his consequent perpetual occupation in matters of State had dried up the fountain.*

It would seem so—but for the sonnets. The succession of *these* goes on, reaching their highest towards the close ("Avenge, O Lord" and the "Late Espoused Saint") and is a witness to the way in which his fires were divinely nourished.

Oh, yes! Some God protected this man—the God of Poets protected the Poet in this man. And the sonnets spaced out over nineteen years of aridity like rare water-holes, now almost dry, now brackish, now strong and living fountains along the desert track, are standing witnesses to such favour from the Heavens.

. . . .

We may sum up our conclusions on the sonnets as verse in some such list as the following:—

First among them by far, the one and only very great sonnet written by Milton, is that on the massacre in Piedmont. But side by side with it stand two others which, though they are not its equals, are also great sonnets. These are, in their order, the sonnet on his second wife after her death, the sonnet which he intended to put on his door when there was danger of attack from the Royalist Army threatening the City of London. The sonnet upon his deceased wife suffers from one fault, which is the absence of contrast between the beginning and the end, but it has the merit of continuity and of ending at its highest. The sonnet when the attack was intended on the City is wounded by one line containing a very bad misplaced spondee,

* There is indeed one small possible exception, a translation of Horace's Ode, *Quis multa gracilis*. It has one phrase deservedly famous; but it does not get off the ground; and when he tells us that it is written in the metre of the original he tells us something that is not true.

Tennyson did the same thing when he said that he was writing in the metre of Catullus a piece of verse which was not in that metre at all.

There is however in English letters one supreme example of an exact Latin translation in spirit and in truth and also in metre. It is Thackeray's

"Eheu, fugaces, Postume, Postume!
Oh, for the years that are lost to me—lost to me!"

but for the rest it presents the true contrast between octave and sextet that a sonnet should present, and it rises at the end as a sonnet should rise. These three are the great sonnets of Milton.

Next, not a little inferior, are the sonnet on his blindness, and the sonnet on his twenty-third year. That on his blindness begins well and ends well, but is insufficiently broken in the middle. It is not Milton's fault that the excellent last line should have become a sort of pious proverb, nor should its repetition for the wrong reasons blind us to its value as verse. The sonnet on having reached his twenty-third year, influenced, as we have seen, by Shakespeare, is thoroughly well constructed; but it reaches no great height of poetry. That on the Nightingale which is commonly printed before it (Milton's own order) is much on the same level, but perhaps more lacking in substance.

Next, far below the preceding, come the ten personal sonnets. None of them are good; they decline in value from that addressed to Cromwell, which is the best, to that addressed to "The Religious Memory of Mrs. Thomson, my Christian Friend." The sonnet to Cromwell is a united piece of work, of which the two best known half lines ("peace hath her victories, No less renowned than war") have also been over quoted as a piece of moralising. The sonnet to Vane, unworthy as was its subject, must be put next after that to Cromwell among the personal sonnets. If it had all been written on the level of its best line ("the fierce Epirot," etc., etc.) it might have deserved the first place. But it does not preserve such a level. We may put the sonnet to a virtuous young lady next, for the sake of its construction, and because it preserves for us that admirable penultimate line: then the one to Fairfax, then the one to Lady Margaret Ley, which would deserve an even lower place but for the rhythm of the two central lines:—

> "At Chæronea, fatal to liberty,
>   Killed with report that old man eloquent."

The second sonnet to Cyriack Skinner cannot be wholly condemned because it contains the lines already quoted: "Nor to their idle orbs," etc.

But the first sonnet to him is on a lower level, and so is the sonnet to Lawrence.

The sonnet to Lawes is among the best of the bad ones, and the sonnet "On the religious memory of Mrs. Catherine Thomson, my Christian Friend" among the worst.

But the very worst of all without doubt are the two on the *Tetrachordon* and the caudiferous ones against the Presbyterians to which last we owe the famous epigram (for it can hardly be called a line of verse), "New Presbyter is but the old Priest writ large."

It is difficult to assign the lowest place among these three, but perhaps upon due reflection that prize should be awarded to the first of the *Tetrachordon* sonnets. There is not one line that is not bad, and the three last are execrable. They would shame the worst sonneteer now alive—and one cannot say more than that.

Such are the eighteen.

Part Six

Epic

Epic

RESURRECTION

NOT only had Milton's whole cause, all the business of his hitherto great life, fallen into ruin; but that life itself was forfeit.

The vengeance taken against those who had subverted the English state was, one may say, insignificant. The populace would have been glad enough to see full execution done: but the rebellion had been a rebellion of wealth against the Crown, and wealth had conquered for good and all. The Crown was not really restored. The merchants and squires were the real victors, for no one can take full reprisals against wealth when it is organised and established in the places of power.

But to this inability of loyal England to express itself there was an exception; the regicides at least, those who had urged or voted the death of the King's father, should be sought out and pay the full price. The rage of the public would stand nothing less.

And among these necessary victims John Milton's name stood prominent. He had argued with all his force for the execution of his King. His had been the most potent voice, the one which had been heard throughout Europe. He, the author of the *Tenure*, the man who had not only urged the deed before it was done but afterwards excused it before all Christendom and

[237]

gloried in it, made it his continuous theme—*he* must surely die. Whoever else should be spared *he* should not be spared.

He had completed more than fifty-one years; he had been blind for the last seven of those years; his fortune was forfeit. While all England and London around him was roaring in a frenzy of release, and shouting for all that meant to him in person death, he went into hiding.

Yet he and his goods were saved. He was for some time under arrest; he lay also in terror of assassination from the hand of any one among those exasperated myriads whom the memory of the recent oppression maddened; the terror robbed him of his sleep; the strain was upon him to the utmost. But he passed through it unharmed, and within eight months was free.

To what or to whom did he owe salvation?

On that problem, perhaps the most difficult to be solved in all his story, we have no evidence. Of all men Milton, it would seem, ought to have paid the price. He was by some influence granted the privilege of life and freedom.

Where there is no evidence, we fall back upon conjecture. As it would seem to me, in a matter where every man must judge for himself on probabilities, the influence that saved him was that of the new King.

Clarendon must also have had a good deal to do with it; he was the head of the administration; at the very least he must have been consulted and quite possibly he had the initiative in the matter. But Clarendon had good reason from his administrative experience in exile to feel strongly about Milton, to carry in his mind a permanent impression of hostility between them. Whether a certain respect for letters which Clarendon certainly felt (his own literary talent was remarkable in its way, with a good power of telling a clear historical story, often false) had anything to do with it or not, it would be less easy to determine. But one thing is certain—that of all the characters involved that of Charles the King was himself the most detached and the most open to toleration.

Andrew Marvell, himself a poet and one who had been secretary with Milton, is mentioned in the later traditions as having helped, as also a group of men round Sir Thomas Clarges. And there was also Sir William Davenant, who owed gratitude to Milton in his own case—for his life had been saved ten years before by Milton's intercession. But there was the King in the background, and upon the King finally it depended. That temper of his which has led so many to blame him for a sort of indifference, and which has even made the ignorant accuse him of laziness, was exactly suited for such an occasion as this.

Milton was not yet what he has since become, but he was already a great literary figure. He was known in Europe for other things besides the great political quarrel of the immediate past; and the King was sensitive to European opinion. He was much more sensitive to literary and cultivated opinion than to the official attitude of the Princely Courts. What the other Monarchs thought about the death of a Monarch no one knew better than Charles—but then no one knew better than Charles how mean and narrow were the courts of Kings.

He had had personal and bitter experience. Impoverished and driven from their presence, abandoned, he was in no hurry to fall in with any demand of theirs through sympathy with them. Moreover Charles was strongly national in feeling; almost as national, though not as limited or Jingo, as his brother James. The idea that this or that particular policy would please official opinion abroad would tell strongly with him *against* such a policy. Conversely, he consistently desired, throughout the whole of his life, unity among his own subjects. Since he could not obtain religious unity, at any rate he would obtain, if he could have accomplished it, religious peace. And he had a sense of proportion about the arts which was inherited in his very blood. His father would not have put Shakespeare to death, even had Shakespeare been mixed up with rank treason, and the son would not put Milton to death.

I take this to be the true reading of the affair. It is but a surmise, though a surmise not lightly to be dismissed by those who know how much the shade of monarchy still meant in 1660, and what personal power remained attached to the name of King—especially in the pardon of individuals.

To proceed from surmise to known facts, the sequence is as follows:

It was a little more than a fortnight before the landing of the King that Milton's younger advisers and contemporary friends —a considerable and affectionate group, though not a large one —judged it prudent that he should withdraw from public view. He left his house in Westminster and took refuge with a friend in Bartholomew Close, in the City. That was his first move. What other shifts he made to keep out of public notice we do not know, and that hiding of his was to last the better part of four months, during which came those panic fears of sudden death from enemies, the insomnia, and all the rest of his woes; whereat a lively tradition remained a lifetime after him.

Nearly six weeks after he had thus fled from his known address in Petty France to unknown lurking places in the City, came the discussions upon the Indemnity Bill. The critical date for Milton was the 16th of June 1660. Upon that day it was ordered by Parliament that two of his books, the *Eikonoklastes* and the first *Defensio*, in which he had replied to Salmasius and approved abundantly the killing of the King (covering Charles's memory moreover with contempt and false accusations as a private man) should be burnt by the common hangman.

At first sight one might say that this date, the 16th of June 1660, was critical as being the moment of chief danger, because it was a first open and official condemnation which might lead to so much more. But upon a closer examination we shall see that, on the contrary, the condemnation was framed after a fashion designed to save the poet.

There were three writings of Milton's which were specifically regicide; which could have been made a basis for his destruction. These were, in order of time, the *Tenure of Kings and Magistrates*, the *Eikonoklastes* and the *Defensio*. We remark the singular fact that the *Tenure of Kings and Magistrates* was left out.

Now the importance of that calculated omission—by whomever it was ordered—lies in this: that the other two were apologies for the crime *after* it had been committed, but the *Tenure* was an incitement to the crime written *before* that crime had taken place.

The *Eikonoklastes* and the *Defensio* were only major examples of what was common after the revolutionaries had sealed their victory with the King's blood: but the *Tenure* was a plea for putting Charles to death written while Charles was still alive, and published as a sort of challenge immediately after the execution, in order to show that Milton had been on the side of those who had determined upon the act even before it was accomplished.

There is all the difference in the world, not only in morals but in law, between the two positions. Whether or not approval of a deed involving punishment by the criminal law makes the approver an accessory before the fact lawyers must determine: but it needs no knowledge of any particular legal code to perceive that a man urging another on to do a criminal act necessarily makes that man amenable to the rigour of the law. If I hear that my rich neighbour's house has been burgled, and say out of spite, "I am glad of it!", that is one thing—but if before the burglary took place I should write to the burglar and say, "I hope you will burgle that house," that is quite another.

Had the point been brought forward Milton would have had only one ground of defence; he might have pleaded that technically the *Tenure* had not been published until just after the killing had been done. That would hardly have availed him. His motive for such reticence would have been too clear, and the fact that the plea and urging had been advanced before the trial and sentence was obvious from the body of the book itself. The whole thing had been written to justify *before* the event the final act of the 30th of January 1649.

In many accounts of Milton's escape the House of Lords is represented as seeking out all possible evidences, and omitting the *Tenure* by chance, as though that omission were merely a piece of good luck for the poet. It seems to me impossible to hold that view. The *Tenure* was all the better known for its brevity and its definite pronouncements. Though not as many people may have bought it as bought the official *Eikonoklastes*, and though it may not have been read so widely in Europe as the *Defensio*, it was familiar to everyone who counted and to the public at large. There was no oblivion for such a burning thing after the brief space of eleven years.

Well, the *Tenure* was left out of the Indictment, and Milton thus saved.

He was committed to the custody of the Sergeant at Arms (a certain Norfolke), and did not obtain his release until ten days before Christmas, though the hangman had burnt the books publicly in the last days of August. The Attorney General had expressed the opinion (but not as a public pronouncement) that he deserved hanging—and that was all. It is significant that his escape caused a general astonishment. To this Burnet is our witness; a hostile witness and therefore the more reliable.

Though John Milton was thus a free man just before the Christmas of 1660, he was still at the heavy charge of the fees claimed by the Sergeant at Arms for his custody; he was being asked to pay something like £600. And here again it is Marvell who (according to tradition) helped him; for we are told it was by Marvell's action that the claim was reduced.

The thing was of importance, for the violent counter-revolution had heavily stricken Milton's fortunes. At the end of the Commonwealth, having been a well-to-do man all his life, he was in a better financial position than at any other period. He had parcels of property in the country, notably at Wheatley; houses and land that had come to him from his first wife. He was the owner of at least two and perhaps three substantial houses in London, the most valuable of which was presumably the ancestral home in Bread Street, out of Cheapside, where he had been born and passed his early youth. He had what would be to-day £20,000 capital in money, or the equivalent; something like £700 to £800 a year from rents; and over £1,000 a year paid him as a servant of the State, even after he had ceased to be acting Secretary. He had some £10,000 laid out (as he thought securely) with the Treasury at perhaps 8 per cent—the current rate of the day. He was a man with the equivalent of what we call to-day nearly £3,000 a year.

Most of that income had gone. What he had invested on loan to the Treasury he lost, of course; he also lost his official income; and his nephew tells us that part of his liquid property had been mismanaged and dissipated. We may regard him, say two years after the return of the King, as a man with not much more than what we should call to-day £1,000 a year. He had had to give up to his first wife's brother, not for nothing but almost certainly at a loss, the land in Oxfordshire, and the cash dowry of £6,000 which he had been promised at the Powell marriage and which was confirmed in his father-in-law's will, had never been paid. He was not a ruined man—far from it—but he was in nothing like the position he had been.

In reputation as in wealth, in social status as in hope, he was a broken man. But he was indomitable and he was to re-arise.

It is of the greatest moment to our understanding of Milton, both as a poet and as a man, that in all these vicissitudes he proceeded steadily with what he had so long intended to be the chief work of his life, his epic, which appeared in due time under the title of *Paradise Lost*.

It came first with him. It was his task and his concern. He had the right to claim the reward of such magnificent fortitude and devotion to what is in any poet the chief temporal business of life.

It had filled his thoughts for more than twenty years, it had slowly taken shape in his mind, transformed from a drama to the long narrative poem it became; and this digesting and maturing of his intention took place during those heavy years of controversy when, in any other man, public affairs and violent personal emotion would have eclipsed and perhaps stifled the underlying, main, inward purpose.

He had sat down at last to begin the successful composition of the great thing two years before the King's return; and now, while all this turmoil was battering round him, he steadily continued. After four years of such unclenched grasp upon the helm he brought his argosy safely, triumphantly, in through the narrows and cast anchor.

Even while the Plague was raging in 1665 and he himself taking refuge from it at Chalfont St. Giles, he was dictating the last lines and having read to him for the purpose of revision the completed manuscript.

It was perhaps a little before the outbreak of the Great Fire, that is, somewhere in the late summer of 1666, that the manuscript was submitted for licensing and was in the hands of Tomkyns, the Archbishop's Chaplain, to whom the Primate's authority for this purpose was delegated. In the first days or weeks of the next year, 1667, all was ready; and on the 27th of April the agreement for publication between author and printer was signed. By the August of that year, towards the close of the month, for say twelve or fifteen shillings of our money, some first purchaser was possessed of the new, small, rather thick, quarto book—nearly 350 pages of it—on the title page of which he would read, "PARADISE LOST, a POEM written in Ten Books, by John Milton."

.   .   .   .   .   .

The man who would write of *Paradise Lost*, however superficially, however briefly, should approach his task with awe.

Such an attitude will be ridiculed to-day by many and misunderstood by more. It will be said that one's reverence for the enormous poem comes from emotions or habits which have nothing to do with its excellence. We shall be told that it grew in half a century to be the accepted National Epic, that it enjoyed this title for two centuries more, that the inheritance of so long a tradition rendered men uncritical, and that a clear mind also appreciative of the highest beauty in verse would not be so confused. We shall further be told that the subject of the work was at once so familiar and so sacred to our fathers that they were bemused by its treatment in a huge book of versification, and tended to put *Paradise Lost* side by side with, on the same shelf as, that Authorised Version, the English Bible which was the idol of their idolatry. We shall be told that but for so strange a worship the fortunes of the interminable composition would have been very different. We shall be told that the thing is a hotch-potch of incongruous episodes and imaginations in which the absurd and the dignified elbow each other— with the absurd predominating. We shall be told (what is true enough) that on a steady and continuous reading it palls, that there are whole deserts of dulness in the midst of what is passable, and that the rare episodes of real beauty are like patches of cleared land in a tangled verdure, which only here and there opens into a memorable glade. We shall be told that such merely customary reverence cannot hold, that *Paradise Lost* is now evidently doomed, and that the future will forget it.

The last is a point which will be dealt with at the end of this study. A right decision on it is of importance to our judgment not only of the poem itself, but of our civilisation and its future. This attitude of contempt for *Paradise Lost*—clearly a mere reaction—is not only an empty reaction but an uncritical one. The epic deserves the reverence which it has received, though not an exaggeration of that reverence. It is mighty. It is extravagant in its proportions, and verbose, but it is a unity, and a unity of very high station in our letters. An Englishman well acquainted with *Paradise Lost* is much the fuller for his acquaintance; one who has neglected it is the poorer.

We begin by noticing its volume, and rightly appreciating the scale on which the thing is built: a construction consecutive, with a beginning, a middle and an end, upon the scale of ten thousand lines.*

"What!" a critic may object, "you count mere volume as an excellence? You would then call sublime or at least respectable any haystack of words, even meaningless, if only there be enough of it?"

Certainly not: had *Paradise Regained*, for instance, been pushed to the length of its great forerunner, it would be even worse than it is. All great literatures, it would seem, are cursed with huge futilities of mere matter, the more abominable for their length.

But construction upon a vast scale when it is achieved, when its main architectural lines are as a whole preserved, when its origin, its development and its conclusion follow an accomplished formula, rightly impresses the mind with an effect of vastness. When to that we add a sufficient luxuriance of detail,

* The actual number of lines in the final form of *Paradise Lost* I make, from Masson's final edition, 10,565.

and that detail sufficiently successful, our admiration is confirmed. And when to that again we add special features of manifest excellence, we are prevented from condemning the whole. But of this, later.

Now all this is true of *Paradise Lost*. Milton made his effort to build upon so great a scale and did build: that effort was concluded, and is solid. The rhythm of development from the opening through the central theme to the close is kept to one sweep of a curve—a form binds the whole.

What is more important in the task is this:—that material most difficult to handle was here handled by a master whose grasp, now stronger, now less strong, never quite relaxes, or, at least, never for a sufficient space to break the sequence of our satisfaction. Those passages which save the whole by their beauty are frequent, those of a supreme excellence even where they are brief are sufficient in number to maintain the whole.

More than one metaphor may be applied to the character which saves *Paradise Lost* from condemnation. It may be compared to a range of mountains, too general in outline, often unbroken, yet presenting such diversity of texture and such occasional towering peaks that the chain, when we have surveyed it in one view, must remain fixed in our memory. Or it may be compared to a net, which, from the weight of its material, might sag, but which is supported by a sufficient number of floats: some of them so buoyant and strong as to guarantee without question the survival of the instrument in spite of neglect or attacking storms. It may be compared to one of those great stone surfaces which have been chiselled into a multitude of subjects; so that, though we may admire the outline as a whole, we distinguish at first nothing of the pattern—but on a closer approach and examination we are astonished by an almost infinite variety.

For indeed Milton's chief work (which is not his greatest) is established if by nothing else by its almost infinite multiplicity of effect in the use of the English language; by the inexhaustible variety of cæsura, of length and emphasis in syllable, of every form interwoven to relieve the too-insistent beat of the iambic, by a very tapestry of trochee and even anapæst; by the deft admission, rare but sufficient, of the redundant syllable; and by the giving, even to the normal "short and long" effect which is the basis of English heroic verse, so many degrees of sound that the ear perpetually awaits a satisfactory surprise, and is not disappointed.

Here and there even, but these indeed are rare, come brief flashes of that pure lyric inspiration which had been the glory of his youth and which, in the early songs and odes and the high summit of *Lycidas*, are the laurels of Milton.

These flashes come more often in single lines, hardly ever in more than three; but when they come they are on the level of the earliest and the best.

> ". . . Sleep on
> Blest pair! and Oh! Yet happiest if ye seek
> No happier state, and know to know no more."

. . . . .

> ". . . All but the wakeful nightingale,
> She all night long her amorous descant sung.
> Silence was pleased. . . ."

Or again:—

> "Imparadised in one another's arms."

Hackneyed, simple and good.

It has been repeated so often that men forget what a discovery it was, that impetuous embrace, the first four syllables, that grasping word "imparadised."

That invocation to the sun, which it is true was the product of his youth (the season of all his most eager work), is almost on a level with his very best,

"O Thou that with surpassing glory crowned
Lookest from thy sole dominion like a god
Of this new world; at whose sight all the stars
Hide their diminished heads,
To thee I call. . . ."

Or again:—

". . . And now went forth the morn
Such as in highest Heaven arrayed in gold
Empyreal; from before her vanished night
Shot through with orient beams."

And:—

"Airs, vernal airs,
Breathing the scent of field and grove, attune
The trembling leaves, while universal Pan
Knit with the Graces and the Hours in dance
Led on the eternal Spring."

That last might have been written between his twentieth and his thirtieth year. Perhaps it was; for we know that poets bring out of their storehouse fragments of their past, which they could not complete while they yet were happy. These fragments, when the fatigue of age has wasted them, they restore and mix in with lesser things.

But the main thing to be said about this great poem is that the reader, to judge it aright, must take it in a large draught; that is, he must deal with it as one, remembering its effect upon him as a whole when he has completed his reading rather than excuse it by admitting the supreme success of particular, and usually brief, passages. And one must take it in a sweep, because the movement of it is essential to its character.

It is not a rapid movement; *Paradise Lost* is not a poem of action; but it is a poem in progression from its beginning to its end. You do not expect an elephant to gallop for your excitement, but you cannot deny the majesty of its progress.

A man having read *Paradise Lost* as it should be read, from beginning to end; a man having had the sense not to interrupt that reading by the reading of other fiction, history or verse; a man having taken it as a great meal (it is a meal that will take him a day or two), does find that he is nourished. He has continually regarded the sublime, and he has followed a slow but living sequence which leaves his mind furnished with an air of satisfaction; he has been filled with sufficient beauty and dignity. Throughout all those thousands upon thousands of lines you feel the fashioner at work, you are dealing with something made and with its maker; you are in communion with an achieved, creative effort of the human mind.

Even regarded in this large way, however, the great epic has grave and most apparent defects. The first of these, which strikes everyone, is the jarring of more than human matter, more than earthly landscapes, with exceedingly terrestrial details.

Milton sets out to attempt (as he tells us) something greater than was ever yet attempted "in prose or rhyme." He gives you his visions—but he fails to maintain them constantly upon an exalted level because his intense imagination calls up images drawn from material things, very limited things within his direct and earthly experience.

He has hardly finished giving you—with just that abstraction, just that softness of outline which the thing requires—the mystic glory of the Garden, when he must add a description of its products—which might be the products of any garden. He has hardly thrown out the high phantasy of the Satanic Palace in its gloom than he must light it up inside suddenly, as a contractor would.

> ". . . Many a row
> Of starry lamps and blazing cressets, fed
> With naphtha and asphaltus."

Note again how this palace, which he so finely calls

> ". . . Pandemonium, the high capital
> Of Satan and his peers . . ."

was furnished with its material. Mammon, because he is keen on gold, gets a gang of his devils to dig for it, and we have a description not only of how the gold is melted and cast, but how the dross is skimmed from it before it cools. Between the vision and such base facts there is discrepancy.

The man who felt these discrepancies in Milton's Epic most strongly was that master of English prose, the sturdy but excessive William Cobbett.

If we wish to see the thing expressed at its strongest, we should turn to his description of the time he passed in America —a little book published in 1819 and everywhere available among Cobbett's works.

Turn to the chapter entitled "Potatoes," for it is under such a title that, characteristically enough, William Cobbett launches out against Milton (he launches out against Shakespeare at the same time, but that is by the way).

If it be asked what Milton has to do with potatoes, the explanation is that Cobbett was inveighing against the use of that root, and lays it down that the praise of potatoes is false and snobbish: the common frailty of praising a thing simply because one hears its praise repeated, without thinking out the matter for oneself. His point is that people go on belauding the potato only because they have heard others do so, and that if they used their own judgment they would discover it for the horrible thing it is—to Cobbett's palate at least. In the same way (says he) men are always making a fuss about Milton, though if they would take the trouble to read him they would find that he is worthless—but they only call *Paradise Lost* a great poem because they have heard other people say so. "The whole of Milton's poem," says Cobbett, "is such barbarous trash, so outrageously offensive to reason and common sense that one is naturally led to wonder how it can have been tolerated. . . . But it is the fashion to turn up the eyes when *Paradise Lost* is mentioned."

Cobbett is particularly annoyed with the presence of iron gates in the spiritual world, and notes with a special anger that they have hinges. He vigorously denounces the use of artillery in non-material spheres—and so had many others before him.

A recent critic, and one of the best, has shown a personal irritation with the Archangel Raphael's weakness for good food. It will be remembered how in the fifth book Eve, to entertain so important a guest, goes busily about framing the menu, and how:—

> "She turns, on hospitable thoughts intent
> What choice to choose for delicacy best,
> What order so contrived as not to mix
> Tastes, not well joined, inelegant, but bring
> Taste after taste upheld with kindliest change."

This is certainly what a good hostess should practise, still more a good cook—but it is not poetry. And Raphael falls upon the food as do his host and hostess, with too much gusto.

> ". . . So down they sat,
> And to their viands fell; nor seemingly
> The Angel, nor in mist—the common gloss
> Of theologians—but with keen dispatch
> Of real hunger and concoctive heat."

It is the same thing when Eve eats the fruit.

> "Greedily she ingorged, without restraint."

She wolfed it down; being (as he has just told us)

> "Intent now only on her taste, naught else."

The origin of such incongruity was Milton's own laudable love of good food—one of the best things about him as a man— but it interfered with him as a poet.

Further frailties in *Paradise Lost*, on which account it is blasphemed, are plain enough. The embroidery of such delicate variations is stitched onto conceptions in themselves ridiculous.

Thus of the beasts which "frisking played" for the amusement of Adam and Eve after luncheon:—

> ". . . Bears, tigers, ounces, pards
> Gambolled before them, the unwieldy elephant
> To make them mirth used all his might and wreathed
> His lithe proboscis."

Or again, of Adam and Eve,

> ". . . He, in delight
> Both of her beauty and submissive charms
> Smiled with superior love."

That word "superior" was not in Milton's ear exactly what it is in ours, but it was unfortunate all the same.

If a man should read who had no ear for English sounds nor for the braiding of English strands into English verse, if such a man should go through *Paradise Lost* (he would weary soon enough) only to discover such lapses, the continual insufficiency of these would be apparent soon enough.

For example, after a sort of ball which God the Father gives (as far as one can make out) in honour of the Second Person of the Trinity, comes a supper—Raphael describes it with longing memory.

> ". . . Evening now approached
> (For we have also our evening and our morn—
> We ours for change delectable, not need),
> Forthwith from dance to sweet repast they turn

> Desirous; all in circles as they stood,
> Tables are set, and on a sudden piled
> With Angels' food. . . ."

These grotesques are not frequent, they do not give the whole thing a savour, but they are present.

It is another frailty in *Paradise Lost*—which one might indeed expect from Milton's character, coupled with his incredible mass of reading—that when he is giving examples of his knowledge he cannot refrain from displaying it even at the expense of his verse, putting in little asides to let the reader know that he is learned enough to gloss a bald statement. For instance

> ". . . Nor that Nyseian Isle
> Girt with the river Triton, where old Cham
> (*Whom Gentiles Ammon call, and Libyan Jove*)
> His Amalthea."

Or again:

> "While smooth Adonis from his native rock
> Ran purple to the sea, *supposed with blood*
> *Of Thammuz lately wounded.*"

Last we must note what has most often been reproached him; an absence of glamour in his description of action by Angels, and even by the Deity.

There is nothing like Milton's verse for glamour in the description of landscape or in the calling up of great visions; but when Michael speaks, and any of his peers, or does this or that, still more when God pronounces and acts, it is too often in a fashion so matter of fact that the reader might blush for the writer. We have found the same thing in one of his early lyric poems, when he sets the Trinity round a table; and you find it again when (a passage in VII. 225 which has been the subject of endless merriment) a depot is opened and compasses are taken out of it to describe the celestial circles.

But it must be remembered that this defect in the great poem is native to the time, and also nearly unavoidable in a man with so vivid, almost violent, a visual imagination as was Milton's. If you see in your mind's eye a great landscape you see something heavenly; but if you see in your mind's eye a personality speaking and acting, you cannot (being a man) see other than a man speaking and acting. And this, working literally, tends to fail where the Deity is concerned—or indeed anything above man.

But if the magnificence in *Paradise Lost* is spoilt by failures in particular themes, there are also other particular themes which, when Milton touches them, move him to his highest.

I have already emphasised the truth of this more than once in the matter of landscape, and particularly do you find it when he calls up before his blind eyes the English woods and fields at evening. Crowds also inspire him and great movements of living things, and architecture, remembered I think from Italy, stirs him also to creation: further, he magnified it.

Then there is another theme, not unconnected with these effects of magnificence, and that is the theme of sound—any great volume of sound.

> "Hell heard the unsufferable noise; Hell saw
> Heaven ruining from Heaven, and would have fled
> Affrighted; but strict Fate had cast too deep
> Her dark foundations, and too fast had bound.
> Nine days they fell; confounded chaos roared
> And felt tenfold confusion in their fall,
> Through his wild anarchy.

Or again:

> "He called so loud that all the hollow deep
> Of Hell resounded. . . ."

Everything martial, combining as such things do both sound and multitude, had appealed to Milton since the Civil Wars, because war (so long as it remained human and was not yet basely mechanical) presented the greatest of pageants. His imagination seized especially upon the call of its music and the splendour of its colour.

A man could make a small book of such military extracts alone.

> ". . . That proud honour claimed
> Azazel as his right, a Cherub tall:
> Who forthwith from the glittering staff unfurled
> The imperial ensign; which, full high advanced,
> Shone like a meteor streaming to the wind,
> With gems and golden lustre rich emblazed,
> Seraphic arms and trophies; all the while
> Sonorous metal blowing martial sounds:
> At which the universal host upsent
> A shout that tore Hell's concave, and beyond
> Frighted the reign of Chaos and old Night.
> All in a moment through the gloom were seen
> Ten thousand banners rise into the air,
> With orient colours waving: with them rose
> A forest huge of spears; and thronging helms
> Appeared, and serried shields in thick array
> Of depth immeasurable. Anon they move
> In perfect phalanx to the Dorian mood
> Of flutes and soft recorders—such as raised
> To height of noblest temper heroes old
> Arming to battle. . . ."

And again, in the sixth book, where the Host of Heaven gets sight of their distant enemy advancing against them:—

> ". . . At last
> Far in the horizon, to the north, appeared
> From skirt to skirt a fiery region, stretched

> In battalious aspect; and, nearer view,
> Bristled with upright beams innumerable
> Of rigid spears, and helmets thronged, and shields
> Various, with boastful argument portrayed,
> The banded powers of Satan hasting on
> With furious expedition. . . ."

And then just before, the advance of the others:—

> "Nor with less dread the loud
> Ethereal trumpet from on high 'gan blow
> At which command the powers militant
> That stood for Heaven, in mighty quadrate joined
> Of union irresistible, moved on."

But that one of Milton's excellencies which is almost personal to himself, that which he discovered latent in his native language and put to use so often and so incomparably well was the harmony, the concord, the spell of place-names.

Since his day one English poet after another has been inspired by this example, but none have so much as approached him. This use of place-names was a function of Milton's endless erudition, and a poetic reward for the toil of his youth. Maps had always pleased him, because his classics had taught him the titles of seas and rivers far away, and of mountain chains —great kingdoms, and the tribes of men. Even when his blindness had come upon him he begged for maps, and must have had their configuration described to him by those whose eyes replaced his own. He delights in the outlandish as well as in the civilised; it is no doubt in great part the desire to make us admire his inexhaustible learning, presented by his most vigorous memory. But whatever the motive the result is unique and invaluable. It is Milton's most characteristic gift to English letters.

A man wandering through *Paradise Lost* to mark those points in which Milton plays this best of his cards, the rhythm and noise of place-names, is like one wandering through an upland field in the spring mountains, picking flowers. Later that un-failing gift of his failed; in *Paradise Regained* it plays him false; perhaps he had become too conscious of it, yet it reappeared strongly enough in the *Samson*.

When he strikes that note, especially in *Paradise Lost*, the timbre of it stands out separate from the rest—sometimes in but half a dozen words:—

> ". . . the sea that parts
> Calabria from the hoarse Trinacrian shore."

And again:

> "From Oran eastwards to the royal towers
> Of great Seleucia, built by Grecian Kings
> Or where the sons of Eden long before
> Dwelt in Telassar. . . ."

And again:

> "Nor where Abassin Kings and issue guard
> Mount Amara . . . under the Ethiop line
> By Nilus head. . . ."

And here I have suppressed the equivalent of a line, because Milton has spoilt his own passage by one of those bits of pedantry he found it so difficult to avoid: the original reads of course:

> "Mount Amara (though this by some supposed
> True Paradise) under the Ethiop line."

Of what advantage was it to drag in his knowledge that some people thought the earthly Paradise to have lain in the Abys-sinian mountains—just as General Gordon thought that the fruit of the Tree was the double coco-nut, or something of that sort! Then there is the more famous

> "As, when to them who sail
> Beyond the Cape of Hope, and now are past

Mozambic, off at sea north-east winds blow
Sabean odours from the spicy shore
Of Araby the blest, with such delay
Well pleased they slack their course, and many a league
Cheered at the grateful smell old Ocean smiles."

All these are of course from the fourth book; of which it may be said that if a man has become too poor to travel he can still replace that pastime by reading to himself the fourth book of *Paradise Lost*.

And here is something more from the ninth:

". . . Sea he had searched and land,
From Eden over Pontus, and the Pool
Mæotis, up beyond the river Ob;
Downward as far antarctic; and, in length,
West from Orontes to the ocean barred
At Darien, thence to the land where flows
Ganges and Indus. . . ."

It is a pity that the Devil, ranging about the globe, should have come across the river Ob, or that, if he did, Milton should have recorded such a monosyllable—but here again, he could not bear to hide his knowledge! The rest is fine enough, and it is particularly pleasing to find the two rivers Ganges and Indus commanding a singular verb, "flows." Elasticity of that kind is excellent in poetry, and even refreshing to prose.

It will also I hope give joy to all honest men to learn that Milton also could split an infinitive like any of us. I will bargain that there is not one great English writer who has not done it, if a search be made. It is native to the language. And if it be asked where that infinitive is split, I answer in the central glory, in the *Lycidas* itself. You will find it in the sixty-sixth line, cunningly hid away, lurking but present, and looking at you with its sharp little eyes.

> "To tend the homely slighted shepherd trade
> And strictly meditate the thankless Muse."

"Strictly" is the wholesome and manly splitting of an infinitive in apposition.

But, to return to the place-names: here is something from the tenth book:

> "As when the Tartar from his Russian foe,
> By Astracan, over the snowy plains
> Retires, or Bactrian Sophi, from the horns
> Of Turkish crescent, leaves all waste beyond
> The realm of Aladule, in his retreat
> To Tauris or Casbeen. . . ."

But when it comes to Milton's play on place-names one might go on for ever.

.   .   .   .

Such is *Paradise Lost*. For generations Milton's fellow-countrymen have regarded it with the reverence due to something sacred. His foreign co-religionists who speak the English tongue have shared in that unquestioned worship; it has even powerfully affected men outside such a field, wide as that field is. It has stirred, in translations, the most unlikely of foreign audiences: popular, I am told, with Russian peasants. It has moved the creative power of painters and engravers, to whom the original and its deep grandeur of utterance were unknown. It has produced an exaltation.

Will that exaltation be maintained? Will *Paradise Lost* stand on the same level of fame, enduring unshaken through the coming generations?

Many would say not, and for this reason: the English Bible is read more and more rarely, and even less believed than read.

Indeed the mental picture of its cosmogony, which Protestant English-speaking men and women had come to possess and carry with them wherever they wandered throughout the world, has faded altogether. Your modern adolescent as he enters life, stamped by our modern mass education, sees the beginnings of his race in the mirror of a new mythology, which he calls (and believes to be) "scientific." His ancestors, he is sure, were brutish and disgusting. There is no element in it of majesty, there is no tragedy, no Fall, and therefore no distant vision of redemption. In the place of Paradise with god-like Adam and delicious Eve, he sees a wild peopled by cretins uncouth and hairy: inarticulate as well. There is no Eden for the youth of to-day, there is not even a Hell—there is only a sort of nasty fog from which he doubts whether he shall ever escape.

With such a mood *Paradise Lost* jars violently, if it be seriously read. And indeed such a mood would seem to make *Paradise Lost* unreadable. The interest of its thesis has gone; it is no longer the putting into metrical form of what was in all men's minds; it has become archaic nonsense. It will soon no longer count. The judgment is false: what those forget who argue that the prestige of the great epic will fail and with it the crown of Milton, is an element unfamiliar indeed to many to-day but always powerful and of its nature immortal: Beauty.

We have seen passages in the prodigious body of *Paradise Lost* where the grotesque falls sometimes to the absurd, and where song is suddenly replaced by the prosaic and the literal. But, perpetually recurrent, comes sounding in throughout the Miltonic chord, the unmistakable accent of high verse: the Voice.

For indeed Milton's effect is the effect of a voice once somewhere passionately loved, now heard again, and recalling beatitude. He that has ears for the poetic revelation knows how truly it proclaims itself over and over again in the luxuriant forest of *Paradise Lost*. He that has appreciation for form feels the strength of form perpetually as he reads; he that knows what landscape can do for the mind is granted, in *Paradise Lost*, vision of such landscape as we hardly find in the real world.

For all these reasons this epic and the renown of the name attached to it must endure.

Paradise Regained was intended by John Milton to be a pendant and conclusion of *Paradise Lost.* Instead of that it is a foil. The difference between the two poems is startling to those who come on them with a fresh eye. A young ingenuous reader who had never heard the history of them, might well believe that they were from different hands.

Indeed I have often wondered whether a useful trick might not be played on such a reader. Let the lad be told, before he begins his reading, that after *Paradise Lost* had appeared and had had the success we know, some clumsy forger had put forward under the name of Milton something which purported to be in his manner, but could be seen at once, by every lively critic, to be none of his. I am sure that such a youthful unsophisticated reader would believe the story at once, for it jumps exactly with the fact.

The true word for Milton's *Paradise Regained* is "Bad." It is a thoroughly bad exercise. It contains no quite first-rate line, hardly a couple of dozen good ones—and that is not enough to float nearly two thousand mean and flat.

It is an awful proof of the power which association in ideas has to confuse thought, that because John Milton's name is attached to the stuff—and perhaps because the subject is sacred and solemn—it should be treated with any respect at all.

Why the *Paradise Regained* sinks to this level it would be difficult to say. It is, presumably, nearly contemporary to the *Samson Agonistes*, with which, bound up in the same little book, it was published—and certainly the *Samson Agonistes* rises again and again to Milton's highest. The suggestion occurs to the reader, as he breaks through that morass of blank verse on the Temptation in the Desert, that the failure is due to some such combination of circumstances as the following:

[263]

Milton during most of his active life had been ruminating *Paradise Lost*, first as a play and later as an epic. Now when poets do that, when they pass years thinking about, wishing to complete, some considerable piece of verse, they are perpetually flashing out detached lines and short passages of it in their minds; most of these lines they remember and as a rule set down; and all that kind of work will have been done when they were at their most vigorous. Later, with more leisure and less self-torture, more complacency and less strictness of taste, the poet sets out to finish the affair once and for all. Then, when the thing has to be thus completed, the old stuff belonging to the vigorous years supports the later stuff, and also helps to inspire that later stuff.

But if the aged fellow start *de novo* and cannot rest until he has written another epic; if he has the itch to be off again because he cannot stop—then all the weakness of his age will be upon him. He has already been spouting too much, Heaven knows; now he would spout uninterruptedly and without restraint. He will go on pouring out line after line in a spate without discipline, and for whole pages almost without variety.

There were already in *Paradise Lost* any number of flat pages, the product of such a method—in *Paradise Regained* they swamp the whole affair. If we represent good verse by solid land and bad verse by water, *Paradise Lost* may be compared to a country like Finland, full of lakes but still on the whole firm ground and granite at that. *Paradise Regained* is like an unbroken sea out of which stand one or two small islands, of no very hard rock, and here and there a few banks hardly reaching the surface.

Moreover it is worth noting that the subtle changes of metre which are the wonder of the greater poem, and by which Milton above all other writers and almost alone managed to save blank verse from monotony, are not present in *Paradise*

Regained. In this regular iambic beat runs on, sometimes, for nearly a page unbroken.

In *Paradise Regained* we further notice with interest something that happens often enough to poets in their old age—and that is, repeating themselves. We also notice that the second version is not as good as the first.

> "Thus passed the night so foul, till morning fair
> Came forth with pilgrim step in amice grey."

It is a pity to have written that after fifty, when at thirty one could write the lovely line near the end of the *Lycidas,* one of the jewels of English on which we have already lingered:—

> "While the still Morn went out with sandals grey."

A good way of contrasting the failure of the one poem with the success of the other is by that method of openings and conclusions. Note the sonorous opening of *Paradise Lost* and see how splendidly it is concluded: contrast *Paradise Regained.*

Here is the opening of the first book, beginning with the ninth line:—

> "Thou Spirit, who led'st this glorious Eremite
> Into the desert, his victorious field
> Against the spiritual foe, and brought'st him thence
> By proof the undoubted Son of God, inspire,
> As thou art wont, my prompted song, else mute,
> And bear through height or depth of Nature's bounds,
> With prosperous wing full summed, to tell of deeds
> Above heroic, though in secret done,
> And unrecorded left through many an age:
> Worthy to have not remained so long unsung."

It is so with all the four books. Here is the opening of the second book:—

> "Meanwhile the new-baptised, who yet remained
> At Jordan with the Baptist, and had seen
> Him whom they heard so late expressly called
> Jesus Messiah, Son of God, declared,
> And on that high authority had believed,
> And with him talked, and with him lodged—I mean
> Andrew and Simon, famous after known,
> With others, though in Holy Writ not named—
> Now missing him, their joy so lately found,
> So lately found and so abruptly gone,
> Began to doubt, and doubted many days,
> And as the days increased, increased their doubt."

This is deplorable!
And the opening of the third is not much better:—

> "So spake the Son of God; and Satan stood
> A while as mute, confounded what to say,
> What to reply, confuted and convinced
> Of his weak arguing and fallacious drift;"

And here is the fourth:—

> "Perplexed and troubled at his bad success
> The Tempter stood, nor had what to reply,
> Discovered in his fraud, thrown from his hope
> So oft, and the persuasive rhetoric
> That sleeked his tongue, and won so much on Eve
> So little here, nay lost. But Eve was Eve:"

And now with the noble concluding cadence of *Paradise Lost*, contrast this conclusion of *Paradise Regained*:—

> "Queller of Satan! On thy glorious work
> Now enter, and begin to save mankind.
> Thus they the Son of God, our Saviour meek,
> Sung victor, and, from heavenly feast refreshed,
> Brought on his way with joy. He, unobserved,
> Home to his mother's house private returned."

Contrast that last line with

"Through Eden took their solitary way,"

and you have the gulf between the older and the younger brother of these twins.

There are exceptions. A touch of poetry appears in the mention of Athens:—

> "See there the olive-grove of Academe,
> Plato's retirement, where the Attic bird
> Trills her thick-warbled notes the summer long;
> There, flowery hill, Hymettus, with the sound
> Of Bees' industrious murmur, oft invites
> To studious musing; there Ilissus rolls
> His whispering stream. . . ."

In that short passage beauty does put out its head a little: puts it out shyly and takes it back again, but still, puts it out of window. "Trills her thick warbled notes the summer long" is true Milton; and everybody would be glad to have written "there Ilissus rolls his whispering stream." But if you want a contrast, you get it just over the page, when Our Lord is very rude to the Devil.

> "Whom thus our Saviour answered with disdain:—
> 'I never liked thy talk, thy offers less.' "

Or observe a little earlier a dreadful piece of bathos in his own special line of place-names:—

> "The realm of Boccus to the Blackmoor sea."

Men who praise *Paradise Regained* (and it is delightful to remember that Wordsworth praised it, it is what one would expect; though less pleasing to remember that Coleridge did the same thing—after his collapse, I hope) praise it for things that have nothing to do with beauty in general or high verse in

particular. They may say that it argues rightly upon theology
—a matter also doubtful; they may say that it has unity, which
indeed it has—so has a block of wood; but the point of unity
in art is to give framework to what is filled with creation, and
personality to what is alive; it does not of itself do anything to
inspire or to create.

When the reader does discover in it some passage which
slightly moves him (such as the Parthian battle in Book III,
lines 322-29:

> "He saw them in their forms of battle ranged,
> How quick they wheeled, and flying behind them shot
> Sharp sleet of arrowy showers against the face
> Of their pursuers, and overcame by flight;
> The field all iron cast a gleaming brown.
> Nor wanted clouds of foot, nor, on each horn,
> Cuirassiers all in steel for standing fight,
> Chariots, or elephants indorsed with towers,"

he is moved only by contrast with the utter lethargy of the
rest. Even the long list of place-names coming just before this
passage falls badly below the true Miltonic level. A line like
"Chariots, or elephants indorsed with towers" arrests the ear
for a moment, and gives something of a picture—but such lines
are rare therein. More common are such monotonies as:—

> ". . . Persepolis
> His city here thou seest, and Bactra there:
> Ecbatana her structure vast there shows,
> And Hecatompylos her hundred gates."

I have said that bad history makes good verse. If you want
to read how good morals may make bad verse, consult the conclusion of the second book, where Our Lord in answering the
Devil instead of ending his speech where it would naturally end
—and that also would be a bad ending—makes it worse by
putting in an afterthought. It is a consolation to remember that

[268]

it was not Our Lord's afterthought, but Milton's. For the speech in condemnation of power in man and pride in Government has tacked on to it these six lines, like a piece of lead at the end of a wet and sodden string:—

> "Besides, to give a kingdom hath been thought
> Greater and nobler done, and to lay down
> Far more magnanimous than to assume.
> Riches are needless, then, both for themselves
> And for thy ruin when they should be sought—
> To gain a sceptre oftest better missed."

Those bad lines are made the worse by that spondee "oftest" in the middle of a line already hissing with sibilants and chattering with dentals.

Quite apart from the matter of beauty or the matter of poetry, there is in *Paradise Regained* one considerable literary interest of an historical sort, coming near the end in the fourth book. It is the speech of Satan on the origin of Our Lord—the speech of which the second line opens the theme:

> "Even Son of God to me is yet in doubt."

The Devil is puzzled, as Milton was, by the full Christian doctrine of the Trinity, since the Devil (like all Milton's other characters) is Milton himself even in this minor form, just as he was Milton in the grander Satan of *Paradise Lost:*

> "Thenceforth I thought thee worth my nearer view
> And narrower scrutiny, that I might learn
> In what degree and meaning thou art called
> The Son of God, it bears no single sense.
> The son of God I also am—or was
>
> .   .   .   .   .
>
> All men are sons of God."

To these questions the Devil in *Paradise Regained*—A.D. 1665 at earliest—gives no answer. But Milton in his great secret at-

[269]

tack on the Trinity had given the answer to his own satisfaction at some unknown date—almost certainly earlier and possibly much earlier. We shall find it in the *De Doctrina* at the end of this book. If Milton had launched his attack on the Trinity here publicly in *Paradise Regained* he would have betrayed his inmost heresy to the multitude—and that he dared not do. But it is pertinent to the understanding of him to note that he could not keep off the subject.

So much for *Paradise Regained*. One may sum it up by saying that if Milton had written nothing else in verse he would be utterly unknown, in spite of here and there a successful line or two, here and there a successful epithet, as "bowing low his grey dissimulation."

The *Samson Agonistes* is, take it by and large, the strongest monument to Milton's genius. I had almost written "highest," but there is a difference between height and strength. We mean by height an approach to perfection, to the ideal: something which, when we shall have read it, makes us say, "This thing in its entirety compels unmixed admiration; it has, as one thing, touched the mark of the gods." Now in Milton's work such a crown belongs of right to the *Lycidas;* next after it to the Ode on the *Nativity;* and perhaps next after these to the Vaudois sonnet.

But such excellence, such "height," can only be affirmed of a unity, of a thing all one in quality, possessing, as it were, personality, and keeping its character to an unfailing level. Therefore as a rule it can only be affirmed as a rule of limited pieces (though the Ancients are here an exception) for height connotes a measurement of levels.

But "strength" connotes rather the texture of a created thing, the grain of it. We can say of even a long piece of verse or prose, uneven and suffering from tedious interludes, that it is strong if this quality of hardness be present in it. Another way of putting the difference is to say that the highest things survive through their excelling; the strong things through the durability of their material. Thus some towering (limestone) peak will not be worn down in ten thousand years, because it was originally so exalted, but its lower neighbour of granite will equally endure because it is of a stuff upon which the elements break themselves. So will it be with the *Samson Agonistes:* not because it is supreme, still less because it is uniform, but because there runs through it a packed intensity.

It is a great part of the glory of Milton that he should have ended that long, combative, curiously unequal life upon a note of triumph. It is to his glory, because that note owed nothing to chance, but was the final reward of his most considerable quality—his courage and endurance. His perseverance had carried on until it touched the heroic. It is not often that a human life in which this virtue has been practised finds any temporal reward: but Milton found it. It is a great thing to do some of one's very best work at the end.

The *Samson Agonistes* is in contrast with the two epics and clearly superior to them. That it is superior to *Paradise Regained* need not be laboured; it will be self-evident to anyone who has spent an hour or two in reading them both. The one has passages at the summit of Milton's genius; the other is the basest thing he ever printed under the guise of poetry. What will be less freely admitted but is none the less true, is that the *Samson Agonistes* is superior to the *Paradise Lost*.

In both poems there is a muddle of the sublime and the flat; of the poignant and the dull; in both poems there is an occasional piece of mere absurdity, a grotesque line or group of lines. Now and then there is even horrible bathos. For example: That very fine speech of Manoah's, a speech of dignity and consolation, is about to end; the old man has already described what a funeral monument he will build for the hero his son, and how to that monument the young men and virgins shall come on festival days to visit his tomb with flowers. So far, so good. Then comes the horrid shock, the flop:

> ". . . only bewailing
> His lot unfortunate in nuptial choice,
> From whence captivity and loss of eyes."

Yes, there are "pockets" like this in *Samson* as in *Paradise Lost*, but the point to note is that the proportion of good to bad is all in favour of the *Samson*.

The main reason for this is that in the *Samson Agonistes* from the nature of the case Milton was compelled to unity. He had one character and one only to handle; the few other personages were wholly subsidiary to that central figure; and that central figure was his very self. It is more utterly *himself* than is his main theme in any other poem.

He put a lot of himself into Satan, in both the two epics, and especially in *Paradise Regained;* and something of himself of course into everybody else including Eve; but Samson is altogether Milton, without overlap and without exception. He is Milton in every particular—the man fallen upon evil times, the man gone blind, the man impoverished, the man disappointed in women, and their victim.

Milton feels this identity between himself and Samson so strongly that in one passage he goes into medical details, remembering his own trouble of insomnia which took him when he began to grow old, as it takes many men. It seems that John Milton the poet had recourse to drugs to get a little artificial rest under that strain. Therefore Samson follows the same prescription:

> "Sleep hath forsook and given me o'er
> To Death's benumbing opium, as my only cure;
> Thence faintings. . . ."

The *Samson Agonistes* also contains one of Milton's rare obscurities. It is where the hero speaks of his first Timnean wife:

> ". . . In this other was there found
> More faith, who also in her prime of love,
> Spousal embraces, vitiated with gold
> Though offered only, by the scent conceived
> Her spurious first-born, treason against me?"

Let the reader make what he can of it; I can make nothing, though no doubt it has been explained, or an explanation attempted.

Now and then a deplorable line in the *Samson* is due to that fatal temptation felt by men who are good Greek scholars, the temptation to copy what are faults in the classics, as well as their virtues. Because a Greek tragedy will often present a flat line—put in on purpose, one may say, from an affected simplicity—therefore do scholarly poets deliberately put one in when they are writing English.

It is something like that abuse of unornamented blank spaces in architecture. All the arts are in peril from this cause—"False Good Taste"—deliberately making things too simple in order to show that you can extract a subtle poesy from the prosaic.

We all know how the old gentleman of a Greek chorus will make some such remark as "Excessive anger often has disastrous consequences"; or, after some appalling piece of bad news, "We cannot say that this household is fortunate." So Milton, in the *Samson*, when the hero's father says to him, "I cannot praise thy marriage choices, son." There is an element of *meiosis* in this phrase which is not without attraction, but it is a little overdone. A gentleman has come a cropper over two wives. The second has had him betrayed, bound, blinded and enslaved. One might expect something a little stronger from an affectionate and even admiring parent than "I cannot praise thy marriage choices." Moreover Samson was the specially chosen of God—he was the greatest, because the strongest, of the champions of righteousness; his matrimonial troubles deserve a more dignified description.

I have said that the main cause of this poem's excellence was the identity of its theme with the poet's own personal tragedy. His embittered pride inspired him, so that Milton could pour his entire self into this verse, as a man fills a jar with wine.

There were lesser reasons supporting this main reason for the triumphant close of Milton as a poet in the *Samson Agonistes*. He had not only the unity of subject, and the exact parallel with himself, he had also a model upon which to work —a model with which he was acquainted, and one handy in size;

the Greek drama. As in the sonnet, so here it is always good for a poet to be working on a model, to be bound by a known scheme.

But it is odd that, having the Greek tragedy as a model upon which to work, Milton, who had been—after Shakespeare—the greatest by far of the English lyrists, should miss that lyrical opportunity. For the choruses of the *Samson Agonistes* are much too long and still more too formless. They are not carried on, as were the Greek choruses, by a surge of metre. They almost read as though the writer were trying to show how he could write irregular verse because he had seen the thing done in a dead language. But the effect he produces is quite different.

Compare the opening of his chief chorus with the opening of a Greek chorus, such as the "Polla men deina," etc., of the *Antigone*.

> "Many are the sayings of the wise
> In ancient and in modern books inroléd,
> Extolling Patience as the truest fortitude;
> And to the bearing well of all calamities,
> All chances incident to man's frail life,
> Consolatories writ
> With studied argument and much persuasion sought," etc.

You can sing the Greek, you cannot sing the English—at least it does not sing itself. We all know that Handel put it and the rest to music; but there is no music arising naturally in the ear of the man who reads it. That chorus happens also to be prosaic excessively, but I speak rather of the chaotic lack of metre in it.

There is a story, now nearly fifty years old, of a young man who sent in some verses to an editor. The editor, returning them with a kindly letter, added, "Your verses will not stand alone; they should be set to music." Most of the verse of the *Samson Agonistes* stands well enough alone, and some of it magnificently; still for most of the choruses there is need of music artificially tacked on to give this stuff sufficient body.

Every now and then Milton will try to save a failing passage in one of his choruses by the introduction of rhyme; one never knows when it is coming nor when it is going to stop; as for instance:

> "Thou rulest (*says the Chorus addressing God*)
> The angelic orders and inferior creatures mute
> Irrational and brute,
> Nor do I mean of men the common rout
> That, wandering loose about,
> Grow up and perish like the summer fly."

And again, a little further on in the same much too long chorus:

> "Not only dost degrade them, or remit
> To live obscured, which were of fair demission
> But throwest them lower than thou didst exalt them high
> Unseemly falls in human eye
> Too grievous for the trespass or omission."

Yes, that chorus is too long; its wings were not strong enough to carry it. Yet it is that same chorus which ends up with the magnificent passage, only too justly familiar because it is one of the finest things in the English language—I mean of course that comparison of Delilah to a ship in full sail:

> "But who is this? what thing of sea or land—
> Female of sex it seems—
> That, so bedecked, ornate, and gay,
> Comes this way sailing,
> Like a stately ship
> Of Tarsus, bound for the isles
> Of Javan or Gadire,
> With all her bravery on, and tackle trim,
> Sails filled, and streamers waving,
> Courted by all the winds that hold them play;

> An amber scent of odorous perfume
> Her harbinger, a damsel train behind?
> Some rich Philistian matron may she seem;
> And now, at nearer view, no other certain
> Than Dalila thy wife."

And the conclusion, after one line of Samson's interrupting, is almost on the same level:

> "Yet on she moves; now stands and eyes thee fixed,
> About to have spoke; but now, with head declined,
> Like a fair flower surcharged with dew, she weeps,
> And words addressed seem into tears dissolved,
> Wetting the borders of her silken veil.
> But now again she makes address to speak."

The second most famous passage in the drama, the concluding speech of the hero's old father Manoah, is (as far as the opening goes at least) almost as high; and though it has been quoted so often I will quote it again here:

> "Come, come; no time for lamentation now,
> Nor much more cause. Samson hath quit himself
> Like Samson, and heroicly hath finished
> A life heroic, on his enemies
> Fully revenged—hath left them years of mourning."

But perhaps the strongest thing in the whole poem is in the three and a half lines at the end of Samson's reply to his father's protest:

> ". . . Nature within me seems
> In all her functions weary of herself;
> My race of glory run, and race of shame,
> And I shall shortly be with them that rest."

That last line is of oak.

It is not true of the *Samson Agonistes* that it ends—as we have seen other successes of Milton's end—at its best. That is a pity. Still, the last short chorus (of only fourteen lines) is of a fine full flow, which would have been more satisfactory had it not lapsed into rhyme.

> "All is best, though we oft doubt
> What the unsearchable dispose
> Of Highest Wisdom brings about,
> And ever best found in the close.
> Oft He seems to hide his face,
> But unexpectedly returns,
> And to his faithful champion hath in place
> Bore witness gloriously; whence Gaza mourns,
> And all that band them to resist
> His uncontrollable intent.
> His servants He, with new acquist
> Of true experience from this great event,
> With peace and consolation hath dismissed,
> And calm of mind, all passion spent."

These less than 2,000 lines (1,758, to be accurate) make something of a length that can be dealt with by an eager reader in one turn; they have as much unity for him and his receiving mind as they had for Milton producing them. It is the more pity that, the thing being so conveniently short, Milton should here again have been unable to avoid the ridiculous—the grotesque. Take for example the passage where he talks of Jephtha:

> "Who by argument
> Not worse than by his shield and spear
> Defended Israel from the Ammonite."

Having said so much, which is tolerable, he suddenly breaks out into a quatrain of verse which is not tolerable at all:

> "Had not his prowess quelled their pride
> In that sore battle, when so many died
> Without reprieve, adjudged to death
> For want of well pronouncing 'shibboleth.' "

And it is the *Samson* which holds the most unforgivable piece of rubbish in all the collected works of Milton. It is a gem of absurdity already quoted; and here to be quoted again. It is the very depth of bad verse: yet we find it coming plumb in the midst of such a poem as the *Samson*—and at the opening of a chorus which he intends to be sublime.

> "God of our fathers! What is man,
>   That Thou towards him with hands so various—
>   Or might I say contrarious?"

It is startling! It is not decent to admit such a five words as "or might I say contrarious" into anything short of open farce.

I am afraid however that one must be in two minds about that other remarkable opening, Samson's greeting to his wife: "Out! Out! Hyæna!"

It makes one laugh, but it is vigorous and natural, nor is this naturalness quite on the level of the ridiculous. A tortured man, betrayed, and exasperated into vivid anger, may call a lady a hyena without quite tumbling off his poetic perch; it can be read as a shriek; and if one be sufficiently excited by the tragic circumstances one would rather stare in horror than grin.

One little piece of affectation must be noted in passing, because—if we accept the reading—it seems so characteristic of our man. Five times he spells Hebrews, the substantive, whether in the plural or the singular, without an "h": "Ebrews." Masson thought this was done deliberately and (though he does not put forward this argument in favour of such a judgment) had it not been done deliberately it would hardly have been done at all.

Everybody then wrote the word Hebrew with an "h" as we invariably do to-day, whether of the substantive or the adjective; it had been, I think, a universal practice in England for more than a hundred years, and common practice long before that; ever since "The Revival of Learning," that is, from the

Renaissance. But the French and the early English form inherited from the French had no "h." Now it may be suggested that Milton, who loved to put his learning forward, chose of set purpose to print the archaic form here when he was dealing with the noun (a Hebrew person or persons) in order to differentiate it from the adjective, to which he left the "h." The "h" is of course the right spelling, the Greeks put a strong breathing on to the original epsilon, and they got the word from the Aramaic, so that Milton in using the unaspirated "e" —if he did use it—did not do so in order to show off his knowledge of the earliest Biblical tongue (as he might have done, for he possessed that knowledge), but his knowledge of early English (and Franco-English) spelling in the days when the educated classes in England had only recently ceased to be French speaking.

To conclude by a return to praise, where praise is so amply due: the *Samson Agonistes* succeeds, coming as it does at the very end of Milton's life, largely through that which had been present with Milton as a gift from the very first years—the vivid visual concept, now at its height after twelve years of blindness. And that concept enhanced by the right noise of words, in which also this master (as we know) excels. Take this passage, where Samson is challenging the giant Harapha:

> "Then put on all thy gorgeous arms, thy helmet
> And brigantine of brass, that broad habergeon,
> Vant-brace, and greaves, and gauntlets; add thy spear,
> A weaver's beam, and seven-times folded shield."

All these are details to be excused by curiosity. In the large *Samson Agonistes* triumphs. Strange text! Acted on a stage today it strongly moves the modern man—though he finds the choruses too long.

This grand organ recital in blank verse, the *Samson*, with which Milton topped his business as a poet should also fitly have come before a complete silence: that pause which best concludes the business of life. But the angry activity of that soul could not repose even at the very end. In the very year before his death, he must needs publish one last tract in English prose, and cast one more dart into the battle-confusion of that seventeenth century English turmoil. It was in the midst of the new excitements upon toleration, and the rising anger of all that was anti-Catholic in London—certainly a majority of the citizens, and, if you count in the less violent, a large majority—that Milton in 1673 published his final broadside.

If it was the last, so it was the clearest of his attacks by the pen. And what emotion guided him may best be judged by the title:

Of

TRUE RELIGION, HERESY, SCHISM,
TOLERATION;

And what best means may be used against the

GROWTH OF POPERY

The last line gives the note of the whole. It was this growth of Popery in Carolingian England, the nightmare haunting the last fifty years, which pinned on to Milton's great body of literary life so incongruous a tail. By the next autumn John Milton was dead.

The tract is short—about the length of a not too extended magazine article; more than 4,000 and less than 5,000 words. Its clarity (which is its most remarkable feature) depends upon that principle which he had more and more emphasised as controversy had grown upon him in the past—that only one authority in religion exists for all men, which authority is the Protestant text of the Hebrew Scriptures and the New Testament.

We must do violence to our reason as we read, and compel ourselves not to argue, but to accept this attitude. It was adopted rigidly as an axiom by the strongly Protestant Englishmen who became increasingly from Milton's youth onwards the normal type of Englishman. Their minds reposed therein; and refused to accept anything from outside the family Bible as having voice in the matter of religion.

"Is this or that in the Bible? Can it be argued from the Bible? Then it is admissible. If not, not. Whatever is ascribable to tradition, whatever is drawn from the corporate authority of the Church, is an addition and therefore a heresy."

By this plain rule it stands to reason that there must be toleration for everyone who so bases his faith upon the known text of the Old and New Testaments; they were all of one body, the body of true Christians renovated by the glorious Reformation, for they all refer to the same fount of teaching and to the same principle of private interpretation.

It follows by an iron logic that in the body of those to whom the Scriptures are the one infallible guide there is only one true heretic—in the West at least—and that heretic is he who professes as being of Faith things not to be found in the oracular writings: who accepts a rival infallibility. Hear Milton on this:

"The Lutheran holds consubstantiation; an error indeed but not mortal; the Calvinist is a believer in Predestination, not without plea of Scripture; the Anabaptist is accused of denying infants their rights to baptism; again they say they deny nothing but what the Scripture denies them. The Arian Socinian is charted to dispute against the Trinity. The terms 'Trinity,' 'Trinimity,' 'Co-essentiality' they reject as scholastic notions not to be found in Scripture. The Arminian is condemned for setting up freewill against free grace, but grounds himself upon Scripture only."

Therefore all these, and any others of the same sort that ground themselves upon Scripture only, are to be taken for brethren. But Popery does not ground itself upon Scripture only—therefore it must be destroyed.

"Popery as being idolatrous is not to be tolerated either in public or in private; it must be now thought how to remove it and prevent the growth thereof."

He concludes against corporal constraint, or fines, "more than what appertains to the security of the State." This, as is usual with Milton when it comes to practical policies, is left utterly undefined. The Catholic may be gradually exterminated by successive cuts in his fortune: one-third of a man's property or if necessary the whole of it at once; he might be even driven by long or short imprisonment, by anything you like: on all that he is vague. But on one point he does come to a definition, "We must remove their idolatry and all the furniture thereof, with their idols, or the Mass wherein they adore their God under Bread and Wine. . . . We have no warrant to regard conscience which is not grounded on Scripture."

He then asks whether you should ever argue with a Papist, and decides against such waste of time, very logically, "For," says he in effect, "if they do not admit our first principle of unique Scriptural authority, we start from different premises."

He is less consistent when he allows Romish books to be published, on condition that they are only so published in Latin.

He ends by the pragmatic advice that true believers in the Book will have most effect of all against their opponents by the example of their worthy conduct—"the last means to avoid Popery is to amend our lives."

But there is a special reason in this case; England, observes John Milton, has grown since his group lost political power, "excessively vicious," suffering from "pride, luxury, drunkenness, whoredom, cursing, swearing, open atheism everywhere abounding: where these grow no wonder Popery also grows apace." For Popery, when you fall into a fit of depression after the aforesaid extravagances, consoles you with "confessions, absolution, pardons, indulgences, Masses, Agnus Deis, relics and the like"—and that is why, when people overdo it, they tend to fall into the snares of Rome.

A contemporary has said, "It is always sin or sorrow" which leads men thither. The judgment is insufficient. More than one adherent to that Communion would plead other sources of conversion: such as intelligence, vision, experience, and even historical learning. But for John Milton the case was clear; and he has put it as simply as it can be put.

In his penultimate words he remarks that God sometimes gets tired of chastising sinners with pestilence, fire, sword, and famine, because these might possibly do them good; so he takes up against them "his severest punishments, besottedness of heart and idolatry, to their final perdition." And he ends with the earnest adjuration that his readers should follow the courses he prescribes, "lest through impenitency we run into that stupidity . . . the worst of superstitions, and the heaviest of all God's judgments, Popery."

And these were the last and solemn words of John Milton to his England.

Part Seven

Epilogue

THE *DE DOCTRINA*

The "De Doctrina"

IT is 1674, nearing the end of that year, and John Milton is dead. We have had before us the sum of his life.

We are sure we know all about him. He is apparent and public altogether. He is the voice of Puritan England save in his passion for beauty. He is the great national Poet, high above the rest. He is all that the English are, especially in religion, save perhaps on his peculiar crotchet on divorce. He is the exponent of English orthodox Protestantism and its champion, while the glory of his verse confirms him on his throne. He is manifest. There is no ambiguity about that figure. It stands fully lit before posterity and complete in our eyes.

So was he taken, so is he, by most men, still taken, and the image is fixed.

Well: it is a false image. The real Milton, lying beneath all this and unrevealed, was other: far more intriguing; of a very different conviction; growing steadily, but secretly, into quite another thing from the Milton of his biographies and of his legend.

For there had been running, like a subterranean river, beneath all this outward apparatus of orthodox English song, statement and worship, a hidden and awful protest. He had diverged from all those about him. He had created a mighty new denial all his own. He was apart and in a final opposition to it all. He had renounced the Creed.

His great denial of the central Christian doctrines was in silent process during all those years when men saw him so simply for what they took him to be. He had been at work, since we know not when, upon a refutation of the Trinity, of Monogamy, of the absolute Creator, even of the immortal soul. He in his heart had come to deny the godhead of the Lord, the family with one wife for its shrine, the calling forth of all things visible and invisible from nothingness by the Omnipotent, even our triumph over death: and this he set down at great length and with a wealth of argument (but carefully concealed) in that testament and confession which he called—in a title not without irony for us, though for him it was sincere—"A treatise on Christian Doctrine," *De Doctrina Christiana*.

The *De Doctrina* he kept profoundly secret. None suspected its existence. Save for an accident we should not have it to this day. It was discovered barely a century ago, and it has not yet disturbed the false popular conception of that great soul: perhaps it never will.

I cannot believe that the *De Doctrina* was completed in the very last months of his life. It is often spoken of as though it were the final achievement, the last development of Milton's progressive rebellion. It is argued that so extreme a departure from what all Protestant England held sacred could not have been reached in the middle of his life; it must have been (they say) the very last of his progress away from the certitudes of his youth. But the thing is on too large a scale to be the product of his very ending, when his health had at last begun to break up and even his fierce energy to decline.

I shall give other reasons, in the discussion of this extraordinary piece of work, to show that the whole basis of it must have been worked up before he lost his sight. I cannot but take it from the general tone of the thing that voluminous notes at least had been made, and probably the bulk of it already clandestinely written, in those years of violent reaction against authority which followed 1642. It may well have continued—supplementary work on it—for many years; he may have dictated even a considerable body of revision in his blindness before he closed the pages. But the mass of the labour involved surely fell during the period of the Civil Wars and, I suggest, during the interlude when he was not burdened with public work nor as yet deprived of his power of reading and writing. In other words, it would seem presumable that the bulk of the *De Doctrina* belongs to the seven years between the first breakdown of his marriage and his sudden appearance as a pamphleteer crying out for the death of the King.

All the tone of its extravagance against marriage fits in with that and all the circumstances under which alone so closely knit and lengthy a thing, so packed with reference and proof, could have been made.

It must have been about this time that he collected and put together the material for something startlingly different from the mass of his open and public work.

It purports to be a general examination of what a man may, or rather must, believe if he takes Scripture for his sole guide. It is an elaborate, intensive plea against Monogamy and the Incarnation. It is more than that, it is a considered plea in favour of a limited God: a God who did *not* make all things visible and invisible, but with whom matter was co-existent, who worked upon matter, but who was not himself the conscious author of the stuff whereof the Universe is made. It proclaims the death of a man to be absolute, soul and body both ceasing in one end.

Had the *De Doctrina* been familiar to the men of the eighteenth century they would have claimed Milton as something of a champion for their attacks upon the Christian religion as a whole. It would have shocked, it would have offended the mass of Englishmen; but it would have made the name of Milton more vivid, luridly vivid—that of an arch-rebel.

[289]

The *De Doctrina* stands, then, by itself amid all the works of Milton; it is, I say, still half unknown—and yet if we are to understand the inward mind of the man it should be better known even than his verse: for it is Milton in his very self; the heart of his mature conviction. It has never come to its own.

It is true that no one reading *Paradise Lost* fully and closely can fail to mark a certain odd note in the relations of the First and Second Persons of the Trinity, but the reader of that epic who feels either shocked or amazed may say to himself—"This is poetic necessity. The Person of Christ is crudely presented because the image has to be salient, and the Son, as agent of the eternal Will, presented in the portrait of a man instead of abstract theological definitions." This being so Milton cannot but take somewhat from his divinity, as indeed he does from that of God the Father. The reading of *Paradise Lost* might make some men suspect Milton's orthodoxy on the doctrine of the Trinity; as the reading of Wordsworth will make most men suspect Wordsworth's orthodoxy on the transcendence of God —for though the spirit of Wordsworth is pantheist, that does not prevent people regarding Wordsworth, or Wordsworth regarding himself, as thoroughly Christian. Why not Milton?

Well, Wordsworth is pantheist in tone, but not *declaredly* so. It would be another matter if Wordsworth had left a solemn treatise behind him proving that in old age he had come to doubt whether God were personal at all. Now that is just what Milton did in the matter of the Trinity. Probably in middle age he compiled, certainly in old age he completed a carefully thought out, closely written Latin document, far clearer and more thorough than any of his other tracts—something representing his deepest thought quite lucidly. And that something beyond all question denies the Trinity.

The *De Doctrina*, I say, is neglected; yet not only in our judgment of Milton, but as a landmark in the break-up of European religion, it is of the highest moment. It shows on the surface of English Protestantism like the first thin crack one finds on the ice of a frozen pond, which will soon grow to a broad fissure, until the general ruin of the whole surface in the full thaw.

For Milton's final philosophy, firm and thoroughly thought out, is a forerunner of all that breakdown in certitude upon religion which has marked the modern world. There was of course plenty of scepticism, and that of the broadest sort, long before Milton closed the last page of this singular secret work in his old age; the Renaissance had been full of it, it was not absent from English letters. A current of it runs right through the Middle Ages. Indeed scepticism is necessarily present side by side with religion in any strongly organised Catholic society. It appears in dozens of tracts and speculations during the chaos of the seventeenth century.

But the particular point of the *De Doctrina* is that this challenge to the central doctrine of the Incarnation, of God's creative power, of the immortality of the soul, has come from the pen of a champion—and a champion on the other side. Milton stood in the eyes of the Commonwealth as in the eyes of all Europe for the voice of English Protestantism in its extreme form—and that extreme, be it remembered, was not only an extreme of opposition to the claims of the Catholic Church, it was also an extreme of fixity, rigidity, in the matter of those main doctrines which Protestantism had chosen to retain out of the body of Catholic definition.

Calvin had burnt Servetus (it is only fair to remember that he tried to save him) for saying what, in secret, Milton was to say. The rebel Parliament of England a century later had most horribly tortured a man who set forth to deny the divinity of Christ—which Milton denied. In between, James I had burnt the Unitarian of his day. Here, after two-thirds of the seventeenth century had run, the greatest public writer upon the Protestant side was shaking the foundations of the Trinitarian

Creed, undoing the work of Hilary and Athanasius, and adding to that denial after denial of the prime dogmas.

First, then, the *De Doctrina* is Unitarian. Let whoever doubts that read the fifth chapter of the first book, where Milton denies with close and serried argument the Divinity of Our Lord.

This should be sufficient to show what the new heresy was which had taken shape in Milton's mind. But the whole book must be read to appreciate the attitude into which Milton had with undoubted sincerity reasoned himself. I shall never forget the impression which it made upon me when I first read it myself, late in life, and was struck full by the compact Arianism of it leading on to all the rest. Everyone, I think, should thus read it through who desires to know not only the mind of John Milton but the curve of European thought upon the most important of all subjects. This thing, the *De Doctrina*, was a blow struck at the very root of that which is, above all other doctrines, the essential doctrine of a Christian man—that Jesus is God: and therefore went on to demolish the rest of that on which our culture still precariously reposes.

Did Milton ever intend it to be published? That he was intent on its publication sooner or later has been held. It had leaked out that he was busy with something theological, a whole examination of the foundations, and his appetite for fame would necessarily lead him to desire its publication: but are we certain that he was willing to risk the universal outcry, the violent attack that would follow?

The story of its salvation from obscurity, as also the story of its early concealment, are significant.

Two bodies of manuscript were sent off into hiding; one the State letters which Milton had written for Cromwell, and the other this powerful and hostile treatment of the central truths of the Christian religion.

Let us note that the first MS. was certainly regarded as most dangerous. The Government of Charles II desired to suppress those letters, or at any rate to allow them to be forgotten, and any number of men prominent in public life after the Restoration felt more strongly on the matter than the King. That there should be put into one and the same category of hidden work those letters and the *De Doctrina* looks as though the publication of the latter was to be postponed as much as that of the former.

The dangerous documents had been deposited in Holland, with the Elzevirs of Amsterdam; someone thought it urgent that they (or the letters at least, which was the only part of the *cache* that people were then worrying about, for the *De Doctrina* was unknown) should be returned to England lest the opportunity for printing them abroad should prove too great a temptation, and Sir John Williamson was the man into whose custody they were to be delivered. The Elzevirs writing from Amsterdam to Williamson said that they thought it better not to print, and that was a relief. But one never can tell; at any moment the indiscretion might take place, and for the money there was in it someone might publish those letters broadcast on the Continent. As a fact they *were* published; the effort to suppress them came too late and they became public property. Moreover after a comparatively short period phrases which men still living dread to see published cease to be scandalous and become merely of historical interest.

Anyhow the bundle of manuscript was made up and sent back to England, to Williamson. It contained not only the State letters which Milton as secretary had written, but also packed up with them (though wrapped in a separate paper) a Latin script which may still be consulted in the Record Office. This bundle was the *De Doctrina*.

If it were opened at that time (and it presumably was in order to discover what relation it had to the letters) it seems to have been put up again when it was found to be merely some

[293]

dull stuff about Divinity, full of Biblical quotations. So there it lay, forgotten for 150 years. Milton rose to be the great national poet, the great voice of English Protestantism; he sat on that throne, he exercised that function increasingly as the seventeenth century gave way to the eighteenth, and during the eighteenth he was at the height of his posthumous power— and still the *De Doctrina* lay buried awaiting resurrection. It was not till 1823 that Lemon, going through the papers in the old State Paper Office in Whitehall, found the parcel docketed with its date, February 1677. He opened it, and what followed is due to the culture and initiative of George IV. That man, who understood so well the difference between what was important and unimportant in literature, ordered the document to be translated and published.*

The curious treatise bears on its title these words:

"Johannes Miltoni Angli de Doctrina Christiana ex sacris duntaxat, Libris petita, disquisitionum libri duo posthumi."

Note the "posthumi" for though the command is ambiguous, yet it may have been made in the recollection of his secret determination communicated to one or few that the thing should see the light, but not until he were out of range of its effects.

More important are the four words, *"sacris duntaxat, Libris petita."* "Sought out with exactitude from Holy Writ." The word *"duntaxat"* (there might be preferred *"dumtaxat"*) connotes not only precision but integrity; the refusal to add anything by way of speculation or glossing over. It is as though Milton had said in plain English, "I got every bit of these doctrines of mine from Holy Writ, from the Bible, from nowhere else; and if you consult your Bible alone those doctrines will be manifest to you also."

This is of the utmost importance. The Protestant Reforma-

* Let all remember that George IV was the man who said, "Is he a gentleman? Has he any Greek?"

tion had based itself upon the Hebrew Scriptures, and that Canon of later Greek books which the Church accepted and which came to be called the New Testament. The old basis of authority in doctrine had been the Church corporate, her voice expressed in Councils through the universal Episcopate, to which was added in the Christian West, from which the Protestant Reformation derived, the admitted authority also of the chief Bishop, the Pope of Rome.

But there stood, all through the development of Christian doctrine, an appeal to another authority, which could hardly be called subordinate, but which was summoned as a witness—and this was the authority of the Scriptures, Hebrew and Christian. Since it was the very business of the Protestant Reformers to question and reject tradition, which they said was corrupted, hierarchic authority which they said was usurped, it became their central affirmation that the sole authority for doctrine was Holy Writ. Since they denied the right of hierarchy or Council, let alone Pope, to interpret Holy Writ, leaving that business to the individual man, a man's business on the Protestant side in advancing this or that to be true was to say, "You will find it here, in such-and-such a place, in the Old or the New Testament, set out in words which, if you use your plain reason, cannot mean otherwise to you than what I have said they mean."

Conversely, anything that was not thus plainly set forward in Holy Writ, in so many words, was not to be accepted as doctrine.

In all this there was of course one exception. The cardinal words of the Sacrament, "This is my body . . . This is my blood," *they* were not to be taken as they stood but were to be regarded as metaphors, at least by the most Protestant section of the Reformers who by their enthusiasm gave the driving force to the whole movement.

[295]

The whole point of the *De Doctrina* therefore lies in its arguments from the Bible. On that all depends.

"Read the actual texts," is Milton's attitude, "read them as though you had never read them before; ask yourself to what conclusion they lead you if you eliminate all tradition, all superimposed ideas, and you will agree with me that the Son is not co-equal or consubstantial with the Father."

The long argument is summed up in more than one clinching phrase, to be discovered up and down this fifth chapter of the first book. Here is one:

"Who can believe that the very first of the Commandments was so obscure that two other persons equally entitled to worship should have remained wholly unknown?"

("*Primum omnium mandatum duas personas ignotas divino honore . . . caruisse quis credat?*)

The reader who is curious in such things will at once inquire how Milton deals with the Johannine comma. It will be found that he deals with it characteristically—that is, with his characteristic scholarship and his characteristic close argument.

The Johannine comma is that passage, I John V. 7.), of the "Three witnesses." "There are three that bear witness in Heaven, the Father, the Word and the Holy Ghost, and these three are one." Everybody knows that these words are not found in certain of the most ancient manuscripts. Milton notes that they are absent from the Syriac, and two other Oriental versions, and that they are absent from what he calls "the greater part" of the ancient Greek manuscripts.

That phrase "greater part" is disingenuous. The point is one of priority, not of counting sources. Milton also notes that in the Greek texts where the words appear the readings sometimes vary. He knows of course that Erasmus boggled at it, and Beza. But, again characteristically, although he depends wholly on Scripture and rejects tradition (for such an attitude had been the whole basis of the Protestant attack upon the Church for more than a hundred years) he founds his central argument—just as he does his plea in favour of polygamy—upon an unexpected negative. "What," says he, "if the Father, the Son and the Holy Ghost are mentioned in Scripture? Does that mean that they are co-equal and all one God? There is no specific mention of *that*."

Let anyone who has the leisure read the whole chapter, with its wealth of quotation and its passionate industry, devoted to getting rid of the central doctrine upon which the Faith is founded—it will leave him with an image of Milton's religion very different from the conventional picture of our text-books.

This fifth chapter, "De Filio Dei," covering nearly a hundred pages of print, filled to the brim with citation, allusion, reference, argument, is the strongest thing written against the Divinity of Our Lord—the strongest, at least, for those who, like Milton, base themselves upon the Bible only. Instead of that title "De Filio" he might rather have put at the head of his enormous charge against Christ's Godhead the words which the Mohammedan conqueror had carved upon the Church of the Redeemer in Jerusalem. On the front of this Church the Christians had inscribed the phrase "To the Son of God." And Omar (I think it was) had inscribed in its stead "God has no Son."

All this argument against the Divinity of Our Lord is sober, rational and extensive. He builds it up from text after text, and though the shock to his orthodox fellow-Protestants would have been enormous had Milton published it while he was alive, though the shock was considerable even in the first third of the nineteenth century when it most belatedly appeared, though in such a shock there is something comic, yet the adherents of "the Bible only" could not complain.

In another matter of the *De Doctrina* there is high comedy—

I would almost say farce. I mean the amusing plea for polygamy just mentioned.

Milton was in dead earnest here also, and that makes it all the funnier. He really did want to see Englishmen and the members of "all the Churches of Christ" going about with a bunch of wives. He was for Mormonising us thoroughly. And again he was—on Old Testament premises—perfectly right. Those to whom he was addressing his arguments, and who were for him "The Churches of Christ," that is, the reformed bodies up and down Europe, with all their infinity of vagary, at least agreed on this—that Scripture was the only authority, and certainly if you make Scripture the only authority and rely especially upon the Old Testament, polygamy is not only obviously but enthusiastically taken for granted. Milton holds all the trumps. He has no need to play them with particular skill, he simply sweeps trick after trick off the table.

He plays Deuteronomy XXIII. 2, Leviticus XVIII. 18, Genesis XXVI. 31, Canticles VI. 8, Esther II. 12, I Kings I. 4, Canticles VI, 8, II Chronicles XXIV. 2, Ezekiel XXIII. 4, Judges VIII. 30, I Samuel XXV. 42, II Samuel XXV. 12, Nehemiah XXIII. 26—and lots of others. I only quote this brief category, because, if I went on, it would fill a page and more.

Where there is a text which seems doubtful he batters it down with counter argument. Such texts are naturally to be found in the New Testament rather than in the Old; but even Genesis says that a man shall keep faithful to his wife and that they are one—an idea which is repeated, as we all know, in the reported sayings of Our Lord, notably in Matthew XIX. 5.

"Ho!" says Milton. "Let not that trouble you! I admit that to use such texts as argument shows a certain cunning (acute sane), but I can easily expose that cunning. Are we not actually commanded not to covet our neighbour's house nor his he-slave nor his she-slave nor his she-donkey? How ridiculous it would be if we were to read into that text a proof that a man was not allowed to own several houses, oxen, and slaves and she-donkeys! And that is that—and let us hear no more nonsense about it."

The innocent might imagine that, seeing how excellent is Milton's case from the Old Testament, he would have shirked the very great difficulties of the New in this matter, elsewhere than in the passage quoted. Far from it, he delights in the battle. He picks out every Christian text that might seem to support the horrid idea of having one wife only, and expounds its true sense with glorious confidence. Thus among the other reported sayings of Our Lord (also in Matthew X. 23) is the statement that if a man put away his wife and marry another he commits adultery. It is quite plain to Milton that there would have been no adultery if he had *kept* the first wife side by side with the new one instead of divorcing her; otherwise she would not have been dragged into the question at all. To argue monogamy from this text, says he, is *"protinus repudiandum"*—"it is an altogether illogical conclusion."

In the same way when St. Paul says (Milton quotes the Latin of Geneva rather than the Greek), *"Suam quisque uxorem habeto"* (let every man possess, or cleave to, or hold, his own wife) clearly (says Milton) he does not mean that the worthy fellow should not *also* possess, cleave to or hold many other wives. As for the text in Timothy that a Bishop should have only one wife, that makes it all the more obvious that the Apostles were in favour of any number of wives for the generality of man.

Yes, it is true (says Milton) that Bishops (and Presbyters too for that matter) are condemned not only in Timothy but in Titus to monogamy—but why? Because in this fashion they may better carry out the tasks of their office. But even that he only puts forward as probable—*"opinor"* says he; and anyhow, the very fact that Bishops and Presbyters were not allowed several wives is an irrefutable proof that lay Christians were not only allowed them, but almost commanded in the matter.

"Indeed," says Milton (carrying on as people often do when they are drunk with argument), "*satis declarat polygamiam in ecclesia iis temporibus fuisse usitatem*"—"it sets forth fully that in the Church of those days polygamy was common form." You would have been quite surprised, dropping in to supper with an early Christian, not to find half a dozen of his ladies at the board.

All this I say is comic, and stands out with a vigour of its own in the great mass of Milton's new creed. But when he goes on to show that Scripture allows divorce he falls back again to the obvious.

He quotes at large; but there is no need to multiply instances, one text of his alone is quite enough—it is straight out of the heart of the Jewish law in Deuteronomy. "*Si duxerit quis uxorem, eritque ut non inveniat gratiam in oculis ejus, scribet ei libellum repudii, etc.*"—"If anyone has married a wife and comes not to like her, let him write out for her a writ of divorce." And the Jewish law goes on to say that having done that he can turn her out of his house.

So the Old Testament allows divorce, and the trouble with the New Testament can be got over. The conception of divorce on occasion was familiar to our European tradition in pagan times and lingered in the codes of the early Christian Emperors. Divorce to us to-day is familiar and comprehensible, and the plea for polygamy only makes us laugh because it is unusual. When we have got on a little further and are still more civilised we shall no doubt agree with Milton and the Mormons, and there will be nothing odd (as there still is to-day) about this department of the *De Doctrina* and the Mohammedans. Our rich men will establish their harems publicly!

It is in connection with these passages on divorce in the book that we are able to discuss the date of its composition—not an unimportant question when we are considering the develop-

ment of Milton the man during his life. It may be fairly concluded that the treatise, with its continued attack upon orthodoxy, this prime piece of novel and daring heresy set down (but
carefully not made public) by the most representative Protestant voice of the mid-seventeenth century dates from his years
of greatest vigour. We cannot regard its material as compiled
before 1642, nor much of it after 1652 when he went blind.
That is, it was presumably written when Milton was in his
thirties, or completed at the latest shortly after he had passed
his fortieth year. It was at the age of thirty-four that Milton
got his severe shock in the matter of matrimony—a matter upon
which he had not been in a position to receive a shock before.
It was in his thirty-fifth year that he launched out for the first
time, and obviously under the effect of that shock, in favour
of divorce. It was then that he must have turned his more than
human industry on to the task of collecting texts and arguments, and the first of these in the *De Doctrina* must therefore
belong to that year at the earliest.

On the other hand, shortly after his fortieth birthday Milton's
blindness was threatening him, and within a few weeks of his
forty-third birthday it had become total.

Milton blind was able to draw upon the vast store of his
learning, and perhaps upon a body of notes. But the mass of
citation and close comparison of texts not only Latin but Greek
and not only Greek but Hebrew which fills the *De Doctrina*
could not possibly have been the work of a blind man. Even
supposing a blind man to be able from memory alone to send
a secretary in search of these hundreds of citations, the time
required would have meant a devotion to nothing else for years
—and it is not credible that any memory should be of such a
quality.

Open the book at random in that part of it where he is not
driven to very close argument, being that part most orthodox,
the later part; take for instance the twenty-third chapter, which

[301]

deals with God's adoption of those who are justified by Faith. He has nothing to say that would not be agreed with by the whole mass of Protestants, and very nearly all of it by the whole mass of Catholics and Greeks. It is only three short pages; yet it has twenty-five separate quotations from Scripture alone, all taken from the Latin version, of course.

One may say that the very texture of the book—and it is a long book—is citation, and that there is as much citation in its sixty thousand words as there is of his own comment. He quotes individual Greek terms from the Greek tragedies and from Thucydides, arguing on the unity of God. He uses detailed discussion of Hebrew words that are to his purpose. He quotes them in the original, not even transliterating, but writing the Hebrew letters with their vowel points.

Here is a passage on the Divine Unity and against the Trinity of which I give the essential, to show how improbable it is that such matter could have been dictated by a man after he had lost the use of his eyes.

"Similar to this is the use of the word 'the Lord' [This word is given in Hebrew characters] in the plural number with a singular meaning, and a plural affix according to the Hebrew mode, and [another Hebrew word] with the vowel *patha* to signify one man, and with the vowels *kamets* to signify one God. The same may perhaps" (*fortasse*) "apply to the proper names" [Here two names in the original Hebrew].

He then goes on to quote examples from the Greek, using the plural for the singular not to indicate more than one person but merely as a sign of respect; and refers in particular to a passage of Euripides, from the *Iphigenia*, which he quotes; and he makes further reference to the *Rhesus* and the *Bacchæ*. The whole page is a mass of such detailed, minute, literal comment, letter by letter. Nor is this page exceptional. The whole Latin treatise—much the longest piece of prose Milton ever wrote—is a mosaic of such.

Again, take such a passage as this from the first book when he is arguing against the creative omnipotence of God.

"Our moderns, most of them, will have it that all things arose from nothingness. The same may be said of that very opinion (that is based on nothing). For in the first place it is certain that neither the Hebrew verb used nor the Greek word nor the Latin word 'creare' mean 'created out of nothing'! Indeed each of these words always means to make something *out of* (pre-existing) matter, i.e., to fashion, not to create."

John Milton proceeds to quote Genesis I. 21-7 in proof of this; and then Isaiah LIV. 16; then II Corinthians IV. 6; then Isaiah XLV. 7; and after that he quotes from Wisdom and again from Maccabees and Matthew—all word for word from the Junius Latin version, which he used in his contempt of the Vulgate.

One may say that the man who thus writes down his Greek and his Hebrew and his Latin, and citation after citation from the Scriptures did it from dictation, though blind, because he could tell his amanuensis where to lay his hands on passages carefully filed for reference. But when one considers the time involved, let alone the effect of memory, it is most unlikely. One cannot but be morally certain that such passages—and there are scores of them—were written while he could read and write and commentate. A little further in the same chapter (Book I, Chapter VII) upon the nature of Angels fifty-two references to the Old and New Testaments are crammed into thirty-three lines. That is not conceivable as the work of a blind man.

But this chapter, the seventh of the first book, which should be famous, has a more profound significance in our study of Milton than the witness it bears (with so much else) to the way in which the *De Doctrina* was written. For it is an argument in favour of something *approaching* (but not merging in) materialism.

[303]

Milton's attitude on that prime question is all his own; he is not materialist in the silly modern sense of that term, he does not regard consciousness as proceeding from matter. But neither does he regard God as the creator of matter. He would have the material universe to be a necessary emanation of God: i.e., as to its essence if not its form coeval with God: he would therefore have God *finding and fashioning* matter: inseparable from matter but not bringing it into being by his direct word—wherein once more he not only breaks away from but contradicts the foundations of the Christian faith.

Mark that in all this Milton is not Pantheist; what he seems to envisage is rather a dualism between God acting with purpose, and matter acted upon. He separates the one from the other. But, though it is not just to call him a Materialist, he was on the way to materialism; it was this "half materialism" in his new creed which led him to deny the immortality of the soul.

He held to the old Catholic doctrine that the soul and the body are not strangers. That a man is soul *and* body: that each is necessary to make up a true and complete human being: but he rejects the Catholic argument for the special survival of the soul until it is reunited with the body at the resurrection. When a man dies he dies altogether. God will (or *may*) by a special act call him back to life, after this annihilation, at the last day. But in the meanwhile, and (if God so chooses) *forever*, the man is no more.

But to return to the question of date. Could such passages have been the work of a blind man? They might have been if they were exceptional, but there are scores and scores of them. He probably touched the thing up by dictation after his blindness, he may even have somewhat expanded it, but the bulk of the book must have been written while he could still consult texts himself and make notes on them.

In this connection, and before leaving what is by far the most interesting to history and for an understanding of the man of all Milton's prose works, let everyone pause and admire the gigantic erudition here at work. It is apparent throughout the whole body of his writing, it fits in strangely well with his lyrical inspiration; it appears by implication in every tenth line or less that he wrote from his first boyish days at college until the mixed hours of disappointment and triumph which introduced his death.

In all that grinding life, nearly sixty years full of writing, wrangling, proclaiming—with divine song flourishing in the midst—he ceased not to learn, to learn anew, to keep alive what he had learnt of old, to proclaim and use his learning both old and recent. If we were to make no other monument to Milton than the mass of his quotations and allusions these would already half explain the man and raise him beyond the measure of his contemporaries.

To sum up on the date of the *De Doctrina*. The presumptions upon it might be set forth as follows:—

(1) It is a long book which could only have been written under conditions of leisure.

(2) It is a book very closely reasoned, which could not have been written other than quite slowly. Especially as:

(3) It is built up of an immense number of quotations from Latin, Greek and Hebrew and from the text of Scripture.

(4) It is written in strong opposition to current orthodoxy, and is in part concerned with his revolt against Christian marriage.

(5) It is in a very packed close style, quite different from the flowing and often confused style of his dictated Latin.

These five considerations put together point strongly to the years between 1642 and 1649. Though he was writing pamphlets he had sufficient leisure, and he was through all that time still in possession of his sight.

On the other hand, there are the following considerations:—

(1) The MS. as we now have it is not in Milton's hand, and therefore it is either copied or dictated.

(2) The views against the Trinity, against the creative Power of God (materialist in character) and in favour of polygamy are so extreme that they do not harmonise with what we know of his character in the middle years of his life. Those extreme views are only put at their fullest in a certain number of places, they are not the bulk of the book, but such as they are they do not square with the middle part of his life, and are quite different from his early orthodox youth previous to his marriage.

(3) The title put on the MS. includes the word "posthumous." This may be interpreted as meaning that Milton had ordered them to be kept from publication until after his death; or as meaning that they were finished too late for him to give orders and that he left no choice for his amanuensis to explain the situation save by using the word "posthumous."

(4) The common, the almost universal opinion is that the *De Doctrina* was written at the very end of his life, almost up to his death. This last point is of no great value, for it is in the very spirit of modern historical writing and, particularly, of modern textual criticism, to copy from what has been said before, and to avoid general reasoning and common sense.

(5) The whole book turns upon a clear-cut and almost violent affirmation that the canon of Scripture in the Old and New Testaments is the only authority for doctrine, and that anything outside it such as tradition or post-Apostolic work is without authority. Now this is the exact position of his last tract, published the year before he died, and is not, I think, anywhere put forward fully during his middle years, though of course it lay at the back of his mind as it did at the back of the mind of all the left-wing Protestant writers.

EPILOGUE

What are we to make of these two contradictory sets of evidence? I would suggest something like this:—

Milton's mind began to turn against the body of orthodox tradition (in so far as this remained with the Protestant side of Europe at the time) after the violent shock of his ruined marriage in 1642. During the seven years that followed, when he was unoccupied by any public duty, was in full possession of his sight, and at the height of his energy, with his books all round him for consultation at any moment, he collected his material, increasingly confirming the doubts that had arisen in him. He probably also actually composed the greater part of the text of the book in those years.

But when with the year 1649 he had become plunged in heavy public work he could not continue it or complete it; though he kept by him the enormous magazine of references from which he drew his material.

With a return to leisure towards the end of the Commonwealth he took on the completion of the work and the putting of it together, and though he was principally occupied with his Epics and the *Samson*, yet had especially towards the end of the period opportunity for amplifying and rounding off the whole. Further towards the end of that period he may have added as the MS. was read to him the passages which are strongest in their departure from orthodoxy, and finally gave orders when the thing was read to him again in its fulness that it should not be published until after he was dead.

This, it seems to me, would be the process fitting in best with the known facts. The period between 1642 and 1649 though morally disturbed and full of half a dozen violent tracts was on the whole a period of leisure. The only other similar periods he enjoyed were towards the end of the Commonwealth and in the intervals of his epic work in his very last years.

Thus we should have for the *De Doctrina* three main periods—no doubt joined up by notes and jottings. First the collection of the material and probably much of the actual writing, between 1642 and 1649. Second, perhaps the last two years of the Commonwealth—1658-60—though he had already begun *Paradise Lost*. Third, for the interpolation of special passages and the rounding up of the whole, the last years after the completion of the *Samson Agonistes*—1667-74.

With that we leave Milton the man, and even Milton the Prose Writer—though not the Poet: for the poet stands apart. The *De Doctrina* is a conclusion in the fullest sense: the ultimate result of his philosophy and the last testament of his pen. He died no longer believing the omnipotence of his Creator, the Divinity of his Saviour and the native immortality of mankind.

Index

INDEX

[312]

INDEX